DYNAMICS OF SOCIAL FORMATION AMONG THE LEPCHAS

DYNAMICS OF SOCIAL FORMATION AMONG THE LEPCHAS

D.C. Roy

AKANSHA PUBLISHING HOUSE
NEW DELHI - 110 059 (INDIA)

AKANSHA PUBLISHING HOUSE
R-37B, Vani Vihar, Uttam Nagar
New Delhi - 110 059
E-mail: ektabooks@yahoo.com

Showroom
4649/21B, Ansari Road
Darya Ganj
New Delhi - 110 002
Ph.: 23263193, 9811582579

Dynamics of Social Formation among the Lepchas

First Published, 2005

ISBN 81-87606-93-2

PRINTED IN INDIA

Published by M.P. Misra for Akansha Publishing House, New Delhi - 110 059 and Printed at Tarun Offset Press, Delhi.

In the Loving Memory of

My Elder Brother

H.C. Roy

PREFACE

Enlistment of Scheduled Tribes in India is primarily an administrative affair guided often by pragmatic and political considerations. Categorisation of Scheduled Tribe, therefore, need not and cannot be identical to that of the theoretical concept of tribe. As a result many a time conflicting results are obtained by the simultaneous application of these two principles. The question of what is tribal (from an academic point of view) about Scheduled Tribe (as per administrative decision) can therefore be taken up for more serious consideration.

Most of the academicians in India have accepted Constitutional branding of Scheduled Tribe as tribe. The economy of these Scheduled Tribes has been widely cited as examples of tribal economy of the respective tribe without judging their corresponding theoretical concepts. Other related tribal studies (like tribal culture, tribal demography, tribal history, tribal law, tribal politics, tribal religion etc.) centre around the people recognised as scheduled tribe presupposing their tribal identity.

The present book is departure from the existing trend. We have tried to identify a tribe after critically examining the nature of its society. Two theoretical concepts have been considered relevant: 'social formation' or 'socio-economic formation' (as propounded by Marx) and 'social embeddedness' (as developed by Polanyi).

Although Marx propounded the concept of social formation but he did not specify details about the tribal social formation. However, combining the existing literature on tribes and the Marxian mode of production, we have tried to reformulate the concept of tribal social formation. Karl Polanyi's concept of social embeddedness is much relevant in the distributional aspect of society. Economy does not determine society; society does not determine economy. They are mutually dependent. Karl Polanyi's concept of reciprocity and redistribution are connected with pre-industrial economy while market exchange is related to industrial economy. Concepts of other social scientists particularly economic anthropologists like Malinowski, Firth, Sahlins, Dalton, Bohannan, etc. have also been discussed in brief.

From the simple binary classification of capitalist and non-capitalist societies, we have ultimately classified any agriculture based society as capitalist farming and peasant economy. Depending on the modes of production (i.e. forces of production and relations of production) a peasant economy can again be classified into tribal peasantry, feudal peasantry etc. In this book we have examined both the components of modes of production of agriculture-based economy of the Lepchas. Different aspects of agriculture like land, labour and capital have been critically examined. The distributional aspects of agricultural produce have also been carefully discussed in order to identify the market orientation and the nature of the society.

The theoretical aspects of the nature of the society have been examined with the Lepchas, a lesser known scheduled tribe of Darjeeling district of West Bengal. Existing literature on the Lepchas are neither systematic nor sufficient in the sense that they are nothing than the preparation of an economic catalogue of the people who have already been officially recognised as tribe. The present study on the Lepchas is intended to be a departure from the established trend where we have not plotted merely the present state of their economy but tried to examine the concept of social formation with them. Without pre-supposing their tribal identity, the present study examines the production and distribution of the agriculture based Lepcha economy and came out with some interesting results.

The book as a whole is undoubtedly challenging in handling both the theoretical aspects of tribal social formation and examining it with field data collected from among the Lepchas of Darjeeling district. It is interesting to come out with some new aspects of tribal society. I would appreciate the readers for realising the spirit of challenge and innovativeness as carried out in the book.

The researches and the scholars on tribal studies might find some new angles in the book while handling the problems associated with the tribes. The book is diagnostic and ends with some areas where further studies on tribes in general and on Lepchas in particular can be carried out. All my efforts will be fruitful if someone tribes to enhance the work in the direction initiated in the book. Suggestions are heartily welcomed whereas all limitations were with the author.

D.C. ROY

ACKNOWLEDGEMENTS

In connection to my service I have been posted at Kalimpong, a sub-division of Darjeeling district of West Bengal in 1987. Since then, I felt keen interest about the land and the people of the region. Among the different communities (Nepalis, Tibetans, Bhutias, Limboos etc.) living in this hill track, Lepchas attracted me the most and I started enquiring and writing about them for different magazines, newspapers and seminars. My haphazard and unsystematic work got a concrete theoretical shape under the efficient guidance and supervision of Dr. Bani Prasanna Misra, retired Professor, Centre for Himalayan Studies, North Bengal University and Dr. Rajat Subhra Mukhopadhya, Professor in the Department of Sociology, North Bengal University. Without their proper guidance, constant encouragement, untiring efforts, sympathetic advice, the present work could not have been completed in the present form. Although I could not fulfil their aspirations, still I like to keep on record my sincere respect, gratitude, honour and indebtness to both of them.

While conducting my doctoral research, a number of persons helped me in a number of ways and I like to acknowledge them by heart.

I am grateful to all the staff members of the Centre for Himalayan Studies, North Bengal University for extending their help as and when required.

I am grateful to Ren. D.T. Tamsang, President; Ren.L.S. Tamsang, General Secretary; Ren. N.T. Lepcha, Secretary, Thom Shezon; Ren. L.T. Sadamoo, ex-President; Ren. C.D. Simikmoo, ex-General Secretary and other members of the Lepcha Association, Kalimpong for their valuable information and suggestions.

I desire to express my gratitude to Lapon Sonam Tshering Tamsang, Sangeet Natak Academy Awardee and Ren. Passang Tshering Simikmoo, Bhasa Samman Awardee for sharing their expert knowledge on different issues connected with the study. I must mention and express my gratitude to Runue Mayel Clymit Sangdyangmoo for her help on a number of occasions.I am really thankful to Dorjee, Ong Tshering, Dongmit, Sangden of Mani Gumpa; Ezra, Sevastin, Mikma Tshering of 5th Mile Lepcha Gaon; Pascal, Suk Tshering, Sanumit of Pochaok for accompanying me and working as interpreter during my field survey in their respective villages.

I like to thank all Lepcha members of my study area particularly the heads of the households for their whole-hearted cooperation.

I am thankful to my ex-colleagues Tapanda and Ashutosh with whom I had actually started working on Lepchas.

I am grateful to Dr. R.K. Sprigg for allowing me to use his personal library when he was in Himalayan Hotel, Kalimpong.

I am indebted to my parents, brothers and other family members for their constant support to the work. I like to keep on record my thanks to my wife Ranju, daughter Dona and son Rishi who remained as a constant source of my inspiration during the work.

I must thank Mr. M.P.Misra of M/s Akansha Publishing House, New Dehli for taking keen interest in publishing the book.

D. C. ROY

CONTENTS

LIST OF TABLES

LIST OF SKETCHES

LIST OF DIAGRAM

LIST OF MAP

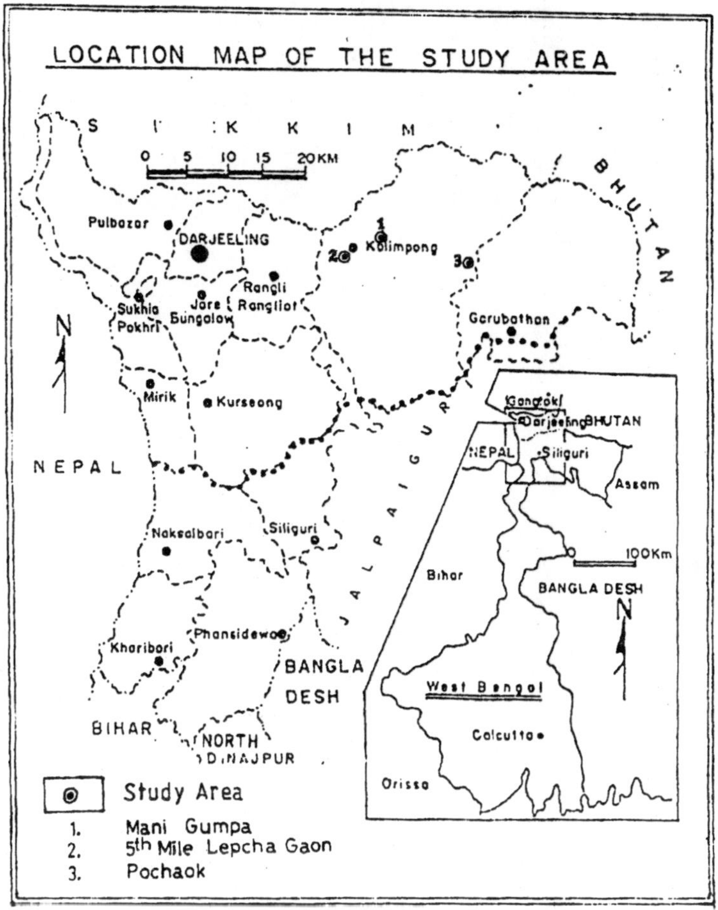

Location Map of the Study Area

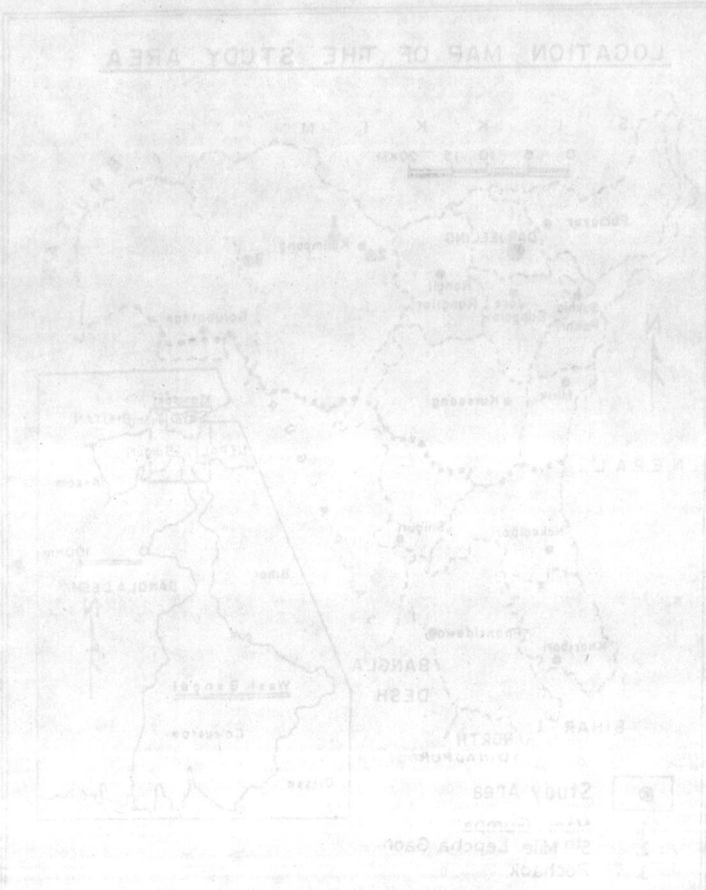

Location Map of the Study Area

CHAPTER ONE

INTRODUCTION

The Lepchas are found mostly in the state of Sikkim and in the adjoining hilly region of Darjeeling district of West Bengal. The Constitution of India has categorised Lepchas as 'Scheduled Tribe'. The expression 'Scheduled Tribe' may mean either of the following two things. First, it may be held to imply that, in India, all tribes are scheduled or listed under the constitutional provisions. Alternatively, it may imply that some of the tribes are scheduled for the purposes of preferential treatment while others are not. The second possibility is further suggested by the analogy with the other important category of 'scheduled castes' where some of the castes, and not all, are scheduled. But, be whatever it may, there cannot be any denying of the fact that the scheduled tribes are 'tribes'.

Now, the problem of identification of tribe lies with the problem of its definition. Tribe, as is the case with many other terms, may be broadly defined from two different angles. In an instrumental or purposive definition, much about the properties or characteristics of the 'object' is of secondary importance when compared with the objective or interest of the 'subject' who defines it that way. Looked at the other way, when an essentialist definition of tribe is made, there has to be attributes or characteristics or properties or substance inherent within the community so as to identify them as tribe. The administrators are more likely to be preoccupied with the instrumental or purposive definition of tribe while the academicians are usually concerned with the essentialistic definition of tribe. Since Indian categorisation of scheduled tribe is more an administrative business than academic one, many a times conflicting results are obtained by the simultaneous application of these two principles. The question of what is 'tribal' (from an academic point of view) about the 'scheduled tribes' (as per administrative decisions) can therefore be taken up for serious consideration.

In India much of the discussion on the subject has been presented against the perspective of a 'tribe-caste continuum'. In the western writings on the subject, the binary classification of 'status and contract', 'community and association' or 'mechanical solidarity and organic solidarity', and the like have offered from time to time useful insights. However, even without entering into the debate of whether the tribes should be viewed as a type of society or a stage of social evolution, one may attempt a serious examination of the social formation of the tribes so called. Without being deterministic in a mechanical sense of the term, it is agreed that the economic activities and organisation of any community play a decisive role in the determination of its social formation. At present the mainstream economists appear to be little concerned with the social formation or such kindred questions. Their lack of concern appears justified because the study of comparative economic system has lost their relevance in the face of pervasive homogenising tendencies of capitalism all around. Further, diachronic studies have been handed over to the historians, for, the economists are overburdened with their concern with the present. Also, the classification of economics into micro and macro leaves little space for serious enquiries into the vestiges of earlier formations at the local or regional level.

In the present work, our main objective has been to study the social formation among the Lepchas. In the study of social formation, we start by ignoring people's beliefs and ideas and, instead, look at who produces what and who gets what is produced. "Society viewed as a system for production and distribution, conceived of independently of the actors' representations or justifications of the system, is what has been called the 'social formation'". [Bloch, 1985: 23]. The social formation is to be understood not by just one 'mode of production' but by an articulation of several. For example, in a colonial situation a communal mode of production may coexist with a capitalist one but the capitalist one will dominate over the communal mode.[1]

The study of social formation is, thus, not simply a study of economy[2] of a particular people isolated from the rest. In fact, in many otherwise laudable efforts at studying the tribal economy, this very perspective of social formation is ignored, thereby making a weak representation of the whole. Also, oftentimes, what passes in the name of 'tribal economy' is nothing more than the preparation of an economic catalogue of a group of people who are officially recognised as 'tribe'. The irony is that, in the same or adjoining areas, the same type of study may pass under various labels, such as rural economy, peasant economy or tribal economy depending upon the type of people being studied. The present study of the social formation of the Lepchas is intended to be a departure from the established trend. It is not meant in any way that this is absolutely a new idea. Rather, we shall derive in our present exercise useful insights from whatever literature is there on pre-capitalist economics and those offered by some of the classical economists or economic anthropologists.

TRIBAL SOCIAL FORMATION

'Tribal social formation' as one form of various other types of social formations (like slavery, feudalism, capitalism, socialism etc.) is supposed to be prevalent among the tribes. There may be as many forms of social formations as the types of society. As most of the academicians in India have accepted constitutional branding of scheduled tribe as tribe, the economy of these scheduled tribes have been widely cited as examples of 'tribal economy' of the respective tribes without judging their correspondence with the concept of tribal social formation. It also poses a conceptual problem where different tribes constitute different types of tribal economy. The good number of other related tribal studies (like tribal culture, tribal demography, tribal history, tribal law and justice, tribal politics, tribal religion etc.) centre around the people recognised as schedule tribe presupposing their tribal attributes on the basis of constitutional recognition.

Literature under the heading 'tribal social formation' is rare either in the field of economics or in the other branches of social science. Even Marx who propounded the concept of social formation did not illustrate the application for the tribes in his later writings [Marshall, 1998: 612; Bottomore, 1983: 444]. The Marxian literature did not specify details about the tribal social formation even 'it does not provide a comprehensive description' of social formation [Bottomore, 1983: 445].

Even then, it is not difficult to attempt a reformulation combining the existing literature on social formation on the one hand and primitive or tribal economy on the other. Often the concept social formation poses some sort of confusion as 'at all events, in actual usage (social formation) refers to two phenomena which are quite familiar to Marxist, and to sociologists of all persuasions–namely the type of society (e.g. feudal society, bourgeois or capitalist society), and to particular societies (e.g. France or Britain as a society) [Bottomore, 1983: 445]. But usually by social formation for all practical purposes we mean the type of society.

In the classical Marxian literature economy is characterised by its mode of production[3], which again is constituted by forces of production[4] and relations of production[5]. The mode of production determines the base[6] of the society, which together with the superstructure[7] determines the social formation.

The first (or earliest) and original (or natural) form of social formation, in Marxian ideology, is primitive communism. Social formation under primitive communism can be viewed from production and distributional angles. In the production front, the mode of production is based on communal ownership of land and other means of production while the products are distributed on the basis of need. There may be some private property in the form of tools, weapons and personal effects but it denied the presence of money, price, exchange and market. It is a simple type of society where communal ownership, work and living together are attributed by the primitive method of production.

Beside Marx and Engels, some other social scientists particularly economic anthropologists have dealt with the attributes of primitive and tribal economy mainly from distributional angle. The most notable western scholars on the subject are: B. Malinowski, Karl Polanyi, Raymond Firth, Marshall D. Sahlins, Paul Bohannan, George Dalton etc. Some of the Indian scholars who worked on tribal economy are: Andre Beteille, K.S. Singh, S.C. Dube, B.K. Roy Burman, Jaganath Pathy, Ajit K. Danda etc.

The views of some of the above leading scholars can be shown in some kind of morphological continuum[8]:

B. Malinowski (1922):	Urigubu	Kula	Gimwali
Karl Polanyi (1946, 1957):	Reciprocal	Redistributive	Exchange
Raymond Firth (1965):	Primitive	Peasant	Industrial
Marshall D.Sahlins (1965):	Generalised Reciprocity	Balanced Reciprocity	Negative Reciprocity
George Dalton (1968, 1971):	Marketless	Peripheral Market	Markets

The initial distributional criteria of the above classifications (like Uriguba and Kula of Malinowski, Reciprocal and Redistributive of Polanyi, Primitive of Firth, Generalised and Balanced reciprocity of Sahlins and Marketless and Peripheral Market of Dalton) may be reconciled to get the modern day tribal economic attributes.

Malinowski challenged the existing popular economic view that all human being aimed at maximising their gains describing it applicable only for western developed societies.[9] In primitive societies, on the other hand, products are used to fulfil the moral obligation rather than maximising individual gain. From his experience with the Trobrianders, Malinowski noticed three types of distribution and exchange–Urigubu, Kula and Gimwali. "The first was a form of payment in kind to women and children who had rights in the property of the matrilineage; the second was gift or ceremonial exchange, which might also accompany the third; only the third, simple trade, which was carried on largely with strangers and constituted a very small part of economic activity, could be said to be governed by the motive to maximise gain. Culture, not human nature, conditioned men's economic conduct." [Malinowski: 63-65, 81-86, 189-191; Cohen, 1967: 92].

Polanyi introduced the concept of social embeddedness in primitive societies. It has been established that there exists a close relationship between economy and society. "Economy does not determine society; society does not determine economy. They are mutually dependent" [Dalton, 1971: 16]. Economy is embedded in any society and there exists a close relationship of economic activities of individuals with the social institutions to which they belong.

Polanyi's reciprocity and redistribution (as shown in his famous book Trade and Market in the Early Empires) are connected with pre-industrial economy while market exchange to that of industrial economy. By reciprocity, he refers that material gift and counter gift giving induced by social obligations derived typically from kinship. Redistribution refers to the channeling upward of goods or services to socially determined allocative centres (usually king, chief or priest) that after receiving the materials redistribute them to others.

Polanyi's reciprocity and redistribution form the 'socio-economic transactional mode' and express the ways in which social organisation relates the economy to its contextual society. The other 'economic mode of market transaction' is purely economic having no social relationship. In pre-capitalist society the first mode is more dominant and the economy is more embedded in the society.

Firth differs from Malinowski and thereby rescued and channalised economics in the same line with Robbins. Malinowski by putting the case of Trobrianders argued that economic activities are not always carried on the basis of maximising profit. Firth, on the other hand, starts with the assumption that all men in all societies are faced with the same economic problem: how to allocate scarce resources between alternative uses, given that some uses are more highly valued than others. Firth argues that most primitive and peasant economies lack specialised economic institutions like factories, banks and commodity exchange but they are guided and carried out by some concepts like family, kinship and community. Without being explicit on the matter we can say that tribals as such are qualitatively not different from others. They are also of the same kind and apparently the difference is a matter of degree and not of kind.

Firth out of his experience with Tikopia society discussed more about primitive and peasant societies. Regarding primitive societies he wrote, "The term primitive is a relative one. More closely applicable to an economic than to a social system, it has no very precise defining character and is variously used" [Firth, 1965: 17]. "They use simple non mechanical technology with little or no innovation, directed to maintenance rather than increase of capital assets; payments for services and rates of exchange are fixed by customs and scarcely fluctuate in the short run, though they may alter in the long run with changes in the relative scarcities; and gift giving is the most important form of distribution and exchange. These and other characteristic function as part of a system of moral involvement and familiarity, and notes that there is relatively little economic activity outside of the moral community" [Firth, 1939: 347-361; Cohen, 1967: 94].

In his later book *On the Sociology of Primitive Exchange*, Sahlins moves away from his earlier (1958) political classification of society (in the category of band, tribe, chiefdom and state) to a new classification based on the distribution of material goods. Sahlins rejects the definition of economic conduct given by Lionel Robbins and also accepted by Firth which emphasizes the process of collection of scarce means to alternative uses, and opts for the view that the study of the economy is the study of how men provision their society.

The first two types of reciprocity generalised and balanced, are the norms of primitive societies while the third type of negative reciprocity dominates modern industrial societies. More explicity, according to Cohen, "The first (generalised) exists where goods and services are given by one party to another without any demand for a return at a specified time or of a specified kind; the prototype of this is the nurturant relationship between mother and child. The second (balanced) exists where a return is made which is recognised by both parties as the equivalent of what is given; custom or moral principle defines such equivalence and is unquestionable. The third (negative) exists where there is bargaining, no party is morally inhibited from seeking gain at the other's expenses" [Cohen, 1967: 98].

Generalised reciprocity is the norm within the family but negative reciprocity is found almost entirely outside of the moral community. As the society is bounded within the ties of kinship, the degree of distance is the minimum in the first two cases than in the last case where relationship establishes outside the family or community ties. In both generalised and balanced reciprocity a sense of rootedness of individuals prevails which in all economic activities reminds the belonging of the individuals in the family or community. In this spectrum, we can put the tribal social formation within the generalised and balanced reciprocity and consider negative reciprocity as a non-tribal attribute where the distance between man and man is more.

Bohannan and Dalton's work on *African Market* is a pioneering work in case of study of primitive markets. In the marketless economy, firstly, there is no market place and secondly, the market principles, if any, are present in a few casual, interpersonal transactions. "Societies without market places are marked by a multicentric economy–a characteristic they share with societies having peripheral markets. A multicentric economy is one in which there are several distinct transactional spheres. Each sphere is distinguished by different material items and services, and may be distinguished by different principles of exchange and different moral values." [Bohannan & Dalton, 1968: 3].

In the second category of peripheral market, both the market places and market principles exist but only peripherally. Two distinguishing characters of peripheral market are that (1) the market sales are not the dominant source of material livelihood. Either most people are not engaged in producing for market or selling in the market or those who are so engaged are only part time marketers. Their livelihood comes from non-market spheres of economy; (2) the participants in peripheral markets are sometimes 'target' marketers who engage in marketing sporadically to acquire a specific amount of cash income for a specific expenditure. Beside supply and demand other social factors like kinship, clanship, religion or other status indicators of buyers, traditional norms of just price etc., do effect the price formation.

Reconciliation

The mode of production and social embeddedness together can specify a complete character of tribal social formation. The major focus of attention has been shifted from relation of man with material goods and services to the relations among man with respect to material goods and services. The relation among men is a social relation while their reaction with material goods and services is economic relation. But the social relations guide the economic relations.

Thus, in tribal social formation we consider a little bit more of what Marx had anticipated about reaction between base and superstructure. Alongwith the mode of production, which is more an economic aspect, the social embeddedness that is more social aspect need to be studied for the tribal society. Tribal social formation has two components: production and distribution. The formation of production is more economical than social while its distributional part is more social than economical and yet they are in extricably tied up one with the other[10]. Their mutual existence and interdependence varies in terms of degree and not in kind. High degree of closeness of social ties in both production and distribution separates tribal social formation from any other formations. In case the social formation is individualistic or self-centred, a distance is created between man and man and hence low degree of embeddedness may be the consequence. Embeddedness depends on social formation but not the other way round.

In tribal social formation emphasis has been shifted from the Marxian superstructure to the Polanyi's embeddedness. In the production sector, modes of production prevails while the distributional aspects are dominated by the embeddedness. The modes of production are more external than internal. Embeddedness is more internal than external in the sense that the relation can only be guided and determined by the relations within the internal structure of the society. Tribal social formation is dominated by its characteristic internal structure, which is entirely different from the other social formations.

In all the above-discussed classification, a society [of Marx, Malinowski, Polanyi, Firth, Sahhlins and Dalton] can be grouped under a simple binary classification of capitalist and pre-capitalist societies. Capitalist society is composed of three different sectors: primary, secondary and tertiary. Agriculture is the basic component of primary sector while industry dominates in the secondary sector. The pre-capitalist society, on the other hand, is dependent on nature and is dominated by agriculture. It can be observed that agriculture appears as the common sector in both capitalist and pre-capitalist society. But agriculture under capitalism is better defined as capitalist farming while it is broadly designated as peasant economy in pre-capitalist economy. The binary classification can ultimately turn into a new classification of capitalist farming and peasant economy.

Capitalist farming can be characterised by (1) hired labour and (2) market orientation. Guided by profit motive commodification of agricultural products separate capitalist farming from peasant economy where agriculture operates with (1) non-hired labour and (2) non-market orientation. Capitalism follows division of labour and all the factors are guided by profit motive. Products in capitalist farming may not be used for consumption purposes by any of the factors of production. The producers are hardly the consumers. Labour is used mainly on hired basis and monetary wage is the reward for involvement in productive activity. Under peasant economy, on the other hand, there is hardly any division of labour and the producers themselves are the consumers of the product. The objective of production shifted from profit motive to consumption requirement. (Labour, under peasant economy, is supplied by the family or community and consumption or distribution of products instead of monetary wage, emerges as the main motive behind production.)

All the non-capitalist societies, particularly those who based on agriculture can be brought under the common category of 'peasant economy'. But each type of peasantry can be differentiated from the other on the basis of their distinct characteristics or differentiating attributes. One broad such differentiating attribute may be their distinct mode of production. Each force of production, particularly labour, are specific to specific form of peasant society. In agriculture, land is indispensable and one of the important passive factor of production but the relation of production in respect of owners of land and labour makes one type of society different from the other. For example, the relationship between master and slave, serf and lord, make each type of peasant economy peculiar to itself. However, in each type, the labour, by using land, takes active part in producing agricultural crops but the ownership and management of land alongwith the distributional pattern of agricultural crops varies widely.

The ownership right (viewed either as right of use or right of transfer) of land takes different forms under different types of peasant economy. In tribal peasantry, the community for all practical purposes establishes an absolute right of using even the individual land. The rule of society or convention permits all individuals within the community to enjoy a qualified right of use over all individual lands. The individual ownership eventually turned into a community based mutually interdependent right of use of land. Tribal peasantry, thus, carries the legacy of primitive society where individual ownership could not develop and all natural resources including land belonged to the society or community. The right of transfer, another component of ownership right of land is also distinct under tribal peasantry where right of transfer is established through succession among the nearest blood relations on hereditary basis. The other means of transfer like lease, outright sale or the like are the attributes of non-tribal peasant societies.

The relationship between owner of land and labour over the distribution of agricultural products differs widely in different types of peasant economy. In some society, the producers at the individual or communal level use the products they produce. Here the producers are the users or consumers. But in other cases one party (i.e. labour, the most active factor of production) engage in productive activities, but the other party (land lord who do not take part in production except supplying land) got the right to use or consume the products. Profit is the basic motive in non-tribal societies as against subsistence in peasant society.

The distribution of agricultural products follows a variety of patterns (as shown by different writers like Malinowski, Polanyi, Firth, Sahlins, and Dalton etc.) in case of peasant economy. But in all the cases the distribution of products confined either within the family or community. The first two categories of each of the types of distribution, thus, satisfy the peasant economic characteristics from the viewpoint of distribution of agricultural products. Production for the market is a non-peasant character of agriculture.

The tribal social formation[11] or tribal economy because of its pre-capitalistic character can thus be grouped under the broad category of peasant economy. More specifically, we may define tribal social formation as the other name of tribal peasantry, which has its own differentiating attributes.

Beside the basic two characteristic features of peasant economy (non-hired labour and non-market orientation), the tribal social formation possesses the following distinguishing economic attributes.

The tribes subsist by exploiting the natural resources. Land, the basic resource, is owned, managed and controlled either by the individual or community who ultimately use it to cater to the consumption requirement. Individuals may possess land but each operates in a communal milieu within the network of kinship ties. In the non-producing society (e.g. hunting and food gathering stage) land was under the society's command while individual ownership has established gradually in the later stage of settled cultivation.

Tribal society is non-monetised and the laws of reciprocity among the members of family and community happens to be the main distinguishing attributes. Commodities are exchanged as per need of the community without expecting much return from the other party. A sense of belonging to particular clan of the tribe remains the main differentiating marker of tribal economy, which is reflected through the distribution of products among the members. Tribes are more concerned about the present consumption and saving or hoarding for the future is a non-tribal concept. Through reciprocal exchange, the tribal economy is a self-sufficient, self-contained, self-confident small economic organisation without much interaction with the outside world.

Some consider tribal economy as non-producing society, which subsists on gleaning, hunting and gathering forest produce. This 'primitive tribes' is a concept of the past and is similar to the category of 'band' (Sahlins, 1958). But in the modern producing society (consists of primary, secondary and tertiary sectors) tribes participate mainly in the agricultural activities. Tribes use indigenous tools in productive activities. They prefer to stick to their traditional method of production and try to resist all types of changes in respect of modern implements and techniques. Due to low level of technology, the tribal economy is backward and underdeveloped. Non-use of machineries and implements make the tribal agriculture labour intensive where labour is supplied on the basis of mutual co-operation and is done on communal basis. The tribal economy is community confined where all the members of the tribe are mutually interdependent in respect of both production and distribution. Such economic system denies individualism and binds them to live in unity. The tribal villages are autonomous but linked and maintain a sort of internal egalitarianism so they relate to other villages in a non-exploitative framework.

OBJECTIVE OF PRESENT STUDY AND RESEARCH—QUESTIONS

In the light of what we have discussed so far (particularly about the background of the study and the concept of social formation), the principal objective of the present study is to examine the issue of social formation in the case of the Lepchas from the economic perspective. As the Lepchas are basically dependent on agriculture for their sustenance, we proposed to study its production organisation and distributional aspects taking into consideration its economic and social frameworks. The main questions of the present study are:

a) How the Lepchas carry out their agricultural production by combining different forces? What are the patterns of land ownership among the Lepchas? Who enjoy the right over the use of land–the owner or the community? How the lands are transferred? Are there any systems of lease or contract or sharecropping? If so, what are their nature and relations with the landowner?

b) Who supply labour for agriculture? What are the modes of labour payment? Are there any mutual exchanges of labour? If yes, what are their nature and mode of operation? What types of labour are used in the different stages of agricultural operation? Are there any difference among labours on the basis of age and sex?

c) What are the nature and sources of capital used by the Lepchas? What types of tools and implements do they use in agricultural operations? How the animal labours are used and managed? Is there any exchange of animal labour among the villagers? What are the conditions of such exchange? How far the Lepchas adopt the new technology and innovation?

d) How the produced agricultural crops are distributed for consumption and market or non-market purposes? Are there any social obligations to meet with agricultural crop? Are there any religious obligations to meet?

e) What is the nature of Lepcha social formation? How far they fulfil the essentialist definition of tribe beside their administrative recognition and categorisation of Scheduled Tribe by the Constitution of India?

EARLIER ENQUIRIES ON LEPCHAS AND THEIR LIMITATIONS

Lepchas are little known community and the existing literature on them is neither systematic nor sufficient. Information available are ad hoc and piece meal in nature; occasionally romantic or political or administrative.

Anyway, Lepchas are not totally unknown and untouched by the scholars and writers both from within the country and outside. From the information available with us so far, the following research studies have been carried out for the award of different degrees from different universities in India and abroad.

A.K. Das (1978) conducted the first research study on the Lepchas for the award of Ph.D degree.[12] He gave mostly an ethnographic account of socio-economic and cultural condition of the Lepchas of West Bengal particularly of Darjeeling district. In the economic front, the author spared one chapter on the description of agricultural practice alongwith the variety of land and crops used. Beside this by using 1961 census data he briefly discussed about animal husbandry, gathering, fishing, hunting, handicraft among the Lepchas. He grouped Lepchas in five different economic categories– agriculturists, agricultural labour, daily labour, service holder and craftsman. With the aim of constructing a frame of present socio-cultural status of Lepcha society, the study could not devote much on economic aspects of the society. But as a first systematic research work, it is the pioneering study and gives a first hand information about Lepcha society.

The first Lepcha scholar, Sonam Wangdi Lepcha (1979) made a sociological study about the modernisation and change among the Lepchas. Despite the changes, he found that there is a definite persistence of the tribal identity among the Lepchas. Sonam submitted his dissertation for the Ph.D. degree from Bhagalpur University, but his work has remained unpublished till this day, though his supervisor, R.N. Thakur (1988) has brought out a book on the same subject incorporating every thing of Sonam's thesis. Regarding agricultural operations, it is said that Lepchas are poor agriculturists. They still follow bi-cropping pattern; paddy and maize are the principal crops.

Dry lands are used for maize and millet while wetland is meant for paddy cultivation. Although land is important in Lepcha society but on a number of slightest pretext such as marriage, bride price, poverty, religious practices etc., lands are being transferred to the Nepalese. The authors observed that in agriculture Lepchas are less modernised compared to other neighbouring communities. Although some Lepchas do cultivate modern crops like vegetables, fruits and flowers but *Namboon* (Lepcha New Year) and the consequent taboo on agriculture restrict them into two crops a year.

The study is unique in the sense that it is the first attempt to study the types of changes adopted in Lepcha society. It also touches upon some theoretical aspects of modernisation. A number of items like dress, religion, culture, marriage, education, health, political situation, food habit, marriage etc., do occupy some pages in both their studies, naturally, they could not provide enough attention for the changes specifically in agriculture.

Sumit Ghosal (1990) got his doctoral degree from North Bengal University for his work *The Lepchas of Darjeeling and Sikkim: A Study in cultural ecology and social change*. The basic objective of the study was to find the (a) nature of socio-economic, socio-cultural and institutional change, (b) adaptation of change in cultural-ecological situation, (c) inter-relationship of productive technology and extend of behaviour pattern entailed in subsistence activities. Surveying two villages (Nassay and Pagong Gumpha Goan) from Kalimpong and Lingdong (of Zongu reserve) from Sikkim, the scholar discussed elaborately the physical setting, the people and their ethno history, marital culture, economic context particularly agriculture, social organisation, political organisation, religion, cultural ecology and social change.

The study concluded by observing some changes that took place in Lepcha society, Lepchas have transformed from their hunting food gathering to settled plough cultivation. Lamaism has superimposed their animistic religion. Through intermarriage Tibetan culture entered in Lepcha society. Later on, the Lepchas could not resist the influence of Nepalis who settled in large number in Lepcha land. The Bhutias who came earlier and fewer in number are more interested in controlling the politics and the trans-Himalayan trade. The Nepalis, on the other hand, established their control over natural resources, particularly on land. This–immigration changed the ethnic composition, ethnic balance and power structure of the region. Inspite of dynamism in economic and religious sphere, the social structure of Lepchas remained static and quite unchanged. In the religious sphere the scholar has noticed the triangulation of *Bangthingism*, Buddhism and Christianity. Neither of the alien religion has ever taken deep roots. The scholar observed some effort in revitalising and maintaining Lepcha ethnic and cultural distinctiveness under the leadership of Lepcha Association. Ghosal concluded that unless the core element of their economy, the land, is allowed to be retained by them it will be difficult to achieve the target of regaining their ethnic pride and confidence [Ghosal, 1990:220-227].

Without mentioning either in the objective or entering details about the question, the scholar in his penultimate chapter suddenly raised the question of Lepchas in the tribe-peasant continuum. Under the subheading 'Shifting towards peasantry' (pp 208-219), the scholar attempted to show peasantry (following Redfield) from cultural and economic level. Without entering into the details, the thesis hints upon the interaction of Lepcha culture (local tradition) with the Buddhist culture (great tradition of the region). "At the economic level, the presence of market oriented cash economy and a complex land tenure system along with other peasant features bring them nearer to the peasant pole of the continuum. The transformation from tribe to peasantry, outside the Hindu society, has taken without caste being a referent group. The Lepchas who happened to be a member of tribal community in all its intent and purpose show definite signs of peasantry" [Ghosal, 1990: 216]. The thesis deserves some credit in giving for the first time the new dimension of change towards peasantry among the Lepchas. But it could not touch either upon the theoretical discourse of peasant-tribe social formation or their applicability with the Lepcha society.

Based on the first systematic anthropological work among the Lepchas of Lingthem village in Sikkim by John Morris and Geoffrey Gorer (1938),[13] Roshina Gowloog (1995), another Lepcha scholar, has conducted a diachronic study of the same villages after fifty years of original work to earn her doctoral degree from the Centre for

Himalayan Studies, North Bengal University. Beside different social and anthropological aspects of Lepcha life, both the authors deal with some aspects of their economic particularly agricultural practices at two different points of time. Gowloog has noticed some changes in the variety of crops and the methods of cultivation as noted by Gorer. Lepchas started using chemical fertiliser during Gowloog's survey period while Gorer's study was silent about such chemical fertilisers. But both of them observed prevalence of labour exchange in case of rice cultivation while hired labour for cardamom and other domestic purposes.

Beside the above research work, [14] one can find nearly hundred write-ups in the form of books and articles or references by different authors. These works can be found in the form of gazetteers and government reports, travelogues, journals, magazines and newspapers, folk tales and folklore's, ethnic affinity, linguistic and sociological and academic work etc.

However, the worth mentioning writers of Lepcha literature are: A Campbell (1840), J.D. Hooker (1855), Richard Temple (1875), G.B. Mainwaring (1876), H.H. Risley (1891), L.A. Waddell (1899), L.S.S.O'Malley (1907), Maharaja and Maharani Dolma of Sikkim (1908), C. de Beauvior Stocks (1927), John Morris (1938), Geoffrey Gorer (1938), Rene Von Nebesky-Wajkowitz (1956), R.K. Sprigg (1960, 1997, 1998), A.K. Das and S.K. Banerjee (1962), Chi Nakane (1966), H.R.J. Siiger (1967), Iman Singh Chemzon (1969), K.P. Tamsang (1973, 1980, 1983), G.C. Bagchi (1972), Gangaram Chattopadhyay (1982), A.R. Foning (1981), R.N. Thakur (1988), Tapan Chattopadhyay (1990), Lyangsang Tamsang (1997-2002), and the others.

Lepchas for the first time, from their role of guides to the foreigners travelling in this region, become the subject matter of any writings in the hand of A. Campbell (1940) in his article 'Note on the Lepchas of Sikkim with a Vocabulary of their language'. Although the basic purpose of the study was to describe the unknown country and its people to the outside world but it contains detailed information regarding their life and customs. Campbell's observation became so authentic that a number of later writers like Dalton, Hunter, Risley, and Das quoted him in a number of occasions. Campbell observed that

Lepchas were 'poor agriculturists, nomadic in their habits' with no settled land to cultivate and basically depended on forest for their food.

In the same line to those of Campbell authors like Hooker, and Temple viewed that they are 'grass eater' and "have no idea of cultivation beyond clearing a spot of virgin soil, and scrapping up its surface with the rudest of agricultural implements." [Temple, 1875: 19]

G.B. Mainwaring (1876), the first European who took pain in mastering the Lepcha language, developed for the first time a Lepcha grammar based on Latin principles. Before entering into the grammatical part, Mainwaring gave a general description of Lepcha life and their history. He stated about their 'primitive state, living in the midst of the vast, wild magnificent forests'. They usually practise shifting cultivation and 'rice is their stable food.' He also narrated in brief the role of forest on day-to-day life of Lepchas.

H.H. Risley (1891) deals with the various tribal groups of Bengal and could not devote intensively for any specific tribe. Clan, marriage, religion, panchayat system, death rituals are some of the sociological aspects of Lepchas where the author depends mainly on Campbell's study. He described Lepchas as 'poor agriculturists' but found rice and vegetables to cultivate in their non-permanent village set up.

In his travelogue *Among the Himalayas* beside describing precisely the history, physical status, religion, house, food items etc. of the Lepchas, Waddell (1899) narrated their economic life with a little bit of description about their agricultural practices. Lepchas 'represent the state of primitive man where they subsist on 'hunting, fishing and digging roots'. Waddell also observed the case of reservation of forest by the British rulers and its impact on the scarcity of food among the Lepchas. For the first time we find a sort of terrace farming among the Lepchas in Waddells writings. He writes Lepcha hut is "surrounded by a patch of cultivation – a few gourds, turnips and chilies and beyond this a few small crops of maize, barley, millet, for beer and a little terraced land for irrigated rice. This scanty cultivation, if it may be defined by such a term, is usually a mere scratching of the ground, and is done mostly by the woman, while the man did the hunting." [Waddell, 1899: 95-96]. Waddell also observes a barter system of exchange of some forest produce for salt and other articles but money was not a common medium and was used 'around their necks as an ornament'. Famine was practically unknown to the Lepchas as they depend on forest for food, cloth and housing.

In his gazetteer, O'Malley (1901), observes that Lepchas 'had to give up their old nomadic cultivation' due to reservation of forest. Like Waddell he also observes Lepchas to 'make terraces for rice fields' and giving up 'hoe for the plough'. Regarding the types of crop, O'Malley observes, "Lepchas mostly cultivate at the lower levels, and are particularly fond of cardamom cultivation at the bottom of the valleys". [O'Malley, 1907: 65]. They also cultivate wheat and barley.

As against switching over from shifting cultivation to terrace based settled cultivation among the Lepchas in Darjeeling areas, H.H. Maharaja and Maharani Dolma of Sikkim (1908) observed prevalence of shifting cultivation among the Lepchas in Sikkim. The authors for the first time hinted about the system of tax on Lepchas. The paragraph quoted by many on Lepcha agriculture is:

> A new patch of jungle would be cleared every year, and when dried set fire to. On the cleared space, paddy, kodo and bhutta, as well as various white and black grains would be sown. Next year another patch of jungle would be cleared. The virgin soil ofcourse yielded a very rich crop, and people used to gain their living very easily, and also enjoyed a good many sorts of fruits and herbs, which they cannot get now. As they had not much call on them for free labour neither contribution nor much of tax to pay, they were very happy [Nakane, 1966: 216].

Considering their folktales, folklores, myths and legends, C.de. Beauvoir Stocks (1927) made a departure in her study to discuss the life, birth, marriage, burial, death, customs, culture and other social and some economical aspects of Lepcha society. Stocks observed settled cultivation during her time and also mentioned in the footnote a system of tax to be paid by the cultivators:

> Taxes are very low, though they are on an average to what a peasant earns, amounting roughly to Rupees Thirteen eight annas per annum (about an English Pound) which include Rupees Three from every 'basti' claiming exemption from Coolie work. [Stocks, 1925: 476].

Rene Von Nebesky Wajkowitz (1956), the Austrian anthropologist and Tibetologist made an anthropological survey of Lepcha society during his stay in Kalimpong and Sikkim. Although his main concern was that of anthropological study, still he touched upon some agricultural practices like the type of crops and the pattern of cultivation among the Lepchas. His writings on agriculture might have been based on secondary sources and he mentioned about shifting cultivation even during the mid-twentieth century.

A somewhat hazy picture of the economic life of Lepchas can also be found from Chi Nakane's (1966) article – 'A Plural Society in Sikkim–A Study of the inter-relations of Lepchas, Bhotias and Nepalis.' This anthropological study based on three villages (Pubyuk, Phodang and Phensang) of eastern Sikkim. In case of anthropological work, Nakane compares her work with Gorer's findings in *Lepchas of Sikkim* while all information regarding agriculture are collected and quoted from *History of Sikkim* by H.H. Maharaja and Maharani Dolma of Sikkim.

Siiger's (1967) anthropological work published in two parts – I and II. Out of his experience with the Lepchas of Kalimpong and Sikkim, Part I describes mainly the socio-cultural and religious life in length while Part II comprises mainly the collection of songs. Regarding Lepcha agriculture, Siiger observes shifting cultivation from the works of Campbell, Hooker, Waddell etc. But his field survey finds settled terrace cultivation. Now-a-days agriculture, and especially the wet rice cultivation, furnishes the staple food of the Lepchas. The author also marks different varieties of crops like rice, maize, millet, buckwheat, wheat, potato, radish and various grains and fruits. But his study limits by mentioning the names of the crops Lepchas are cultivating.

Two Indian authors Lal Bahadur Basnet (1974) and Kamala Devi Chattopadhyay (1978) as a part of their main works do mention about the socio-economic life of the Lepchas. Basnet is more interested in mentioning the traditional system of shifting cultivation while Chattopadhyay is more concerned about the variety of crops in their contemporary periods.

Tapan Chattopadhyay's (1990) is a travelogue, in which interesting and faithful description of what he saw among the Lepchas in the course of his sojourn is available. In chapter four while describing Rong life cycle, he narrated some of the agricultural aspects of Lepcha society but no indepth study or any theoretical discourse of agriculture took place in his study.

Apart from these[15] a number of articles have been published on Lepchas in different magazines, newspapers, bulletins etc. but none of them deals with the basic question of the present study and hence they are not reviewed here. That the Lepchas are a tribe is implicit in all the works so far conducted on Lepchas. Not a single author engages in enquiring about their tribal identity. None of them attempt to test any hypothesis about their tribal character either from social, political or economic angle.

All the studies conducted so far on Lepchas may conveniently be folded under one broad category of 'ethnography'. Most of them are descriptive or anthropological account of Lepchas with a little bit of information here and there on their economic life and particularly their agricultural practices.

METHOD ADOPTED

In this section attempts have been made to give an idea about the methods, tools and techniques adopted, selection of villages, pattern of analysis, period and limitations of present study.

a) **Sources of Information**: For the present study both primary and secondary sources of information are used. However, emphasis has been given on first hand information directly collected from the Lepchas engaged in agriculture.

Primary data have been collected personally from three villages with the help of field guide. In our study, village is the unit of enquiry and not the object. It is not a comparative study of Lepchas living in three types of villages. The principal aim is to study the Lepcha economy in the context of three villages. The knowledgable persons of each village like the village headman, mandal, panchayat member, educated person etc. acted as our key informants in providing first hand information about the village. In the village all the households are listed. All of them are interviewed with the household schedule containing a set of questions on economic activities of the household.

The office bearers of Lepcha Association, Headquarters, Kalimpong have been interviewed to gather some qualitative information about the community.

Secondary data have been used as and when required mainly to show the status of Lepchas and their economic condition. Census documents have been used for demographic details and industrial classification of Lepchas. Ethnographic details have been collected from the available literature. History of the region and community has critically been examined from the earlier literature, folk tales and hearsay.

b) **Selection of Villages**: Villages for the present study have been selected from Kalimpong sub-division of Darjeeling district. It has been noted that in West Bengal most of the Lepchas are concentrated in the hilly region of Kalimpong. By using different sources (like Census (1991), Rahul Sankrityayana (1941), Lepcha Association etc.) a list[16] of Lepcha inhabited villages was prepared. Considering distance from the town or market place and religious dominance, three villages have purposively been selected on practical consideration and convenience.

Two villages have been taken from nearby areas but each one is dominated absolutely by either of the two major religious faiths – Christianity and Buddhism. The third village located far away from the town is inhabited by the Lepchas belonging to both the religious groups.

c) **Tools and Technique**: To meet our objectives we have collected both quantitative and qualitative information.

Quantitative information has been gathered from each of the household. As all villages are small, although sparsely populated, we have considered census technique most suitable than sampling. All the villages have been completely enumerated with the help of household schedule. Household level primary data have been obtained by direct interview preferably with the head of the family.

During our conduct of household survey we have used the observation technique for recording certain events, practices, material conditions etc. Instead of participant observation, close observation seems to be more suitable and feasible for the present study.

Qualitative information, which is more important in effecting the social formation among the Lepchas, has been obtained through observation. Sometimes we did participate in a variety of socio-cultural, religious and ritual events organised both at the individual and social levels. We, as invitee and non-invitee, never missed any such social, cultural events in any of the three villages. All ethno-cultural activities on the community level observed and performed under the organisation of Lepcha Association, Kalimpong are also attended and investigated most carefully.

d) **Pattern of analysis:** Data collected both from the primary and secondary sources have been later analysed and presented in simple tabular form. No sophisticated statistical techniques are used for the study. Secondary data collected for demographic profile are used to show the status and position of the Lepchas in the state of West Bengal and Sikkim. Industrial classification of Lepchas of West Bengal collected from Census documents are used to analyse their economic condition.

The qualitative information gathered from the field survey, key informants, linkmen and existing literature are analysed and interpreted mostly to judge their social embeddedness of the Lepcha economy. All information provided by the key informants are put to cross-examination and analysed minutely to get the most appropriate result. Observations regarding village or community are being discussed with the field guides and the key informants to get their opinion. The portfolio holders of Lepcha Association are consulted to gather qualitative information and their opinion in a number of cases have been recorded and analysed with due importance.

e) **Period of Study**: We have divided the project in two broad phases, collection cum processing of data, and analysis of data. Secondary data have been gathered much before going to the villages for collecting primary data. Existing literature have been reviewed at the initial stage of the study.

In choosing period for the field survey, we have covered a complete agricultural calendar year so as to investigate the total process of agriculture. Both the quantitative and qualitative data have been collected for the agricultural practices during the period February –

March 1999 to August–September 2001 and, thus, covers a complete circle of agricultural calendar year.

f) **Limitations of the Study**: We cannot claim our study to be a complete analysis of Lepcha social formation. No such study can claim perfection and ours' is no exception to that.

In the present study we have tried to identify Lepcha social formation from the economic angle. Any question centering on social formation needs to be examined from multi-dimensions taking into consideration their economic, political, social, historical, linguistic, religious angles. Economic dimension is only one aspect of such a concept. As the present study is time bound and individually organised and financed, we could not take into account other aspects of social formation.

As most of the Lepchas are primarily agriculturists, we have explained mainly the role of agrarian economy in social formation of Lepchas. Beside agriculture, the nature and composition of other types of economy have not been discussed with equal weightage.

We have purposively selected three villages only from Kalimpong subdivision. By increasing the number of both villages and people, a more extensive work may help to get a complete picture of Lepcha social formation.

As Lepchas are simple and close to nature no sophisticated technique other than census, in-depth interview and non-participant observation seems to be suitable. Many aspects of social relations and attributes peculiar to the society can only be investigated through direct touch with the community. Many aspects of such society may be very symbolic or happens without any apparent causal relation with other: the best method, we consider for such happenings, is close observation and direct inter action. But we could not do justice because of our certain limitations.

PLAN OF PRESENTATION

The Chapters of the present study are planned on the basis of the objectives and the questions raised in the earlier section of the present write up. Chapters are arranged and designed in such a manner that each one deals with a set of questions and tries to find the possible answers connected with the Lepcha social formation. However, the broad frameworks of chapterisation are as follows:

In the introductory chapter, as must have already been noticed by now; we have raised some fundamental problems associated with the recognition of any community as scheduled tribe by the Constitution of India. The study of social formation, we propose, may help in identifying the attributes or characters required for an essentialist definition of tribe. We then discussed the conceptual details, as available, of social formation in general and tribal social formation in particular. Some questions connected with the principal objective of the study are being raised. A brief review of existing literature on Lepchas is conducted with the purpose of showing the relevance of the present study. We concluded the chapter, by narrating the methods adopted for the study.

The basic aim of the Second Chapter is to introduce the people and the study area. The meanings of the name of the community, geographical boundary, history of the people, demographic profile are narrated in brief. Using the census data industrial classification of Lepchas has been shown for the state of West Bengal. The section on description of the study area contains the location of the village, population, number of households, religion, education etc. Involvement of the villagers in agricultural and non-agricultural activities and consideration of agriculture as principal and subsidiary sources of occupation have been discussed in brief.

In our Third Chapter attempts have been made to judge the social formation among the Lepchas with land as the central unit of attention. Land has been focused from a number of angles like types, rent, record, transfer, ownership, genealogy, holding pattern, landscape etc. Detailed discussions have been carried out on ownership pattern of land. A relation between owner and user of land has been investigated. The case of sharecropping or contractual lease has been dealt with. The terms and conditions of sharecropping have been explored with due care.

The core item of discussion of the Fourth Chapter is labour connected with Lepcha agriculture. After discussing some items like type of labour, supply of labour etc., we enter into the typical type of mutual exchange of labour as practiced by the Lepchas in both traditional and contemporary agriculture.

Finance, another characteristic feature, by which tribal social formation can be identified, has been examined at length in our Fifth Chapter. Beside the major institutional sources of capital, the type and pattern of domestic capital have been analysed. The various types of both traditional and modern tools and implements used in agriculture are narrated and shown with sketch. The management of bullock, another important capital item of agriculture along with the nature and method of exchange has been discussed. The chapter ends with the description of adoption of new technique and innovation by the Lepchas.

From production we turn to distribution of agricultural produce in our penultimate Sixth Chapter. How the major agricultural produce mainly the food items, besides being utilised for consumption, are distributed to meet the obligations of kinship, seed, payment to exchange labour etc. have been analysed. We have extensively discussed the major two obligations (social and ritual) for which the agricultural products are distributed. Separate discussion has been made for ritual obligations among the Buddhists and the Christians.

Chapter Seven is our concluding chapter where we have jotted down the major findings of all the chapters. We have tried to establish a link among all the chapters so as to identify the type of Lepcha social formation.

NOTES

1. The two concepts of mode of production and social formation are so interconnected and interwoven with each other that 'some authors have given a broader meaning to the concept mode of production, confusing it, in a way, with a socio-economic formation [Berdichewsky, 1979: 9; Bottomore, 1983: 445]. But mode of production is only one component of social formation. Sometimes the social formation may not be in conformity with the particular mode of production. Social formation of other modes beside the dominant mode of production, whether as hangover from the past or precursor of the future, may be present simultaneously. It has also been emphasised that during the transitional phase of any society, a type of 'hybrid' social formation, combining the attributes of two or more modes of production may be experienced simultaneously.

2 .Economy, the basic component, along with the socio-cultural components gives a complete shape of any social formation. As the social formation centres around economic activity some writers like Bernardo Berdichewsky, Jozet Witezynski, Torn Bottomore etc. have preferred to call it socio-economic formation giving more emphasis on the economic aspects of social formation. Godelier on his study of the Inca Empire in the sixteenth century have used the term 'social and economic formation'.

3. The concept mode of production was first introduced by Marx (in A contribution to the Critique of Political Economy) and later on used by his followers like Stalin (in Economic Problems of Socialism in the USSR). All the key concepts of Marxian thought centre around the concept of mode of production which is constituted by two elements–(i) forces of production and (ii) relations of production. The mode of production, according to Marx, determines the structure of any society, which is affected by the superstructure to give the specific socio-economic formation of any society. With the change of society from one mode of production to another, socio-economic formation also got changed. In antagonistic or class formation, socio-economic formation may be constituted by more than one mode of production, one mode being dominant. Sometimes socio economic formation may not be in conformity with the particular mode of production. Socio-economic formation of other modes beside the dominant mode may co-exist simultaneously.

4. The forces of production are one of the two components of mode of production. In Marxian ideology, the means of production (especially the man-made instruments of production) and labour power applied in the process of production of material goods are termed as forces of production. It shows how human labour power and natural resources are used for production. The natural resources consist of items such as soil, fertility, water power, stream, petroleum even present day nuclear power alongwith scientific and technical knowledge etc.. Of all the forces of production, the instruments of labour are considered to be the most decisive element in production and the development of these forces are always initiated by improvements in the instruments and also determines the level and character of the society. The Marxian analysis stresses the technical aspects of production, which in a sense corresponds roughly to the western concept of factors of production.

5. One of the two elements, which together with forces of production determine the mode of production, is relations of production. It is a social aspect of production, which considers the relationship between the owners of means of production and the management on the one hand, and the workers on the other. For example, the relationship between master and slave, serf and lord, proletariat and bourgeois etc. are known as relations of production. The three factors, which govern relations of

production, are (i) the form of the ownership of means of production, (ii) the position of different social groups in production, and (iii) the pattern of distribution of production and income. The relation affects the distribution and consumption of produced goods and services. Changes in relations of production are conditioned by changes in production forces. In case the two cannot match, a violent social revolution may generate which is more acute in antagonistic socio-economic formation. It is claimed that under socialism, where means of production are in the hands of the state, such contradictions are the minimum.

6. In the Marxian literature base refers to the economic system with its production relations in the material sphere at a given stage of society's development. It is also alternatively being known as substructure or understructure. The nature and relations of base with superstructure determine the social development and class relations. Being dynamic in character base, over the different stages of development may contradict with the relations of production. In capitalist society base refers to the private ownership of means of production and exploitation of hired labour. But in socialism base and superstructure operate cordially without any serious disparities between the two.
7. The superstructure together with the material base constitutes the socio-economic formation of any society. This Marxian concept is used to denote the totality of philosophical, ethnical, cultural, political and legal ideas, attitudes and the associated network of institutions and organisations of any society. The attitude and interest of the ruling class is reflected through superstructure. The base and the society directly determine it. In a class society the superstructure is guided and maintained as per the interest of the ruling class. Under socialism it is utilised on a planned basis to respond and anticipate desirable change in the base by the state authority.
8. Ours is a revised tabular form of Ronald Frankenberg's (p-83) anthropological classification of society. We have categorised the society economically by including Malinowski and excluding Sahlin's (1958) political classification of band, tribe, chiefdorn and state.
9. Inspite of differences one can draw a parallel line between Marx and Malinowski on the concept of aim of production. Both have accepted that the concept of individual profit is applicable for the western developed countries where production is more individualistic in nature. Marx as 'Shopkeepers view of man' has already described Malinowski's 'gimwali'.
10. In tribal social formation the production, distribution and consumption are so closely related that it is not only difficult but almost impossible to separate each of the components from the other. Even then, some social scientists for experimental purposes go on trialing and separating production from distribution or consumption. In the present study we

have also attempted with a separate discussion just to show whether such type of separation in the watertight textbook pattern is possible or not.

11. Marx and Engels rarely used the terms 'tribe' and 'tribal' and never defined or analysed the 'tribal social formation' as a distinct type of society. The concept "tribe should not be used with reference to the various types of static social formations that have emerged historically (Asiatic, ancient, feudal, capitalistic, and socialistic) but there is no reason to abandon the term with reference to stateless or primitive societies... A tribal society, thus, is a primitive society in its fundamental characteristics" [Bottomore, 1983: 488-489].

12. A.K. Das was awarded doctoral degree for his work on Lepchas by the Calcutta University and later on published his thesis in book form entitled *The Lepchas of West Bengal in 1978*. A.K. Das co-authored with S.K. Banerjee published their first book *The Lepcha of Darjeeling District in 1962*. The doctoral thesis of A.K. Das is an enlarged and revised form of their joint earlier work on Lepchas of Darjeeling.

13. *Living with the Lepchas* by Moris and *The Himalayan Village* by Gorer have been published in 1938 and are so far richest ethnographic texts of the Lepchas. Both Morris and Gorer, the two British anthropologists, stayed together in Lingthem village of Dzongu reserved for the Lepchas in Sikkim. Gorer has used psychological or personalistic categories to understand the Lepcha culture while Morris depicts the life and culture of the village more as a travelogue than a scholarly treatise [Gowloog, 1995: 9]. Both the authors spend much time in discussing Lepcha family life, sex, festivals, magical practices, religious ceremonies etc. and find little space in elaborating their economic activities and hence are not much relevant for the present study. But as an anthropological study these are the best books and are so important that even after 50 years Roshina Gowloog got her doctoral degree on diachronic study of these books.

14. The above four research studies are to some extent relevant for us. Beside this some scholars carried out their study on Lepcha language, literature and religion for their award of doctoral or other degrees.Prabhakar Sinha received his doctoral degree from Deccan College in Pune in 1966 for his work on *Descriptive Grammar of Lepcha*. [H. Kloss: 1073]. Helen Plaisier conducted her research work on Lepcha language and literature and collected information during her stay in Kalimpong. Details of Helen's work are not available but the information that she is working on Lepcha literature can be available through Internet www. lepcha.com. Paul Lepcha submitted his thesis *A Study of the Scottish Mission work in Kalimpong – Subdivision with special reference to the Lepcha Tribe* to the faculty of the Union Biblical Seminary, Pune, Maharashtra for the completion of his degree of Bachelor of Divinity in 1999. The study highlights the

Scottish Missionary work among the Lepchas, their contribution to the socio-economic, cultural, religious life and the aspect of future evangelism of non-Christian Lepchas. Anthony Lepcha has submitted a dissertation on *The Lepchas and their language and culture in the Darjeeling and Sikkim hills*–A Study for partial fulfillment of his master degree in Nepali under NBU in 2001. The dissertation written in Nepali tries to show the importance of Lepcha language in the region. All these religious or linguistic studies are not directly relevant for the present study.

15. Two Lepcha authors describe the past and present account of their own culture, K.P. Tamsong (1983), a Buddhist by religion was well acquainted with the traditional Lepcha culture and customs. He touched upon the language, religion, culture; house etc. of Lepcha society without any single reference to their economic reference. Readers can smell the author's ethnic touch in all his writings. A.R. Foning (1981), who himself is a Christian Lepcha, wrote another insider's account of the social practices of the Lepchas, particularly their rites de passage and religious beliefs. The work gained some popularity among the outside readers but the Lepchas particularly the Buddhist Lepchas outrightly rejected it on grounds of using the word vanishing and also some customs not original for the Lepchas.

16. The following table shows Sankrityayana's [1950: 56-57] break up of Lepcha and Bhutia population for 30 villages of Kalimpong *Khas Mahal* area.

Rong, Bhutia Population of Kalimpong *Khas Mahal*–1941.

Sl. No.	Village	*Rong* (Lepcha)	Bhutia
1.	North Kalimpong	540	11
2.	Bong	234	10
3.	Dungra	111	317
4.	Bhalukhop	187	27
5.	Sindepong	194	35
6.	Echhay	96	163
7.	Sangsay	285	51
8.	Dalapchand	85	105
9.	Lolay	339	06
10.	Pala	128	04
11.	Santuk	109	46
12.	Peyong	89	357

(contd.)

Sl. No.	Village	*Rong* (Lepcha)	Bhutia
13.	Sakyong	284	495
14.	Kagay	120	25
15.	Pedong Bazar	84	243
16.	Kerchang	331	34
17.	Ladong	67	19
18.	Lingsekha	260	26
19.	Lingsey	137	94
20.	Seokbir	155	-
21.	Kangeybong	391	02
22.	Sinjee	238	-
23.	Samalbong	135	-
24.	Samthar	248	-
25.	Suruk	105	-
26.	Yangmakung	281	-
27.	Gitdabling	665	07
28.	Gitbeong	123	28
29.	Nimbong	141	90
30.	Todey Tangta	163	182
31.	Others	384	29
	Total	6609	2406

A perusal of the above table reveals the following:

Lepcha population is 2.75 times more than Bhutia population in Kalimpong *Khas Mahal.*

There is no village without Lepcha but there are at least 7 villages where no single Bhutia is found.

Village-wise Lepchas are dominating over the Bhutia population in all the villages except only 7 such villages.

Bhutia dominated villages are located on both the sides of the main road from Kalimpong to Oodlabari via Lava, Garubathan. These hamlets might have been settled during the Bhutan rule in the area during 1700–1865.

Lepcha population is concentrating more in the far-flung villages, which are lacking in any approachable road or any other communication. In search of safe places during the oppression of Tibetan, Bhutan and

European reigns, Lepchas might have preferred to corner themselves in these remote areas of Kalimpong *Khas Mahal*.

The highest concentration of Lepchas is found in Gitdabling village, which may be termed as the present day *Mayal Lyang* for the Kalimpong Lepchas. If the government of West Bengal or the Darjeeling Gorkha Hill Council attempts to reserve any area for the aboriginal Lepchas of Darjeeling district like that of Dzongu in Sikkim, Gitdabling will be the best choice.

Instead of any village level information regarding any specific tribe like that of Lepcha, the census department has published information regarding the Scheduled Tribe population for the year 1991. Any intensive study of this figure may help in gathering a working knowledge of Lepcha population in different *mausas* of Kalimpong.

Population of Kalimpong Developmental Block-I as per Census–1991

Sl. No.	*Mouza*	Total population	Total Scheduled Tribe	Scheduled Tribe as percentage of total population
1	2	3	4	5
1.	Bong	3303	724	21.92
2.	Dungra	4642	434	4.44
3.	Sindcpong	3256	544	16.71
4.	Pundung	1776	100	5.63
5.	Echhey	3200	528	16.5
6.	Bhalukhop	3791	288	7.59
7.	Dr. G. Homes	2656	251	9.45
8.	Tashiding	6720	1254	18.66
9.	Teesta	2203	78	3.54
10.	Rambi Bazer	643	06	0.93
11.	Reyong	204	-	-
12.	Suntaley	212	-	-
13.	Seekbir	1057	216	20.44
14.	Yok printem	914	34	3.72
15.	Kafier	978	314	32.11
16.	Kankebong	867	343	39.56

(contd.)

1	2	3	4	5
17.	Samalbong	1884	298	15.99
18.	Lolaygoan	788	44	5.58
19.	Sinjee	1242	460	37.08
20.	Samthar	1682	489	29.07
21.	Suruk	1540	313	20.32
22.	Yongmakum	2548	834	32.73
23.	Nimbong	2860	798	29.90
24.	Pemling	933	411	44.05
25.	Paringtar	1445	60	4.15
26.	Nabgaon	1510	173	11.46
27.	Chunabhati	482	06	1.25
	Total	35166	8985	16.89

Source: Cultural and Information Centre, Kalimpong, Government of West Bengal.

A perusal of table reveals the following: Scheduled Tribes are present in all the *mausas* except two, which are located, near the plains and tea garden areas.

High rate of ST population is inversely related with high rate of total population of different *mausas*. Pembling is having highest (44.35%) of ST population but its total population is as low as 933 only while Dungra processes low population of ST (4.44%) but its total population is one of the highest 4642.

Percentages of ST population are more in those *mausas*, which are located in the remote areas, far away from the sub-divisional town. It has been reported that these *mausas* like Pembling, Yangmakung, Sinjee, Kankebong, Kafier etc. are dominated either absolutely or mostly by the Lepchas.

CHAPTER TWO

THE PEOPLE AND THE STUDY AREA: AN OVERVIEW

The present chapter has been subdivided in two sections. The first section deals with the general information about the Lepchas obtained from census, existing literature or other subsidiary sources. In the second section, we have tried to introduce our study area with the help of survey data.

THE PEOPLE

The basic purpose of the present section is to introduce the Lepchas whose social formation we have intended to identify. The name of the community, area of inhabitation, history of the land and people, demographic profile etc., have been detailed out here.

Name of the Community

Generally speaking most tribes in the world are known by two sets of names–(i) exoethnonym, the name by which the neighbours or outsiders recognise the tribe and remain popular in the outside world and (ii) endoethnonym, the name the tribe use to identify them. Lepchas are no exception to this and there are various explanations to these two sets of names among the scholars and writers. Without entering into the controversy, which may unnecessarily detain us, let us accept their exoethnonym. Be whatever it may be for all practical purposes the community is recognised by their exoethnonym. Even some of them use it as their surname. The Constitution of India for its classificatory purpose into the category of Scheduled Tribe recognises the community by its exoethnonym.

The exoethnonym of the community under consideration is Lepcha. Their endoethnonym is *Mutanchi Rongkup Runkup* or in short *Rong* which means the son of the snowy peak, the Son of God. This may be related to the tribal attribute of 'common name' [Morgan; Singh Grewal, 1992: 5] and original and oldest inhabitants of the land [Pathy, 1984: 6].

Boundary of Lepcha Inhabited Land

From various sources both written and oral, hearsay accounts and folktales, customs and tradition, R.N. Thakur [p.37] demarcates the boundary of Lepcha land in the older days. In the north it was extended upto Kanchenjunga while Jalpaiguri in the south. In the east it was extended upto river Rudok at Paru valley under the Ha province of Bhutan and the western boundary was spread upto Ruchong and Runga (Arun and Tambur) river making boundary with Nepal. Lyangsong Tamsang opined that Lepcha land was extended upto Titalia now in Bangladesh. Titalia is a Lepcha word means 'to retreat'. In a battle between Sikkim Raj and Nepal Raj, the Lepcha battalion chased the Gorkha force upto Titaliya from where they had to come back. Lepchas used to call their own land *Ne Mayal Lyang* or *Mayal Lyang* – the land of the holy and eternal purity having the rule of the honourable people.

The observation of different scholars and authors [like Dozey, O'Malley, Donaldson, Bell, Mainwaring etc.] regarding the intimate relation of Lepchas with all the animate and inanimate objects of Sikkim Himalayas, unequivocally establish that Lepchas are the indigenous people of the region. They were completely dependent on forest for their day-to-day life and were using land without any restrictions imposed from any side. But different alien communities like Tibetan, Bhutanese, Europeans, and Nepalis etc. had overrun the indigenous group, in different periods of time. In the process they have been scattered, cornered and become minority in their own land.

At present, Lepchas, the autochthonous people of the Eastern Himalayas, spread over the hilly regions of Darjeeling, Sikkim, Eastern Nepal and Western Bhutan. Majority of them reside in Sikkim; in Darjeeling spatial concentration is found in Kalimpong sub-division; in Bhutan and Nepal the proportion of Lepchas are very negligible.

Short History of the People

The spread of Lepcha population over the three different countries India, Nepal and Bhutan, is not due to their migratory character but due to the political history of the region. Political change and corresponding reshuffling of boundaries forced the Lepchas to be ruled by different authorities at different times or at the same time by different authorities at different places. Let us discuss in brief the political change in the region historically and see how the Lepchas in their own land got separated among themselves.

Lepcha king *Turvey* or *Turvey Punu* (king), the notable figure in Lepcha history reigned the *Ne Mayal Lyang* during 1420 approximately. After *Turvey Punu*, another if not the last leading spiritual figure was *Thi-Kung-Tek*. The 'Blood Treaty' signed between *Thi-Kung-Tek* and *Khye-Bumsa*, Tibetan counterpart, paved the way for long lasting Tibetan suzerainty over Sikkim. This treaty ultimately paved the way for Phuntso Namgyal who officially ascended the throne of Sikkim in 1642. The historical Blood Treaty, thus, coolly arrested the Lepchas, the yeoman of the soil, under the reign of the Tibetans, the first alien ruler of the region.

With some ups and downs in their relation with the monarch, Lepchas still inhabited in their own land obviously under the rule of Namgyal dynasty, the Tibetan rulers. The Bhutanese made the first artificial cleavage between Lepchas of Sikkim and Kalimpong. Bhutan attacked Sikkim and fought with Lepcha king *Punu Gaeboo-Achyok* at Damsang area and ultimately occupied the entire land including the Kingdom from 1700 to 1707. Later on at the request from Dalai Lama, the religious supreme of Bhutan and Sikkim, Bhutan returned from Sikkim but refused to evacuate the Damsang area i.e. east of Teesta presently known as Kalimpong. Thus, since 1707 Lepchas of Kalimpong permanently came under the Bhutanese rule while the Tibetans ruled their brothers and relatives on the other part of Teesta. Lepchas, although ruled by the Tibetans, were the dominant community in Sikkim while in Bhutan their proportion was very negligible and were treated second-class citizen by the ruler.

The third division among the Lepchas of Sikkim occurred in 1835 through an agreement between the East India Company and the King of Sikkim. Through this agreement, the Rajah of Sikkim presented Darjeeling to the company out of friendship to construct a sanatorium for the British soldiers. All the lands south of the Great Runjeet River, east of the Balasur, Kahail, and Little Rangeet Rivers, and west of Rungno and Mahanuddi Rivers came under the control of East India Company. This grant not only further divides the Lepcha land but also its inhabitants particularly the Lepchas. This political division again segregated Lepchas in their own land. The Lepcha as a community came under three different alien rulers – Tibetans in Sikkim, Bhutanese in Damsang area and British in Darjeeling area.

The fourth political reshuffling occurred in 1865 when Kalimpong and the adjoining areas were taken over by the British from the Bhutan through a war. The British Company administered the entire area of Darjeeling including Kalimpong from its Headquarters at Darjeeling. Due to this political change, Lepchas of Kalimpong and Darjeeling areas came under the same political authority. But some Lepchas across the boundary on the Bhutan still remain under the rule of Bhutanese. They still remain separated from their counterpart residing in present Darjeeling including Kalimpong and Sikkim. Lepchas in Bhutan became insignificant compared to other community. At this stage also three foreign rulers – Tibetans in Sikkim, Bhutanese in Bhutan and Britishers in Darjeeling including Kalimpong ruled Lepchas.

Another political change occurred in August 1947 when India acquired independence. In the state of West Bengal Lepchas remained insignificant (population wise). Even in their own homeland Darjeeling, by this time they became minority due to the then British policy of inviting Nepalese from Nepal. Calcutta or Delhi became the administrative headquarter for the Lepchas of Darjeeling, Gangtok for Lepchas of Sikkim and Thimpu for the Lepchas of Bhutan. Lepchas have no role at all to play in any of these administrative headquarters.

It has been reported that some Lepchas are residing along the western part of Bhutan where the country borders with Kalimpong sub-division of India. But no details regarding the strength of population, attitude of the monarch towards the community, role of the community in administration etc. are available. Hence, we leave any further discussion on Lepchas of Bhutan by recongising their presence in that country.

Lepchas witness another political change when the state of Sikkim from its monarchical rule merged with India as a separate state in 14th May 1975. Sikkim is the only state in India where majority of Lepchas reside. But their population compared to the total population of the state is not appreciable because of immigration of Nepalese and Tibetans during the monarchical rule. Considering the original homeland of Lepchas, the state of Sikkim has reserved Dzongu, an area of 15,845 hectares specifically for the Lepchas. No other community, tribal or non-tribal, is allowed to reside permanently in Dzongu. In true sense, Dzongu is the present day *Mayal Lyang* for the Lepchas where land had not been alienated to any other community. They also use their own language at home and observe most of traditional customs and culture. The total area under the present day *Mayal Lyang* thus confined to 15,845 hectares with a population of 7745 including 3414 seasonal labours from Nepal as per 1981 census. Dzongu falls in the north district of Sikkim, which is bounded by Nepal in the west, Tibet in the north and other three districts of Sikkim in the south. Lepchas of Sikkim, thus, politically changed from monarchical rule to a democratic process. But they are under the same union government like those of Darjeeling areas. At this stage Lepchas were residing in India in the states of West Bengal and Sikkim.

In the recent past Lepchas of Darjeeling district had to face another change when the three sub-divisions came under the direct administration of Darjeeling Gorkha Hill Council (DGHC) since 1988. After violent agitation, DGHC was formed through democratic procedure within the state of West Bengal. In case of policy-making and administration, Lepchas of Darjeeling are at present in a different position than the Lepchas in Sikkim. Here in Darjeeling under DGHC, Lepchas are facing Panchayat at the village level, DGHC at the district level, State Government at the state level and ultimately the Central Government at the all India level.

Beside all these, since long past some Lepchas are residing in Ilam areas of Nepal. Ilam is situated on the extreme eastern Nepal bordering with Darjeeling and Sikkim.

Three arguments may be put for the existence of Lepchas in Nepal. Firstly, it may be inferred that once upon a time the Lepcha land, *Mayal Lyang* might have been extended up to Ilam. Several attacks by the

Gorkhas and counter attacks by the Lepchas or Namgyal Dynasty constantly changed the geographical boundary of both the monarchical states of Sikkim and Nepal. History of the region also witnessed a number of wars organised mainly by the Gorkhas to encroach the neighbouring lands. Ilam might have been seised by the Gorkhas from Sikkim before the Sikkim Puttee Rajah presented the Lepcha populated areas of the Darjeeling to East India Company in 1835. All the lands of Ilam including its inhabitants, thus, separated from their fellow countrymen in Darjeeling and Sikkim areas and were controlled by the monarchical rule of Nepal. Secondly, the simple Lepchas of *Mayal Lyang* particularly Damsang areas could not resist the constant oppression by the Bhutanese from the east. Bhutan occasionally plundered these areas and took away both the assets and women to Bhutan. In search of a safe place, a group of peace loving common Lepchas might have migrated towards the west and took shelter in Ilam areas, which is far away from Bhutan. Thirdly, traditionally Lepchas used to practise shifting cultivation. In the slash and burn methods they usually cultivate a plot of land for 3-5 years and left it vacate to allow jungle to grow for the next 8-10 years. In the process of shifting from one place to another, a group of Lepchas might have been stayed back and settled permanently in Ilam areas of Nepal.

The above discussion on short history of the Lepchas brings two things to note in connection to their tribal social formation. The evidence of the rule of some kings in the Lepcha history negates their tribal social formation. The kings like *Turvey Punu* (1420), *Thi-kung-Tek* (1600), *Gaeboo-Achyok-Punu* (1700) and perhaps others showed the presence of monarchical rule in traditional Lepcha society. But politically tribes deny the existence of such king but there may be some chiefs[1] who may collect some revenues and protect the fellow tribes from external attacks. Secondly, *Mayal Lyang*, the traditional Lepcha dominated geographical area supports the tribal attribute of territorial boundary[2] for the Lepchas. In the earlier days, the region (Sikkim, Darjeeling hills, east of Nepal and west of Bhutan), where the Lepchas are found at present might have been ruled by the same Lepcha chief. In course of time, Lepchas lost their land to the neighbouring countries through war or negotiations. The rule over the region went on changing constantly and different political authorities rule the Lepchas on their own land. But the specific geographical area fulfils one of the basic attributes of Lepcha tribal social formation.

Demographic Profile

Without demographic details, the study of any community remains incomplete. But no systematic records of population over the three countries (India, Nepal and Bhutan) are available and whatever information available is scanty and collected by different authorities at different point of time. However, no demographic details are available for the country of Bhutan. In Nepal, Lepchas are considered as 'minor ethnic group'. Their total strength as per 1991 census is 4,826, which constituted 0.03 per cent of total population. [Niroula, 1998: 15-56].

The demographic profile of Lepchas is available for India and Sikkim only after Britishers occupied the region. Lepcha population remained scanty from the very beginning. When Britishers first came in the place they found the land inhabited only by Lepchas. On 1st Feb., 1835 when Darjeeling was handed over to East India Company by the Sikkim Puttee Rajah, "there was a collection of 20 huts with a population of 100 souls" [Dozey, 1916: 48]. When the Britishers from Bhutanese annexed Kalimpong in 1865, it had a population of 1200 souls but no specification of Lepchas is available.

Table 2.1 shows Lepcha population for the state of West Bengal and Darjeeling.

In the state of West Bengal, Lepchas are concentrated in the district of Darjeeling since the bygone days. But their percentage in their own homeland compared to the total population of the district is not at all notable. Due to large number of immigration, the Lepchas in their own homeland become such a negligible fraction of the total population that a comparative study of Lepcha population vis-à-vis the total population of the district is worthy to mention here.

The percentage of Lepcha population to total population of the district of Darjeeling remained very negligible from the beginning of the last century. In percentage term their proportion is also decreasing over the decades. But when the Britishers came in this region, they found that the majority of population was Lepchas.

Table 2.1: Lepcha Population: West Bengal and Darjeeling District by Census year[3]

	Lepcha Population			
	West Bengal		Darjeeling	
Year	Total	Ten years	Total	% of W.B. Population
1872	3952	-	3952	100.00
1881	26	-	NA	-
1891	9717	2882.5	9717	100.00
1901	10052	335	9972	99.2
1911	9842	-210	9706	98.62
1921	9669	-173	9669	100.00
1931	12719	3050	12101	95.14
1941	12468	-251	12468	100.00
1951	13430	962	13168	98.02
1961	15309	1879	14510	94.78
1971	14568	-741	13536	92.92
1981	23409	8841	22749	97.18
1991	27888	4449	26920	96.53
2001	32377	4489	31210	96.39

Source:

1. For the period 1872 to 1951, Census of India, West Bengal 1951, P.115
2. For 1961, Census of India, West Bengal Part V-A (ii) Special tables on Scheduled Tribe 1961.
3. For 1971, Census of India, West Bengal. Special Table on Scheduled Tribe 1971. P. 268.
3. For 1981, Census of India, West Bengal. Series – 23 Part IX (IV) Special Tables for Scheduled Tribes. PP. 78-90.
4. For 1991, Information received over telephone from the Office of Census Operation, Calcutta, West Bengal.

Lepchas of Sikkim

Any study on Lepcha remains incomplete if we do not take into account the case of Sikkim where the majority of Lepchas reside in the greater part of their original homeland, *Mayal Lyang*. The following Table 2.3 shows Lepcha population vis-a-vis other population in the state of Sikkim during the last half of nineteenth century.

Table 2.2: Total population vis-à-vis Lepcha population of Darjeeling

Year	Total Population of the District	Lepcha Population	Percentage of Lepcha to total population
1901	249117	9772	3.92
1911	265550	9706	3.65
1921	282748	9669	3.41
1931	319635	12101	3.78
1941	376369	12468	3.31
1951	445260	13164	2.95
1961	624640	14510	2.32
1971	781777	13536	1.73
1981	1024269	22749	2.22
1991	1299919	26920	2.07
2001	1609172	31210	1.94

Sources:

1. For 1901 to 1971; Sumit Ghosal, p. 26
2. 1981-1991; Census of India 1991 series 26 Part XII-B, *District Census Handbook. Census of India* – 1981, West Bengal. Series – 23, Special *Istahar* S/T.

It is difficult to explain how Lepcha population has decreased by 500 members during the period 1840–1875. Both Campbell and Temple had collected information on individual levels and there might be some information gap and limitations in collecting population figures by the sources at their personal level. Any way, it is to note that Lepchas in both the individual sources constituted the single largest population in the demographic structure of Sikkim in the early days.

Table 2.3: Lepcha population and other population in Sikkim

Year	Lepcha	Bhutia	Limbu	Other	Total
1840	3000	2000	-	-	-
1875	2500	1500	1000	-	5000
1891	5762	4894	3356	14012	30458

Sources:

1. For 1940. A. Campbell. 'Note on the Lepchas of Sikkim with a vocabulary of their language'. *Journal of Asiatic Society of Bengal* IX. Part I, Calcutta, 1840.
2. For 1875, Richard Temple. 'Two Diaries of Travel in Sikkim.' in S.K. Sharma and others (ed), *Encyclopedia of Sikkim and Bhutan*, Delhi, 1997.
3. For 1891, H. Risley, *The Gazetteer of Sikkim*, Bengal Govt. Secretariat Calcutta.

Table 2.4: Lepcha population in Sikkim

Year	Lepcha Population	Ten years
1891	5762	-
1901	7313	+1551
1911	9031	+1718
1921	9021	-10
1931	13060	+4039
1941	12523	-537
1951	13756	+1233
1961	-	-
1971	22316	+4280
1981*	23234	+918
1991	29854	+6620

Sources:

1. For the period 1891, H. Risley, *The Gazetteer of Sikkim*, Bengal Govt. Secretariat Calcutta, 1894.
2. For the period 1901 to 1951, Census of India, West Bengal, 1951.
3. For the period 1971-1991, Government of India, Language Division.

Note:

* K.S. Singh (ed.) *Peoples of India* (1994) p. 689 shows Lepcha population in Sikkim for the year 1981 as 24952 which is 1718 head more than that shown by language division, Govt. of India.

Table 2.4 shows that the Lepcha population in Sikkim remained at slightly higher level than those of in West Bengal throughout the census period. Like that of in West Bengal, Sikkim also witnessed negative growth of population during 1921 and 1941. But as a whole the growth rates are higher in Sikkim than those in West Bengal.

Inspite of insignificant number (14 as per 1971 Census) of population, Lepchas have been recognised as ST in the state of Tripura.[4] It is a known fact that Tripura, due to political and other reasons in most cases follows West Bengal and hence recognised Lepchas as ST without considering much about their demographic details.

Census documents on Lepcha population for both West Bengal and Sikkim reveal a sort of erratic behaviour and hence unacceptable. The presence of negative growths (in the decades of 1921 and 1941 both in West Bengal and Sikkim and in 1911 and 1971 in West Bengal) makes the population figure very much doubtful. This erratic behaviour needs indepth study, which is beyond the scope of the present study, but some should take up the matter seriously. Surprisingly some scholars [Das, 1978: 28-35; Ghosal, 1990: 23-28] go on narrating such doubtful data without even mentioning any single word about their credibility. It is so much so that some scholars [Thakur, 1988: 62-66, Lepcha, 1979: 162-166],[5] go on finding the causes of such slow growth. The administration for known causes is least bothered and remained silent. The community neither at any individual level nor at Association level ever put any protest against such an unrealistic document. This ignorance can simply be defined as a tribal character of accepting every thing without judging and protesting among the Lepchas. Ignoring every thing we here just note about the insignificant proportion of Lepcha population in their own homeland.

Industrial Classification of Lepcha Population

Data on industrial classification of Lepchas are available with the years 1961, 1971 and 1981. Table 2.5 shows that the percentage of Lepcha workers for the state of West Bengal decreases from 51.59 to 48.69 and 42.23 over the decades 1961, 1971 and 1981 respectively; while it increases from 48.41 to 51.31 and further to 56.26 for that of non-workers. The situation is also more or less same for the Lepchas of Darjeeling district. Against decreasing percentage of workers 51.81, 49.78 and 42.38 respectively, the percentages of non-workers have increased from 48.19 to 50.22 and 56.11 per cent for the years 1961, 1971 and 1981 respectively. But the case is not the same among the Lepchas living in rural and urban areas. The fluctuations in the percentages of both workers and non-workers among the Lepchas of urban areas of the state and the district are due to the corresponding fluctuations in the female population. But for the rural Lepchas a decreasing trend among both the workers and non-workers can be noticed for both the males and females. Over the decades Lepchas, thus, are becoming workless and the trend is more among the females in both the rural and urban areas.

Table 2.6 shows industrial classification of Lepcha population for the state over the census periods 1961, 1971 and 1981. Highest proportion of population is engaged in cultivation (81.91 per cent in 1961; 34.01 per cent in 1971; and 73.23 per cent in 1981 respectively) followed by other services and agricultural labour. The proportion of population engaged in mining and quarrying, household industry, construction, trade and commerce, transport, communication is very negligible.

As cultivator, females are dominating over males for all the three decades. Their role is also important in case of livestock, forestry, fishing, hunting and plantation work. But in all other categories, the role of females cannot be ignored. The higher percentage of female population unequivocally shows the importance of female participation in working group.

Almost same trend has been marked among the Lepchas in the district level classification (Table 2.7) but the corresponding percentages for the cultivators are more than those of state level percentages. As the Lepchas of the state are residing mainly in Darjeeling, the district level statistics basically represent in the state level statistics. Combining cultivators and agricultural labour, it can be stated that nearly 85.16, 62.45 and 81.95 per cent of the population are wholly dependant on agriculture for the census period 1961, 1971 and 1981 respectively. The rest 14.84, 37.55 and 18.05 per cent of workers are engaged in activities other than agriculture. Lepcha economy, thus, can safely be identified as agricultural one. Adding

Table 2.5: Workers and Non-workers among the Lepchas of West Bengal and Darjeeling – 1961-1981

		Population			Worker						Non-Worker					
		1961	1971	1981	1961		1971		1981		1961		1971		1981	
		No.	No.	No.	No.	%	No.	%	No.	%	No.	%	No.	%	No.	%
WEST BENGAL																
RURAL	Male	6946	7526	10795	4292	61.79	4220	56.07	5830*	54.01	2654	38.21	3306	43.93	4857*	44.99
	Female	6883	5847	101333	3172	46.08	2328	39.82	3379*	33.35	3711	53.92	3519	60.18	6512*	64.26
	Total	13829	13373	20928	7464	53.97	6548	48.96	9209*	44.00	6365	46.03	6825	51.04	11369*	54.32
URBAN	Male	631	779	1216	288	45.64	356	45.70	483*	39.72	343	54.36	423	54.30	730*	60.03
	Female	849	416	1265	1471	17.31	190	45.67	193*	15.25	702	82.69	226	54.33	1071*	84.66
	Total	1480	1195	2481	435	29.40	546	45.69	676*	27.25	1045	70.60	649	54.31	1801*	72.59
DARJEELING																
RURAL	Male	6761	7030	10560	4190	61.97	3982	56.64	5707*	54.04	2571	38.03	3048	43.36	4747*	44.95
	Female	6685	5409	9954	3104	46.43	2250	41.59	3341*	33.56	3581	53.57	3159	58.41	6375*	64.04
	Total	13446	12439	20514	7294	54.25	6232	50.10	9048*	44.11	6152	45.75	6207	49.90	11122*	54.22
URBAN	Male	624	708	1070	283	45.35	318	44.92	407	38.04	341	54.65	390	55.08	663	61.96
	Female	840	389	1165	147	17.50	188	48.33	185*	15.88	693	82.5	201	51.67	979*	84.03
	Total	1464	1097	2235	430	29.37	506	46.13	592*	26.49	1034	70.63	591	53.87	1642*	73.47

Sources:

1.Census of India 1961 – West Bengal Part V-4 (ii) Special Tables on Scheduled Tribes.

2.Census of India 1971 – West Bengal Special Table on Scheduled Tribes.

3.Census of India 1981 – West Bengal Series – 23 Part IX (IV) Special Tables on Scheduled Tribes.

Note: Figures with astric indicate those items, which do not tally with their corresponding population figure if workers and non-workers are added together.

Table 2.6: Industrial classification of Lepcha population of West Bengal – 1961-1981.

Categories	1961						1971						1981					
	Male		Female		Total		Male		Female		Total		Male		Female		Total	
	No.	%	No.	%	No.	%	No.	%	No.	%	No.	%	No.	%	No.	%	No.	%
Total workers	4580	100.00	3319	100.00	7899	100.00	4576	100.00	2518	100.00	7094	100.00	6313	100.00	3571	100.00	9884	100.00
Cultivators	3590	78.33	2880	86.77	6470	81.91	1522	33.26	891	35.39	2413	34.01	4485	71.04	2753	77.09	7238	73.23
Agricultural Labourers	146	3.19	92	2.77	238	3.01	1382	36.20	574	22.79	1956	27.57	459	7.27	245	6.86	704	7.12
Livestock, forestry, fishing, hunting, plantation etc.	194	4.24	128	3.86	322	4.08	406	8.87	374	14.86	780	10.99	310	4.91	221	6.19	531	5.37
Mining, Quarring	-	-	-	-	-	-	-	-	-	-	-	-	-	-	-	-	-	-
Manufacturing, processing, servicing, Repair																		
Household industry	29	0.63	6	0.18	35	0.44	10	0.22	8	0.32	18	0.26	23	0.37	12	0.34	35	0.35
Other than household industry	7	0.15	7	0.21	14	0.18	39	0.85	26	1.03	65	0.92	106	1.68	23	0.64	129	1.31
Construction	10	0.22	1	0.03	11	0.14	67	1.46	25	0.99	92	1.30	52	0.82	12	0.34	64	0.65
Trade and commerce	36	0.79	9	0.27	45	0.57	78	1.71	21	0.83	99	1.40	100	1.58	39	1.09	139	1.41
Transport, and communication	37	0.81	4	0.12	41	0.52	113	2.47	41	1.63	154	2.17	109	1.73	7	0.20	116	1.17
Other service	531	11.59	192	5.79	723	9.15	959	20.96	558	22.16	1517	21.38	669	10.60	259	7.25	928	9.39

Sources: Ibid

Table 2.7: Industrial classification of Lepcha population of Darjeeling – 1961-1981.

Categories	1961						1971						1981					
	Male		Female		Total		Male		Female		Total		Male		Female		Total	
	No.	%	No.	%	No.	%	No.	%	No.	%	No.	%	No.	%	No.	%	No.	%
Total workers	4473	100.00	3251	100.00	7724	100.00	4300	100.00	2438	100.00	6738	100.00	6114	100.00	3526	100.00	9640	100.00
Cultivators	3572	79.86	2870	88.28	6442	83.40	1455	33.84	889	36.46	2344	34.79	4463	72.99	2747	77.91	7210	74.79
Agricultural Labourers	84	1.88	52	1.60	136	1.76	1306	30.37	558	22.89	1864	27.67	445	7.28	245	6.95	690	7.16
Livestock, forestry, fishing, hunting, plantation etc.	178	3.98	113	3.47	291	3.77	322	7.49	316	12.96	638	9.47	287	4.69	206	5.84	493	5.11
Mining, Quarring	-	-	-	-	-	-	-	-	-	-	-	-	-	-	-	-	-	-
Manufacturing, processing, servicing, Repair																		
Household industry	29	0.65	6	0.18	35	0.45	10	0.23	8	0.33	18	0.27	23	0.38	12	0.34	35	0.36
Other than household industry	7	0.16	7	0.22	14	0.18	35	0.82	25	1.03	60	0.89	75	1.23	15	0.42	90	0.93
Construction	10	0.22	1	0.03	11	0.14	60	1.39	25	1.03	85	1.26	49	0.80	12	0.34	61	0.63
Trade and commerce	30	0.67	9	0.28	39	0.50	76	1.77	20	0.82	96	1.42	87	1.42	36	1.02	123	1.28
Transport, and communication	37	0.83	4	0.13	41	0.53	108	2.51	41	1.68	149	2.21	92	1.51	7	0.20	99	1.03
Other service	526	11.76	189	5.81	715	9.27	928	21.58	556	22.80	1484	22.02	593	9.70	246	6.98	839	8.71

Sources: Ibid.

engagement of Lepchas in Livestock, forestry, fishing, hunting, plantation and orchard sector, it is seen that as much as 88.93, 71.92 and 87.06 per cent of workers are engaged in activities connected with the exploitation of nature. Irrespective of ups and downs, Lepchas even during the modern periods are continued to maintain a close link and depend largely on nature for their livelihood.

Tables (2.8 and 2.9) on industrial classification of Lepcha population, both for the state and the district, show uniform pattern of positive and negative growth rates. Growths of total workers, cultivators and household industry show negative trend for the decade 1961-1971 while agricultural labour, livestock, construction, transport and other services show negative trend for the decade 1971-81. The negative growth rates are due to 1971 census, which is doubtful for a number of reasons.

The secondary data unequivocally establish the fact that majority of Lepchas are agriculturists and Lepcha economy is an agricultural economy. [6]

General Description of Lepcha Agriculture

Lepchas, in general, live in the hilly areas of Darjeeling and Sikkim. The land morphology of this hill is such that it does not allow plain land cultivation. In the steep hills cultivation is not at all possible. Comparatively less steep slopes are to be converted into terrace of different width as per the availability of land. Lepchas do not get any large valley, like those in Bhutan or Tripura, for agricultural purposes. Lepcha agriculture is, thus, terrace based hill agriculture.

Agricultural land among the Lepchas is classified in two broad categories – wet land (*panikheti*) and dry land (*sukhakheti*). In the upper portion of the hill slope, the cultivable land is of dry land type while in the lower portion it is of wetland type. In dry land no ridge is made on the other side of the hill. Land is made wet by raising earthen ridge of 1-1.5 feet high on the opposite side of the hill so as to keep water inside the land. Lepchas call wetland as *zo-nyaot* where *zo* means paddy, which need more water for cultivation. The dry land is called *moong-nyaot* where *moong* means millet, which do not need much water for its cultivation. Wetland can easily be converted into dry land by removing the earthen ridges on three sides of the land and thereby allowing water to flow out of the field.

Table 2.8: Growth of Industrial classification of Lepcha population of West Bengal – 1961-1981.

Categories	Total Population (Number)			Decennial variation		Percentage decennial variation	
	1961	1971	1981	1961-71	1971-81	1961-71	1971-81
Total workers	7899	7094	9884	-805	+2790	-10.19	+39.33
Cultivators	6470	2413	7238	-4057	+4825	-62.70	+199.96
Agricultural Labourers	238	1956	704	+1718	-1252	+721.85	-64.01
Livestock, forestry, fishing, hunting, plantation etc.	322	780	531	+458	-249	+142.24	-31.92
Mining, Quarring	-	-	-	-	-	-	-
Manufacturing, processing, servicing, Repair							
Household industry	35	18	35	-17	+17	-48.57	+94.44
Other than household industry	14	65	129	+51	+64	+364.28	+98.46
Construction	11	92	64	+81	-28	+736.36	-38.43
Trade and commerce	45	99	139	+54	+40	+120.00	+40.40
Transport & communication	41	154	116	+113	-38	+275.61	-24.67
Other se vices	723	1517	928	+794	-589	+109.82	-38.83

Table 2.9: Growth of Industrial classification of Lepcha population of Darjeeling District – 1961-1981.

Categories	Total Population (Number)			Decennial variation		Percentage decennial variation	
	1961	1971	1981	1961-71	1971-81	1961-71	1971-81
Total workers	7724	6738	9640	-986	2902	-12.77	+43.07
Cultivators	6442	2344	7210	-4098	4866	-63.61	+207.59
Agricultural Labourers	136	1864	690	1728	-1174	+1270.59	-62.98
Livestock, forestry, fishing, hunting, plantation etc.	291	638	493	347	-145	+119.24	-22.73
Mining, Quarring	-	-	-	-	-	-	-
Manufacturing, processing, servicing, Repair							
Household industry	35	18	35	-17	+17	-48.57	+94.44
Other than household industry	14	60	90	+46	+38	+328.57	+50.00
Construction	11	85	61	+74	-24	+672.73	-28.24
Trade and commerce	39	961	23	+57	+27	+146.15	+28.13
Transport &communication	41	149	99	108	-50	+263.41	-33.56
Other services	715	1484	839	769	-645	+107.55	-43.46

Paddy (*zo*) is the main crop in the wet land followed by maize (*kuntsoong*), ginger (*heng*), and vegetable (*bifong*) etc. Maize (*kuntsoong*) is the main crop in dry land followed by millet (*moong*), ginger (*heng*) or vegetables (*bifong*). Paddy is cultivated along with *dal* (*kla*), soyabean (*slyaang*) and *morseom* (*porbeong*, a variety of *dal*) while maize is cultivated along with potato (*alubuk*), beans (*tinbit*), *kerala* (*khaaktik*) and cucumber (*saret*). The only plantation type cash crop is cardamom (*tambrak*), which occupies the land for years together, and no other crop can grow along with it.

Variety of Crops in the Existing Literature

So far as variety of crops is concerned, Campbell (1840) mentioned that they cultivate barely sufficiently for their subsistence. Mainwaring observed self-sufficiency in Lepcha agriculture: "They cultivate their plot of ground, which afforded them rice, their staple food; grains of different sorts; oil cotton from which they span their cloth; seeds from which they expressed their oil" [1876: ix]. As a good friend of Lepchas, Mainwaring could find even production of cotton by the Lepchas which no other writers, both traditional and contemporary could notice.

Lepcha agriculture was enriched with vegetables and was mentioned for the first time by Risley. Besides cultivating rice he wrote about few vegetables "of which the brinjal, cucumber and capcicum are the chief" [1891: 13]. In Waddels write up one could find some more crops ". . . a few grounds turnips and chillies and beyond this a few small crop of maize, barley, millet, for bear and a little terraced land for irrigated rice" [1899: 95-96].

It is O'Malley [1907: 65] who mentioned about cardamom cultivation by the Lepchas beside the other crops like wheat and barley. Stocks [1927: 476] added one extra crop, millet in Lepcha agriculture beside the usual rice, wheat and barley.

Gorer found not only the variety of crops but the variety of lands in the hills associated with different types of land – "there is the sing or field garden against the houses, cardamom fields and rice terraces". Regarding the period of introduction of these crops, Gorer wrote: "Cardamom was introduced at the beginning of the century, rice terraces for wet paddy less than twenty years ago" [1938: 86].

A.K.Das [1978:43-64] grouped land into two: *Panikhet,* suitable for paddy and *Sukhakhet,* suitable for maize. The crops produced by the Lepchas are – paddy, maize, millet, buckwheat, wheat, barley, potato, and cardamom. Among fruits, pineapple, tree tomato, lemon, banana, pear, peaches, plums are important. To name vegetables, peas, cowpeas, beetroots, french beans, cabbage, cucumber, brinjal, raddish, spinach, tomato, onion, mustard etc. are important.

Among the contemporary scholars Sumit Ghosal [1990: 72-74] discussed two types of crops – traditional and contemporary. Among the traditional crops dry rice, millet, maize, buckwheat, barley, cardamom and onion are important. The contemporary crops are: rice, maize, buckwheat, potato, orange, ginger and vegetables.

Variety of Crops in the Study Area

Paddy still remains the main agricultural crop among the Lepchas. The variety and process of cultivation has changed over the passage of time. Some crops altogether vanished for the Lepcha agricultural calendar e.g. buckwheat, dry rice, while some other crop reduces their importance e.g. millet, maize etc. The earlier varieties of maize and paddy have disappeared completely in the present cropping pattern. It has been reported that there was 26 varieties of rice (Gowloog, 199: 43), 17 varieties of maize (Tamsong; 230-31). But now they do not grow all these varieties. Some new crops do enter in the picture e.g. floriculture etc. while other crops have modernised their production – vegetables, cardamom, ginger etc. Monocrop, the usual cropping pattern of early days, has been replaced by multicrop and mixed crop in the contemporary period.

Beside the variety of crops, the process of cultivation has also changed over the time. Shifting cultivation (*Rong-dong*) has become obsolete and is practiced by none; it is now a story of the past. All are participating now in the terrace based settled cultivation. The modern process of ploughing, levelling, sowing, weeding and harvesting has replaced the traditional process of cultivation known as *Zomaal* (digging the earth by pointed rod and inserting seeds).

The picture of contemporary cropping pattern is clear from the cropping cycle (Figs. 2.1 and 2.2). It is evident that major crops in dry land are – maize, millet, ginger, vegetable, floriculture, while wet fields are used for the paddy, ginger, dal, soyabean, vegetables, floriculture, maize, bean etc. The newly included crops (floriculture, vegetables etc.) are at the cost of currently excluded ones (like buckwheat, barley, millet etc.) The timings and process of cultivation have also changed for both sowing and harvesting.

Lepchas now cultivate their land more intensively. Multiple cropping is the call of the day and Lepchas very much responded to the day's demand. There are now three agricultural seasons in a year – each season is used for mixed crop that comprises of more than one crop at a time. Along with paddy, Lepchas cultivate dal, soyabean while maize field is accompanied by bean, *karala*, etc. Nima Dorjee Lepcha of Mani Gumpa said "We can get eight to nine crops from the same field in a year if cultivated properly and carefully. In the first phase, we may get paddy, soyabean, *kala dal*, and *morshem* (a variety of dal). In the second phase in the same field we cultivate wheat and maize. We may cultivate potato and maize in the third phase. Each crop takes 80-90 days to mature and if we are very careful we can get 9 crops from the same field. We have three acres of land and we get the following crops in a year: paddy (25 *muri*; 1 *muri* = 80 kg), soyabean (2 *muri*), *kaladal* (15 kg), *morshem* (9 kg), wheat (120 kg), maize (20 *doko*), potato (26 *mound*, 1 *mound* = 40 kg), millet (3 *muri*), gladioli (Rs.700/-), vegetables (tomato, radish, chilli etc.)".

The indigenous Lepchas are born agriculturists and know how to use the land to its maximum possible extent. Lepchas are not literate but they have emerged as good agriculturists in modern days. They are not only cultivating their land intensively but also introduce new varieties of crops in their field. Lepchas do not allow the land to remain as cultivable fallow and by ensuring the fullest exploitation of the fertility of the land they cultivate at least two and many a times three crops round the year. Dependence on small holdings compels the Lepchas to get maximum return from their land. By the time they also gather much knowledge about agriculture through experience and involvement. This negates the days old popular comment: Lepcha are poor agriculturists [Campbell: 1840; Dalton: 1872, 99].

The sequential cropping pattern as witnessed in the study area can be shown in terms of the following circle:

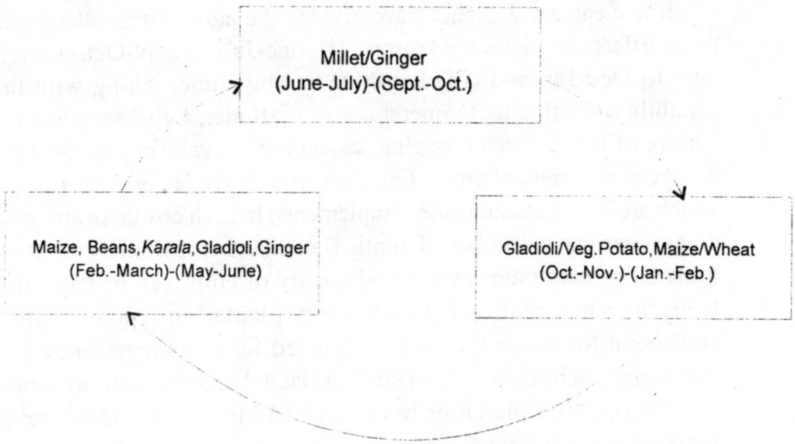

Fig. 2.1: Agricultural Cropping Circle: Dry Land (*Moong-nyaot*)

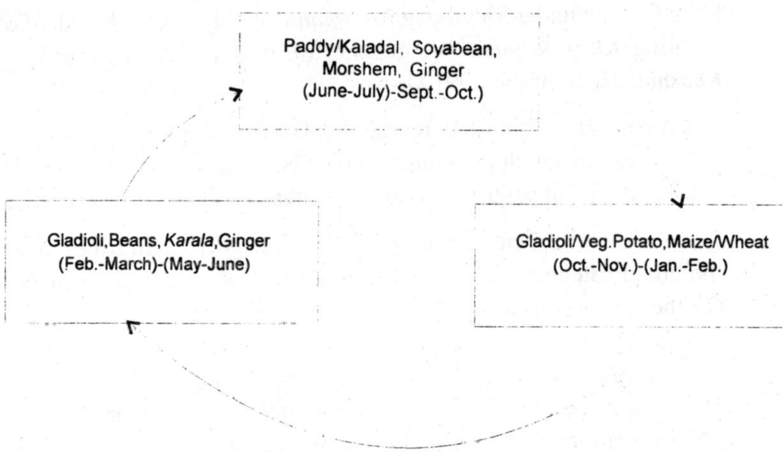

Fig. 2.2: Agricultural Cropping Circle: Wet Land (*Zo-nyaot*)

It is clear that Lepchas have divided the agricultural calendar in three different agricultural seasons: (i) June-July to Sept-Oct, (ii) Oct-Nov to Dec-Jan and (iii) Feb-Mar to May-June. Along with the suitability of climate, temperature, rainfall etc., Lepchas select the variety of crops. Each cropping season is very carefully utilised for the specific variety of crops. Each box in each circle comprises crops, which are both substitute and complements. In each box there are some crops those can be cultivated jointly (i.e. mixed crop) and by selecting these crops maximum variety and quality of crops can be cultivated from the same plot of land. The only plantation type of crop is cardamom for which the land is occupied for years together and no other crop can be cultivated in the same land. Lands are now used most intensively. Multiple crops have replaced Monocrop and wherever possible they use scarce land for mixed crop.

THE STUDY AREA

Information for the present study has been collected from three villages. Of these three, villages namely, 5th Mile Lepcha Gaon and Mani Gumpa come under the jurisdiction of Community Development (CD) Block – Kalimpong I, and village Pochaok under the Kalimpong Block II. 5th Mile Lepcha Gaon falls under Kalimpong *Khasmahals*, Mani Gumpa under Sindibong *Khasmahals* while Pochaok under Git Dubling *Khasmahals*. [7] We get the following facts for the three *Khasmahals* from the 1991 Census:

A perusal of Table 2.10 reveals that Git-Dubling *Khasmahal* occupies largest area with lowest numbers of both households and population. Its density of population is much less than in other two *Khasmahals*.

The District Census Handbook 1991 categorised all tribes under the broad category ST and hence no separate statistics are available for the Lepchas. But as Lepchas are the original and dominant tribe in this region, we can easily infer that Lepchas comprise majority population among the ST category in all the *Khasmahals*. In percentage term, Git-Dubling is having the highest proportion of ST (53.88) compared to the other two *Khasmahals* 16.94 and 21.73 for Sindibong and Kalimpong respectively. This means that Lepchas could still retain their lands more in Git-Dubling than in other two *Khasmahals*. Git-Dubling, thus, can rightly be called the '*Dzongu*' of West Bengal.

Table 2.10: Area, Population, Main workers, Cultivator plus Agricultural Labour and Scheduled Tribe in Three Khasmahals under Study

Name of *Khasmahals*	Area (in ha)	Population	Main worker	Cultivator and Agriculture Labour*	Scheduled Tribe
Sindibong	665.70	3306	1275 (38.57)	983 (77.09)	560 (16.94)
Kalimpong	745.44	6829	2428 (35.55)	1674 (68.94)	1484 (21.73)
Git-Dubling	1281.25	2728	1271 (46.59)	1157 (91.03)	1470 (53.88)

Sources: *District Census Handbook: Darjeeling West Bengal*. Series 26. Part XII-B. Census of India, 1991. Directorate of Census Operations, West Bengal.

Note: Figures in parentheses shows percentage to their respective total population

* Figures are obtained by adding cultivator and agricultural labour together.

Git-Dubling records highest percentage of total workers (46.59 per cent) and majority of them are cultivator and/or agricultural labour (91.03 per cent). This may be because of the fact that Git-Dubling located far away from both the State Highway SH-12 and town areas and hence agriculture remains the main source of livelihood. Sindibong and Kalimpong *Khasmahals* are located near SH-12 and town areas where land is more a scarce factor of production.

Let us now introduce in brief all the three villages we have chosen for our field study. We have selected two villages (Mani Gumpa and 5th mile Lepcha Gaon) from near the town and market place while the other village Pochaok is located far away from the town and main market centre.

Village – Mani Gumpa

Mani Gumpa village comes under Sindibong *Khasmahals* of Kalimpong-I CD Block. It is located at a distance of four km north east of Kalimpong town. From Jore Bunglow of Darjeeling Sadar

Subdivision the SH-12 passes through Peshok, Lopchu to meet NH-31A and after crossing Teesta it passes through Kalimpong town towards north to reach Lava and then towards south for Gorubathan and Maynaguri of Jalpaiguri district. SH-12 passes through Mani Gumpa village from east to west but bulk of the houses lie on the southern part of the road.

The village received its name after an old Buddhist *Gumpa* (monastery) of the locality. It is reported that the monastery was originally located at Dungra Busty where the present 11th mile *Gumpa* is located. But during the Bhutan rule (1700 – 1865), the villagers had to shift the monastery to their village due to clash with the Bhutanese monks. But under the patronage and financial help from the Bhutan Raj particularly Bhutan Queen whose house is just bordering the village, the villagers constructed the present monastery. The hearsay also supports that in 19th century one Passong Namgyel Lepcha had been sent to Thimpu for Lama training who join the *Gumpa* as head Lama. The great grand son of Passong Namgyel Lepcha on hereditary are still occupied the post of head lama and landed property of the *Gumpa*.

Sindipong or Sindibong is the corrupted form of Lepcha word – *Sying-Li-Pung* (*Sying* means a kind of tree, *Li* means house and *Pung* means a hillock), which literally means a variety of tree, found in the village over the hillock and can be used for construction of houses or furniture. The elderly persons of the village still remember the presence of some *Sying* tree during their young days but at present not even a single tree can exist in the village.

The village is surrounded by Upper Sindibong or Tadunchen and SH-12 in the north, Gatte Khola (rivulet) in the east, Ranikhola and Dungra Busty in the west and Relli Road in the south. The village slants sharply from north towards south. The *jhora* or *khola* or rivulet on both east and west boundaries, provide irrigated water for agriculture, run from north towards south. The stony steps passing through the middle of the village connect the two-pacca roads SH-12 on the north and Relli Road on the south. The village got a ridged part at the mid northern part, which slopes downwards slowly towards east and west while slopes sharply towards south. Thus except the stony ridged middle portion, all the other areas are comparatively flatter and suitable for cultivation. All the essential services like schools, college, hospital, medical centre, post office, market, banks, and other government officials are located within the vicinity of 6 km. of the village. All the households except one are Buddhist and they worship in the village monastery.

Village – 5th Mile Lepcha Gaon

The 5th Mile Lepcha Gaon comes under Kalimpong *Khasmahal* of CD Block – Kalimpong I is actually a part of Tashiding Busty. It is situated at the western boundary of the sub-division. After crossing Teesta and leaving NH-31A, the SH-12 starts climbing uphills through zig-zag hilly terrain. The village starts from 3 mile onwards Teesta river towards Kalimpong town and ends where the road again meets the village at 5th mile in the east.

The nomenclature of the village relates its Lepcha origin. *Tashiding* consists of two Lepcha words – '*Tashi*' and '*ding*'. *Tashi* is the name of a Lepcha king probably chieftan of Sikkim. The word '*ding*' means 'to remain motionless or steady on the feet'. Hearsay narrates that once king Tashi on his way from Sikkim on the north stood for a while in the village on a flat piece of land / rock to look around with a bit of leisure. Presence of a flat rock known as '*Choong-ding-loong*' at the extreme south-western part of the village does support the hearsay. '*Chaong*' in Lepcha means south and '*loong*' means leisure. The eastern bordering village Ngasey has derived from the Lepcha word '*ngaa-so*' means refreshing or taking rest after exerting labour. As per the same hearsay king Tashi had a temporary halt in the village for rest. Names of the villages, their Lepcha inhabitants and the hearsay support the characteristics of typical traditional Lepcha villages of the region.

There were six typical Lepcha houses, '*Doo-kye-moolee*' or in short '*Ronglee*' in the village. *Rong* means Lepcha and *Lee* means house. All the *Ronglees* got their typical Lepcha names. They were: (i) *Cholongbong* (organge orchard), (ii) *Ding* (flat land), (iii) *Kankibong* (variety of tree), (iv) *Salbong* (variety of tree), (v) *Siking* (beside), (vi) 5th mile – as per the location of the house.

The typical Lepcha name of the houses, name of the village and their inhabitants unequivocally support the hearsay and establish the Lepcha origin of the village.

The village is bounded by Ngasey on the east, Dara-Gaon and Tanek on the north, Tashiding forest land on the west and 5th mile *jhora* (rivulet) on the south whose other sides is forest land and villages like Bhamse, Poshier and Shiba Church Mission compound areas.

The village slopes from east towards west to meet either SH-12 or Tashiding forest. Beside 5th mile *jhora*, the village also drained by 4 small rivulets which are watering only during monsoon periods. They also help in channelling water through traditional method for irrigation purposes in the neighbouring lands. As almost entire eastern and northern part of the village is bounded by zig-zag SH-12, the village is well communicated. All the three markets, Teesta Bazar on the west, Kalimpong Bazar on the east and Malli Bazar on the north are within 8 km. and well communicated by pucca road. All other essential services like schools, college, medical centre, banks, govt. offices are available within the radius of 8 km. of the village. The only school Tashiding Junior Basic School has established on a plot of land donated by one Lepcha inhabitant, caters the need of primary education in the locality. The village does not have any public place of worship of its own. The nearest Church for the Protestants is one hour walking distance while the Roman Catholic Church is located 3 km. east on the side of SH-12.

Village – Pochaok

Pochaok is one of the largest villages under Git-Dubling *Khasmahal* of Kalimpong II Block. Pochaok is the largest village among all the three villages under the present study. SH-12 passes through Kalimpong town towards northeast to reach Lava and then towards south for Gorubathan and Maynaguri. Before reaching Lava, the road meets a forest controlled metalled road, which via Budhabare reach Kafer, an important tourist spot in the region. Pochaok is around one hour normal walking distance from Budhabare on rough and undulating hilly ridge. The so called road many a times passes through forest like areas and also crosses a number of rivulets which the travellers need to cross by jumping or washing their feet in cold water.

Although Pochaok is around 20 km. straight east of Kalimpong town but one has to cover a total of nearly 55 km. of which 48 km. upto Budhabare are motorable.

The nomenclature of Pochaok gives us Lepcha origin of the village. Present Pochaok is the corrupted form of '*Pazoak*' which in Lepcha means jungle or wild land over grown with dense rank vegetation, often nearly impenetrable. It might have been derived from the Lepcha word '*Po-Chaok*' which literally means joint of bamboo (*Po* means bamboo, and *Chaok* means joint) or *Po-Chaa-aak* means to up-root the bamboo (*Chaa-aak* means to up root). Even today one can witness a variety of *po* or bamboo in and around the village. Whatever may be the original word from where Pochaok is derived but it is undoubtedly been derived from Lepcha word. This origin of the name, its inhabitants unequivocally establish that Lepchas are the indigenous people of the village.

The village is sorrounded by Nokdara, Gitbeong and Pasting villages in the east; Dubling, Pakang, Byang in the west; Chandong, Togang and Pasbong in the north; and Chakkum dara and Luyangshal in the south. The undulating narrow hilly road passing through the village divides it in three different parts – the northern part known as Upper Pochaok, the southwestern part as Lower Pochaok and Mahajandara in the southeastern part. The village slopes from north towards south to meet a river. The upper Pochaok is comparatively steep and there is wide variation of height between the extreme north and extreme south points of the village. The damp weather due both to the height, presence of trees and the abundant water of good number of rivulets make the upper Pochaok suitable for cardamom cultivation. The lower Pochaok and Mahajandara in particular are comparatively hot and the comparatively flatter lands are best for paddy cultivation.

The nearest market place is located at one-hour walking distance from the middle of the village. Beside Wednesday's weekly market when a good number of shops gathered for sale of daily necessities, some permanent grocery and tea stalls remain open throughout the week. Budhabare is the main trading centre in the region, which supplies not only daily necessities, but also exchange of farm products between the villagers and middleman business class. Cardamom and ginger are the two main cash crops of Kalimpong II CD Block and

Budhabare is one of the major seasonal marketing centres for the two cash crops. The only high school including some government offices and religious centres are located in Budhabare. Two buses regularly ply between Kafer and Kalimpong via Budhabare. A few numbers of jeeps carrying both passengers and goods to and from Kalimpong are the main vehicles of communication. But between Pochaok and Budhabare walking through narrow hilly road is the only means of communication.

Basic Statistics

The basic statistical abstract of the three villages under study are shown in Table 2.11.

The map of the study area shows that all the three villages under study lie more or less at the same line passing from east to west of the district of Darjeeling. But their height, landscape, location etc. vary widely from village to village. Location wise 5th mile Lepcha Gaon is located at the extreme western boundary, Pochaok at the eastern boundary of CD Block – Kalimpong I and II while Mani Gumpa is located in between the two villages. The 5th mile Lepcha Gaon and Mani Gumpa are well connected as SH-12 passes through both the villages but Pochaok is located in remote areas far away from the SH-12 and also from the metalled forest road.

The nearest to the subdivisional headquarters and market place is Mani Gumpa (4 km.) while 5th mile Lepcha Gaon is a bit away (7 km.) but its location by the side of SH-12 makes it well communicated. Pochaok, on the other hand, is located far away from the subdivisional headquarters by 55 km. while its distance from the market place is same to that of 5th mile Lepcha Gaon. But Budhabare, the nearest market of Pochaok is a rural and underdeveloped market and there is no communication at all. But being a sub-divisional centre the amenities of human civilisation are present more in the first two villages than in Pochaok, the third village.

Areawise Git-Dubling is the largest among the three *Khasmahals* under the present study and it is the 5th largest among 40 *Khasmahals* of CD Block Kalimpong I and II. Pochaok, like its parent *Khasmahal*, also occupies largest area among all the three villages under study. The total number of households in Pochaok

Table 2.11: Basic Statistics of the Study Area

Name of Villages	Name of Khas-mahal	Name of CD Block	Distance from			No. of Household		Population			LEPCHA						Literate		
											Population			Religion					
			Sub-Div. HQ	Road	Market	Total	Lepcha	Person	Male	Female	Person	Male	Female	Buddhist	Christian	Others	Person	Male	Female
Mani Gumpa	Sindi-bong	Kalim-pong I	4	0	4	22	22	120	54	66	120	54	66	114	6	-	99	44	55
5th Mile Lepcha Goan	Kalim-pong	Kalim-I pong I	7	0	7	24	21	154	80	74	131	68	63	-	131	-	110	62	48
Pochaok	Gitdub-ling	Kalim-pong II	55	7	7	78	76	458	242	216	446	235	211	141	305	-	268	151	117
Total						124	119	732	376	356	697	357	340	255	442	-	477	257	220

Source: Field Survey during 1999-2000.

is also the highest 62.90 per cent compared to only 19.35 per cent under 5th mile Lepcha Gaon and 17.74 per cent for Mani Gumpa. Out of total 124 households 95.96 per cent are Lepchas. Village wise cent percent households belong to Lepchas in Mani Gumpa; while percentage of Lepcha households for 5th mile Lepcha Gaon and Pochaok are 87.50 and 97.44 respectively. Ignoring the negligible proportion of non-Lepcha households, we can safely categorise all the three villages as 'Lepcha villages.'

All the three villages under study are 'Lepcha villages inhabited by Lepcha population.' Among the households 95.96 per cent belong to the Lepchas. They constitute 95.27 per cent of population of the study area.

Among the Lepcha population there are 952 females per thousand males. But their proportions are different for different villages – 1222, 926 and 898 females per thousand males for Mani Gumpa, 5th mile Lepcha Gaon and Pochaok respectively. This unexpected high female 1222 per thousand male in Mani Gumpa is to be noted seriously and could itself be a topic for demographic and sociological research. [8]

The Lepchas belong to two religious faiths, Buddhism and Christianity. Out of total 697 Lepchas in the three villages, 63.41 per cent are Christians while 36.59 per cent are Buddhists. We have purposively selected two villages – each one dominated by either the Buddhists or the Christians, and in the third one there is moderate representation of both Buddhist and Christian Lepchas. The proportion of Buddhists in Mani Gumpa is as high as 95 per cent while it is only 5 per cent for the Christians. The entire Lepcha population is Christians in the 5th Mile Lepcha Gaon. Pochaok is a village where both the religious faiths are present but even here the percentage of Christians is more (68.39) than that of Buddhists (31.61). No other religions except Buddhists and Christians are found among the Lepchas of study area.

The overall literacy rate among the Lepchas of three villages is 68.44 per cent. It is higher than the rate for the district of Darjeeling (48.97 per cent as per 1991 census) and much higher than the same rate for the rural areas (40.79 per cent) of the district. The literacy rate for the study area is higher among the males (53.88 per cent) than among the females (46.12 per cent). The corresponding percentages for the rural areas of Darjeeling district are 63.31 per cent and 36.69

per cent respectively as per 1991 census. We can thus infer that the Lepchas in general and their female counterpart in particular are more literate than the other communities of the district.

But the literacy rate is not uniform for the three villages when they are taken individually. Among the literates 20.75 per cent, 20.06 per cent and 56.18 per cent belong to Mani Gumpa, 5th mile Lepcha Gaon and Pochaok villages respectively. Pochaok, which is located far away from the sub-divisional headquarters lacking in basic human amenities and communication facilities, appears with highest percentage of literates. The highest number of population might have its statistical effect in exaggerating the literacy rate for Pochaok.

Literacy rates of Mani Gumpa, 5th Mile Lepcha Gaon and Pochaok are 82.5 per cent, 83.97 per cent and 60.09 per cent respectively. It is seen that literacy rate among the Christians is more than among the Buddhists. As against highest percentage of literates amongst all the literates of the study area, villagewise literacy rate is the lowest for Pochaok. It can easily be inferred that a remote area like Pochaok should have low literacy rate than the other two villages having better educational facilities. Any way, Lepchas are far ahead in respect of literacy compared to the rate for the district or the state.

Table 2.12: Engagement of Households in Agricultural and Non-Agricultural Activities

Name of villages	Engagement in Agricultural activities (No. of households) activities	Engagement in Non-agricultural (No. of households)	Total
1	2	3	4
Mani Gumpa	19 (86.36)	3 (13.64)	22 (100.00)
5th Mile Lepcha Gaon	18 (85.71)	3 (14.29)	21 (100.00)
Pochaok	76 (100.00)	-	76 (100.00)
Total	113 (94.96)	6 (5.04)	119 (100.00)

Note: Figures in the parentheses indicate percentages.

Literacy rate among the females is more in Mani Gumpa (55.55 per cent) followed by 5th mile Lepcha Gaon (43.64 per cent) and Pochaok (43.66 per cent). This contradicts our assumption that Christians are more literate; on the other hand, females in the Buddhist village are more literate than that in Christian village.

Beside all these village level basic statistical information, let us now concentrate on some economic aspects[9] of the Lepchas in our study area. Secondary data or industrial classification (Tables 2.6 and 2.7) shows agriculture as the main stay of Lepcha economy. Table 2.12 shows the participation of Lepcha households of study area in agricultural and non-agricultural activities.

Table 2.12 reveals that as high as 94.96 per cent of households of our study area are engaged in agricultural operation. In Pochaok agriculture is the only source of livelihood to the people. In the other two villages, which are located adjacent to the town, nearly 85 per cent of households are engaged in agriculture. Lepcha economy can be identified as solely agriculture dependent.

Table 2.13 has been constructed by dividing all the households into three broad categories: (a) Households with agriculture as their principal occupation, (b) as subsidiary occupation and (c) non-involvement in agriculture.

It is evident that economically 66.85 per cent of population is dependent on agriculture either as principal and/or subsidiary source of employment. Females prefer to accept agriculture as subsidiary occupation (52.65 per cent) than as principal occupation (12.65 per cent). Females lag behind males (68.35 per cent) in their involvement and acceptance of agriculture as principal and subsidiary occupation. In Lepcha economy, women play an important role in agricultural operations.

Villagewise Pochaok (68.61 per cent) ranks first in respect of number of population depending on agriculture followed by Mani Gumpa (66.67 per cent) and 5th Mile Lepcha Gaon (61.07 per cent). In all the three villages, the proportion of population engaged in agriculture, as subsidiary occupation is higher than their corresponding figures for principal occupation except the male members of Pochaok whose principal occupation (53.62 per cent) is much higher than subsidiary occupation (17.87 per cent). Very few females of Pochaok consider

Table 2.13: Agriculture as Principal and Subsidiary Occupation

Name of Villages	Agriculture as Principal occupation			Agriculture as Subsidiary occupation			Agriculture as Principal and Subsidiary occupation			No involvement in agriculture			Total		
	Male	Female	Total	Male	Female	Total	Male	Female	Total	Male	Female	Total	Male	Female	Total
Mani Gumpa	13 (24.07)	21 (31.82)	34 (28.33)	21 (38.89)	25 (37.88)	46 (38.33)	34 (62.96)	46 (69.7)	80 (66.67)	20 (37.04)	20 (30.3)	40 (33.33)	54 (100)	66 (100)	120 (100)
5th Mile Lepcha Goaon	20 (29.41)	15 (923.81)	35 (26.72)	22 (32.35)	23 (36.51)	45 (34.35)	42 (61.77)	38 (60.32)	80 (61.07)	26 (38.23)	25 (39.68)	51 (38.93)	68 (100)	63 (100)	131 (100)
Pochak	126 (53.62)	7 (3.32)	133 (29.82)	42 (17.87)	131 (62.09)	173 (38.79)	168 (71.49)	138 (65.41)	306 (68.61)	67 (28.51)	73 (34.59)	140 (31.39)	235 (100)	211 (100)	446 (100)
Total	159 (44.54)	43 (12.65)	202 (28.98)	85 (23.81)	179 (52.65)	264 (37.81)	144 (68.35)	222 (65.3)	466 (66.85)	113 (31.65)	118 (34.7)	231 (33.15)	357 (100)	340 (100)	697 (100)

Table 2.14: Off-farming Remunerative activities

Villages	Mani Gumpa			5th Mile Lepcha Gaon			Pochaok			Total		
Categories	M	F	T	M	F	T	M	F	T	M	F	T
1	2	3	4	5	6	7	8	9	10	11	12	13
Central Govt.	4 (57.14)		4 (57.14)	3 (42.86)		3 (42.86)		-		7 (100)		7 (100)
State Govt.	5 (35.71)	5 (41.67)	10 (38.46)	6 (42.86)	6 (50.00)	12 (46.15)	3 (21.43)	1 (8.33)	4 (15.39)	14 (100)	12 (100)	26 (100)
Pvt. Sector	4 (26.67)	1 (11.11)	5 (20.83)	8 (53.33)	8 (88.89	16 (66.67)	3 (20)	-	3 (12.5)	15 (100)	9 (100)	24 (100)
Business	1 (16.67)	2 (66.67)	3 (33.33)	4 (66.66)	1 (33.33	5 (55.56)	1 (16.67)	-	1 (11.11)	6 (100)	3 (100)	9 (100)
Pension	4 (66.67)	-	4 (66.67)	2 (33.33)	-	2 (33.33)	-	-	-	6 (100)	-	6 (100)
Religious activities	6 (46.15)	-	6 (33.33)	3 (23.08	2 -40	5 (27.78)	4 (30.77)	3 (60)	7 (38.89)	13 (100)	5 (100)	18 (100)
Total	24 (39.34)	8 (27.59)	32 (35.56)	26 (42.62)	17 (58.62	43 (47.78)	11 (18.04)	4 (13.79)	15 (16.66)	61 (100)	29 (100)	90 (100)

Note: Figures in the parentheses indicate percentages.

agriculture as principal occupation (3.32 per cent) compared to Mani Gumpa (31.82 per cent) and 5th Mile Lepcha Gaon (23.81 per cent).

The involvement of villagers in off-farming remunerative activities is shown in table 2.14. Out of a population of 697, the percentage of engagement in off-farm remunerative activities is as low as 12.91 only. The percentage of population in remunerative activities is the highest in 5th Mile Lepcha Gaon (47.78) followed by Mani Gumpa (35.56) and Pochaok (16.66). The largest proportion of population are engaged in State Govt. services (28.89) followed by private sector (26.67), religious activities (20.00), business (10.00), central government (7.78) and pension category (6.67).

Except one agricultural officer in 5th Mile Lepcha Gaon, there is no first or second grade employee among the Lepchas. They are slowly entering into the modern tertiary sector and accepted even computer oriented activities as their way of life. Lepcha economy witness a sort of dichotomy where as high as 20.00 per cent population earns from religious activities while nearly 4.00 per cent engage in sophisticated modern sector. Lepchas have not spared in entering the business sector although the efficiency and the quality of engagement is not at all appreciable. Compared to their early dependence on agriculture or forest, Lepchas have started joining a variety of remunerative activities.

Table 2.15: Household-wise Engagement in Off-farming Remunerative Activities

Name of village	One member	Two members	More than two members	Total	Non-engagement	Total
1	2	3	4	5	6	7
Mani Gumpa	10 (45.45)	6 (27.27)	1 (4.55)	17 (77.27)	5 (22.73)	22 (100)
5th Mile Lepcha Gaon	7 (33.33)	2 (9.53)	8 (38.09)	17 (80.95)	4 (19.05)	21 (100)
Pochak	8 (10.52)	3 (3.95)	-	11 (14.52)	65 (85.53)	76 (100)
Total	25 (21.01)	11 (9.24)	9 (7.57)	45 (37.82)	74 (62.18)	119 (100)

Note: Figures in the parentheses indicate percentages.

Household-wise engagement of population in off-farm remunerative activities is shown in table 2.15. Household-wise engagement is the highest in 5th Mile Lepcha Gaon (80.95 per cent) followed by Mani Gumpa (77.27 per cent) and Pochaok (14.82 per cent). Engagement of more than two members is the highest in 5th Mile Lepcha Gaon followed by Mani Gumpa while no such case is found in Pochaok. Considering the table we can infer that 5th Mile Lepcha Gaon is better placed among all the three villages in respect of remunerative activities. Mani Gumpa ranks second and Pochaok ranks third.

NOTES

1. Tribes deny any organised political party among them. Even their country need not be ruled by any king or like the same person. "It may, or may not, have a *single* chief or a few elders who may wield more or less power within the community." [Nayek, 1988: 36].
2. Andre Beteille outlined some boundaries, which demarcate certain limits of interaction in any tribal society. Geographical boundary is one such important aspect, which can differentiate tribes from non-tribes. While defining tribe Beteille (1971) writes that "tribe is a society the members of which have a common territory." [Beteille: 10-11]. In other words, "there should be a comparative geographical isolation of the people with others". [Nayek, 1988: 33]. "A community, however small it may be remains in isolation from the other communities within a geographical region." [Enrenfels as quoted by Nayek, 1988: 36].
3. Demographic details of West Bengal many a times confusing and information vary with the variation of sources of data. For example, J.H. Hutton (ed) *Census of India, 1931* (P-548) shows the following doubtful Lepcha population of Bengal:

Years	1931	1921	1911	1901	1891
Lepchas in Bengal	25,780	18,690	18,874	19,451	15,507

While A.E. Porter in his Census of India 1931 shows the following figure of Lepchas for Bengal and Sikkim [P-244].

Years	1931	1921	1911	1901	1891	1881	1872
Lepchas in Bengal	25,161	18,690	18,737	19,371	15,479	-	-
Darjeeling	19,909	20,916	17,053	15,693	14,145	7,018	3,157

Census of India 1961, village survey Monograph on Upper Pedong of Darjeeling [P-53] shows Lepcha population in Darjeeling for the year 1961 as 14,910.

As against all these, the Lepcha Association in Aachuley Vol. I. No.2 1999 [P-3] claimed that there are approximately 70,000 Lepchas inhabiting in the district. It is also informed by Loden Lepcha, the General Secretary *Mopelnoboo Totkat*, the Lepcha Youth Wing, which they could collect by this time around 36,000 Lepchas from the two blocks of Kalimpong sub-division for the year 2000.

4. In Tripura, Lepchas are included as one of the 20 tribes who are recognised as Scheduled Tribe in the state. The total number of Lepcha population in the state has increased from 7(as per 1961 census) to 14 (as per 1971 census). Census document (1971) shows that Lepchas live in two districts: West Tripura district (total number 10) and South Tripura district (total number 4). Following table shows negligible proportion of Lepcha population compared to the total strength of tribes in the state and their proportionate variation over the decade.

Statement of S.T. and Lepcha Population in Tripura

	Population		Percentage Variation
	1961	1971	between 1961-1971
All tribes	360070	450544	+ 25.13
Lepcha	7	14	+ 100.00

Source: *Census of India – Tripura 1971*. Social and cultural Table – Part II C(*i*) V.A. Special Tables on SC, ST. Govt. of India. P-22.

It is evident that in spite of 100 per cent growth of Lepcha population in Tripura during the decade 1961-1971, their proportion compared to the total tribes in the state remain as negligible as 0.0031 in 1971 compared to 0.0016 in 1961. Over the decade there has been a marked change in religious faith among the Lepchas in Tripura. In 1961 majority of Lepcha (71.43 per cent) were Buddhist. A large percentage of Lepchas have converted into Christianity from both Hinduism and Buddhism. The following table shows percentage distribution of Lepchas by religion over the decade 1961-1971.

Percentage Distribution of Lepchas by Religion in Tripura

Year	Total	Hindus	Buddhist	Christian
1961	100	71.43	28.57	—
1971	100	57.14	—	42.86

Source: Ibid. P-130.

In Tripura 35.71 per cent Lepchas are literate. The percentage of literacy is more among the male (80 per cent) than among the females (20 per cent). The following table shows educational status of Lepchas in Tripura.

Education among the Lepchas in Tripura – 1971.

Population			Illiterate			Literate		
Male	Female	Total	Male	Female	Total	Male	Female	Total
10	4	14	6	3	9	4	1	5

Source: Ibid. p. 18.

Census document reveals the maximum educational standard among the Lepchas in Tripura is Principal/Junior Basic level. This low education is closely connected with their industrial classification. Out of 6 persons engaged on different activities, 2 are engaged in construction, 1 in transport, and 3 on other services. Out of remaining 8 non-workers 4 are male and 4 are female.

5. According to Sonam Wangdi Lepcha full Lepcha means when both father and mother of a child are Lepcha. Half Lepcha means when one of the parents specially father is Lepcha but mother is non-Lepcha. Quarter Lepcha means when in two generations one of the parents particularly the grandfather is Lepcha.

6. Origin of Lepcha Agriculture:

Debate centres on the question of origin of agriculture in the hills. Some say that at the time of settlement of Nepalis in Darjeeling hills by the Britishers during the 40's and 50's of the last century, there was no agriculture in the hills and it is the Nepalis who brought agriculture with them. But there was not much logic behind such argument. Evidences prove that Lepchas were practicing agriculture before Nepalis settlement in the hills, may be in crude form. Sikkim Raj used to collect revenue from those who were using land for agricultural practices. Mingma Tshering Lepcha of Mani Gumpa is of the opinion that: "It is we who teach agriculture to the Nepalis, not we were taught by them. It is our land, we know it perfectly; we know what to produce at what time, how to produce etc. We are the indigenous people of the region and our forefathers used to depend only on agriculture."

It may be rational to believe that the Nepalis might have been introduced some of the techniques of agriculture in this region. Migration of population not only migrate some souls but also migrates culture, technology, religion and so on and so forth from one place to another. It will be more so if the number of migrants outnumbered the original inhabitants. When British occupied Darjeeling there were only 100 souls but population increased many a times due to settlement of Nepalis. It may be natural that the dominant class might have influenced the suppressed class in agriculture also. In transforming Lepchas from their original shifting cultivation, *Zomaal*, to terrace cultivation Nepalis might have played an important role which has rightly been pointed out by O'Malley "from the Nepalis they (Lepchas) have also learnt how to construct on the mountain slopes the terraces which form such a distinctive feature of Himalayan cultivation"[O'Malley, 1907: 64].

During the original *Zomaal* cultivation, Lepchas used to cultivate paddy in dry land. This variety of paddy has further been substituted by the wet cultivation in *Panikhet*, which may be due to the outside influences. Our brief review about the variety of crop in this chapter reveals that new crops have entered in the Lepcha agricultural calendar with the passage of time. The Britishers have entirely introduced tea cultivation in Darjeeling. After their settlement Britishers might have introduced some crop like vegetable etc. to satisfy their daily consumption requirements.

Regarding the technique used by Lepchas in old days and changes thereof by the Nepalis, A.K. Das comments: "In old days Lepchas had no plough and the implements used by them were mainly meant for scraping and softening the soil for reception of seeds. The traditional type of implements that have been in use for farming is the wide shoved like hoe and it is used for loosening the earth and cleaning it of weeds. There are in addition two or three pronged hoes used for loosening the earth and relieving it of weeds. Now the method employed for cultivation in general is more or less similar to that of the plains areas of the State and use of plough has been borrowed from the Nepalese." [1978: 57]

Quoting Lepcha folk tales, Nima Taknilamov and the party find some source of Lepcha agriculture. Around 1300 A.D. Lepcha King of Sikkim Ranji Pomo married queen Zolosy Pandi, daughter of Raja Deb Chandra of *Zolosy* means Jalpaiguri. *Zolosy* in Lepcha means the country of Paddy. Zolosy Pandi was born and brought up in plains and knew about its agriculture. But when she came up in the hills after marriage, she could not match the timings of crops. She thus, sends a message to her mother through Teesta River requesting her to inform the timings of crops in hill areas. It is told that mother queen send a message through a bird known as *Kurnoak* indicating the time for producing vegetables. It is told that during April-May when the bird comes from the plains, Lepchas consider the period suitable for vegetables. Even now the Lepchas of Main Gumpa belief in the arrival of *Kurnoak* and hurridly complete sowing seeds within times.

7. *Khasmahal* is an administrative classification or division of land and is widely used in the hills of Darjeeling since the British period. C.A. Bell (1905) and H.C.V. Philpot (1925) in their survey and settlement have used the term without any specification of the term. It seems *Khasmahal* has been derived from a Nepali word (*Khas* means main or prime and

Mahal means the dwelling place). Hence, the place where the *raiyats* mainly live and use land for agricultural purposes had been identified as *Khasmahal* during the British period.

8. The sex ratio among the Lepchas in Nepal is highly imbalanced. In contrast to that of in Mani Gumpa there are more males than females in Nepal. The overall sex ratio of population of Nepal counted in 1991 is 99.5 that mean 995 males per thousand female. But the sex ratio for the Lepchas is found to be unexpectedly very high. It is 153.47 that mean 1534 males per thousand female. This rank first among the ethnic groups in Nepal and seems to be very unrealistic [Niroula, 2000: 15-56].

9. Tribal economy cannot and should not be identified in the way it is defined by the Western economists and applied by them for the people of developed Western countries where division of labour and specialisation are proper. But in a tribal society neither division of labour nor specialisation are in application in the proper sense of the terms. People in tribal society simultaneously involve in multifarious economic activities. The person who does farming also engage in other activities like household construction, kitchen garden, livestock rearing, petty business etc. As agriculture is seasonal, farmers during off-season guided by their family requirements and availability of workers perform a variety of work which may not be directly linked with agriculture. Even the full time salaried person helps agricultural activities during the peak season as per availability of time and requirement. The same is true for student whose concentration does not confine to studies only. They contribute farming by providing labour. Even at the cost of study, students do help farming activities during the peak agricultural season. It is very common that both before and after school, students do help farming directly or indirectly. It has been observed that the percentage of absentee students drastically increases during the peak season in agriculture areas. Out of this experience, vacations or holidays in the schools particularly located in the rural areas are scheduled on the basis of agricultural operations.

   The picture remains more or less same with the other members of the family. Children much before becoming adult forced to involve in a number of activities. Children before going to school, on the basis of sex, involve in a variety of both domestic and outside activities. Besides helping her mother in household activities, a girl child also care livestocks, kitchen garden or even minor and less laborious work in agriculture.

   In the event of these situations, it would not be possible to get a clear-cut idea of division of labour and hence occupation as it is applicable in case of developed countries.

   Instead of occupation as such, tribal economy can better be represented on the basis of the involvement of people in different types of activities. Activities on the basis of monetary return can be grouped in two broad categories – remunerative and non-remunerative activities. Remunerative activities are those from where the individuals get direct return in monetary term. Non-remunerative, on the other hand, are those activities from where the individual may not get directly any monetary return but these activities do help in either direct consumption or production of those commodities, which are not meant for marketing. In agricultural activities, production of some commodities one directly linked with market, say cardamom or ginger production in Lepcha society. Production of these two crops may be regarded as remunerative. But production of some other crops likes paddy, vegetables etc. got less direct linkage with market. Surplus, if any, usually sent to market for sale. Market value of a number of activities like kitchen garden, caring livestocks, etc. cannot be calculated in monetary terms. But these activities got direct bearing with consumption and no less important for a family by any means. On the other hand, individuals in a number of cases produce these commodities, which got comparatively much less market value, but they cater to the need of the person.

Activities on the basis of involvement and participation can be grouped as principal activities and subsidiary activities. Principal activities are the main activities where the individual basically involve e.g. study for a student is regarded as principal activity but during the off-study period if he/she helps in household or farming, it would be regarded as subsidiary activity. These principal and subsidiary activities may again be remunerative, non-remunerative or both.

As per the gravity of work some activities are essential while others are non-essential. Labour in agriculture is an essential type of activities the individuals at any cost need to extend at the time of requirement and need. Some works are also time bound and should be performed as and when they deserve, for example, in farming one cannot wait for even a day or so to finish the work. But when a child carries lunch or tiffin for labourers in a mid-day can be counted as non-essential and can be done by other methods. But the activity of the child is no doubt helpful for agriculture and do contribute in total production however negligible it may be.

CHAPTER THREE

OWNERSHIP AND OPERATION OF LAND

Tribal Economy in general is agriculture dependent. In agriculture, in general, land is indispensable factor of production. But as the non-land inputs are insignificant, land occupies a prime and special role in any tribal agriculture. The tribes can be differentiated from non-tribes on the basis of different criteria associated with land. In other words, some characteristics connected with land in any tribal agrarian economy are peculiar to it and can easily be differentiated from other types of peasant economy.

In the present chapter, we have tried to examine some different aspects of the land-management system of the Lepcha in the light of what we have already discussed in our introductory chapter in connection with land. It has been noted that two particular aspects i.e. – management and ownership of land are crucial for the characterisation of tribal peasant economy. The core area of the present chapter is to highlight on three important aspects connected with land: (i) management of land, (ii) the ownership of land and (iii) some other but relevant aspects like land holding pattern, rent, measurement, classification as observed among the Lepchas.

MANAGEMENT OF LAND

Social formation can be viewed from the management of land of any society. In capitalistic society, management or organisation has emerged as a separate and important co-ordinating factor of production. But it is difficult rather impossible to separate management as a separate factor in any tribal social formation. Sophisticated and distinct type of land management directs any society from its tribal nature. In this section, we try to find the management of land among the Lepchas from the point of view of ownership, genealogy and the terms and conditions of share-cropping.

Land Management in the Study Area

The land management in our study area has been shown in Table 3.1. A perusal of the table shows that largest percentage (82.35) of land is managed by the owner cultivator followed by the owner cultivator cum share-cropper (7.57 per cent), agricultural labour (3.36 per cent), non-agriculturist (2.52 per cent), owner non-cultivator (1.68 per cent), share-cropper cum agricultural labour (1.68 per cent) and absentee landowner (0.84 per cent). But share-cropping is not unusual among the Lepchas. Share-cropping is done either by the owner cultivator or the agricultural labour. No household depends absolutely on share-cropping. It may be due to the fact that landowner feels comfortable to lease out his land to those who have land of their own or work as agricultural labour.

Mani Gumpa

In Mani Gumpa, land is managed by all the different categories except absolute share-croppers. Although management of land is spread over but highest percentage (36.36) of land is under the owner cultivator, followed by owner cultivator-cum share-cropper (31.81). Among the three villages Mani Gumpa records lowest percentage of land under owner cultivator and highest percentage under the category of owner cultivator cum share-cropper. Most of the households under the category of owner cultivator cum share-cropper are sharing rent-free *Gumpa* land (details of rent free land are shown separately in this chapter). *Gumpa* is the common meeting place and its property is considered as common village property enjoyed by many villagers. There is no such common land in the other two villages and hence the rate of share-cropping is also minimum in those villages. Absentee landowners and non-cultivating landowners are the two major categories who mostly leased out their land in share-cropping. Some landowners prefer giving land for share-cropping due to non-availability of household labour. The lone household engaged in agricultural labour is a refugee settled in the village on a plot of land donated by a relative and does not possess any cultivable land of his own. Two households settled in the village by purchasing land for dwelling purposes. They are service holders and do not possess any cultivable land. Beside these three, the rest of the households got cultivable land and manage land either by their family labour or by share-cropping.

5th Mile Lepcha Gaon

The smallest village, 5th mile Lepcha Gaon, is managing the land by the owner cultivator, cultivator cum share-cropper and agricultural labour. The owner cultivator managed the largest proportion of land (80.95 per cent) and that is followed by the agricultural labour (9.53 per cent) and owner cultivator cum shareropper (4.70 per cent). Landowners with their presence in the village undertake the agricultural operations. Landowners in the category of absentee or non-cultivator are totally absent. This shows dependence of the Lepchas on land. The percentage of agricultural labour (14.29) is the highest in this village. This is due to the practice of separation of adopted child from the original house without giving any agricultural land except the land for dwelling purposes only. Such families depend for their livelihood on selling of labour force to the agricultural land of others. With reference to share-cropping there is only one household of owner cultivator cum share-cropper. The small landowners prefer to cultivate their land with hired labour than to give it for share-cropping. The comment of Ezra Lepcha is self-explanatory: 'by giving land for share-cropping no landowner likes to invite a permanent headache of the present land laws. The share-croppers do know the present tenancy laws and are ready to withdraw from share-cropping only if they get minimum 8 decimal of land free of cost.' Only in one case, as the present owner does not live in the village, his land is cultivated by its previous owner on share basis.

Pochaok

In Pochaok, land is managed almost absolutely by the owner cultivators. The percentage of owner cultivator is as high as 96.04. There is only one household in each category of owner cultivator cum share-cropper, share-cropper cum agricultural labour and agricultural labour. The table shows that either the absentee landowner or non-cultivator landowner or share-cropper manages no lands. Land is the

Table 3.1: Land Management

Name of Village	Non-Agriculturist	Non-Cultivating land owner		Owner Cultivator	Owner Cultivator cum share cropping	Share Cropper	Share Cropper-cum-Agr. Labour	Agricultural Labour	Total
		Absentee	Non-Cultivator						
1	2	3	4	5	6	7	8	9	10
Mani Gumpa	2 (9.09)	1 (4.55)	2 (9.09)	8 (36.36)	7 (31.81)	-	1 (4.55)	1 (4.55)	22 (100
5th Mile Lepcha Gaon	1 (4.76)	-	-	17 (80.95)	1 (4.76)	-	-	32 (9.53)	21 (100)
Pochaok	-	-	-	73 (96.04)	1 (1.32)	-	1 (1.32)	1 (1.32)	76 (100)
Total	43 (2.52)	1 (0.84)	- 2	98 (82.35)	9 (7.57)	-	2 (1.68)	4 (3.36)	119 (100)

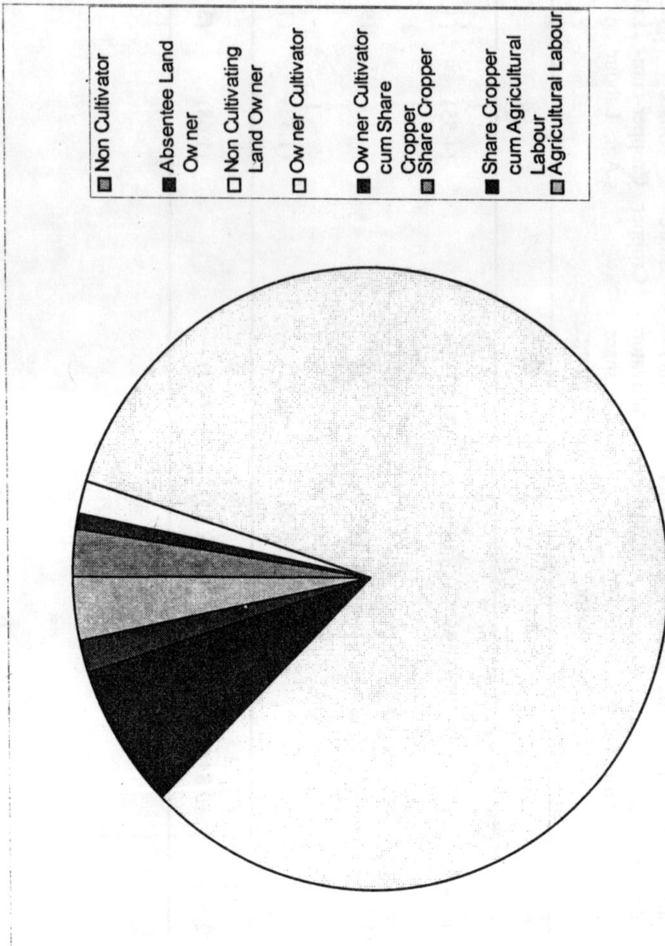

3.1: Pie Diagram showing Land Management

only means of production and lack of alternative source of work compels the owners to engage themselves absolutely on agricultural operations. In Pochaok, the percentage of owner cultivator (96.04) is much higher than that of the average of all the three villages (82.35). Meager entry in the category of agricultural labour shows that no household is without land under their possession and no landowner depends on others for the cultivation of his land. Non-entry in the non-cultivating landowner column shows that owners on the one hand reside in the village and do not keep themselves away from cultivating land.

Table 3.1 has been represented in terms of Pie table and Pie diagram. They show that as high as 296.46° of the circle is engaged by the owner cultivator while the rest 63.54° of the circle is distributed among five categories of management like non-cultivating landowner (9.07°), absentee landowner (3.02 °), non-cultivator (6.05°), owner cultivator cum share-cropper (12.25°), share-cropper cum agricultural labour (6.05°) and agricultural labour (12.10°).

Land Management By *Moo*

Moo[1] is an important ethnic component in distributing land among the Lepchas. It has been seen that Mani Gumpa is dominated by two original *moos*: *Holoongmoo* and *Gauloogmoo*. The four original moos of 5th mile Lepcha Gaon are *Sadamoo, Singthimoo, Karthakmoo* and *Ethanmoo*. Among 17 moos in Pochaok, the dominant ones are *Sangmamoo, Gangtokmoo, Fudungmoo, Gauloogmoo* and *Tamblayangmoo*. Out of 31 *moos* present in the study area, the original 11 *moos* dominate over the land holding. Land distribution among the different *moos* has been important bearing on the pattern of land management. It may be noted that Lepchas rarely sell or purchase land and for all practical purposes land is occupied on hereditary basis where *moo* plays a vital role. As lands are transmitted on hereditary basis, they remain in the hands of the same *moo* for generations together until they are sold to other *moos*. It has also been observed that the original *moos* are mostly orthodox in using their land for traditional crops and techniques. The new comers, whose number is not significant, are more adoptive in new crops and techniques. Crop variety and land management are directly correlated. Lands used for traditional crops are managed traditionally by the traditional or original *moos*. Management of land for the modern crops is more complex and are organised mainly by the new comers who have settled in the village on lands gifted to them.

Table 3.2: Pie Table showing Land Management by the Different Categories

Sl. No.	Categories of Land Management	Percentage	Degree Percentage × 3.6
1.	Non-Cultivator	2.52	2.52×3.6=9.07°
2.	Absentee land owner	0.84	0.84×3.6=3.02°
3.	Non-Cultivating land owner	1.68	1.68×3.6=6.05°
4.	Owner cultivator	82.35	82.35×3.6=296.46°
5.	Owner cultivator-cum-share cropper	7.57	7.57×3.6=27.25°
6.	Share-Cropper	-	-
7.	Share-Cropper-cum-Agricultural labour	1.68	1.68×3.6=6.05°
8.	Agricultural Labour	3.36	3.36×3.6=12.10°

Village-wise land management by the different *moos* in the study area is shown in Table 3.3.

The table reveals that in Mani Gumpa the two original *moos*- *Holocngmoo* and *Gauloogmoo* not only occupy the largest land but also manage the land by themselves. The percentage of owner cultivator and owner cultivator cum share-cropper belonging to these two *moos* are as high as 87.50 and 71.43 per cent respectively. The other *moos* are sporadically spread over the different categories of land management either because of non-availability of their own cultivable land, land on share basis or availability of family labour. The original *moos* are the founders of the *Gumpa* in the village and take advantage of cultivating rent free *Gumpa* land on share basis since the beginning. The other households belonging to *Pheyonglamoo* by virtue of their act as Lama in the *Gumpa* got the advantage of share-cropping on the *Gumpa* land. All other latecomer *moos* in the village are denied the facilities of share-cropping and are engaged in land management through their participation as agricultural labour.

Distribution of land in 5th Mile Lepcha Gaon among the different *moos* is concentrated among the owner cultivator. As high as 80.95 per cent households irrespective of their *moos* prefer to manage their land on their own. Households belonging to the original *moos* (*Sadamoo, Singthimoo, Karthakmoo* and *Ethanmoo*) as well as later intruders keep full control on their land by cultivating it on their own. Sharecropping is rare (only 4.76 per cent) and that too is practised by only one original *moo* (*Sadamoo*) member who had sold the land to an outsider. The households in the category of agricultural labour belong to two different *moos* that actually brought up as adopted child and get land from their pater father for dwelling purpose.

In Pochaok the land is managed absolutely by the owner cultivators. Out of 17 moos, 15 of them irrespective of their number of households are engaged in managing land by themselves. The *moos* (*Yunchungmoo* and *Pachisingamoo*) who involved either as agricultural labour or share-cropper cum agricultural labour are comparatively new households in the village.

Sharecropping is almost absent and only 1.32 per cent of households undertake share-cropping and these households belong to comparatively late settled *moo* (*Sambarmoo*) in the village. The original five *moos* (*Sangmamoo, Gangtokmoo, Fudungmoo, Gauloogmoo, and Tamblayangmoo*) manage their land absolutely by themselves. Finding no alternative jobs, all *moos* keep themselves absolutely engaged in managing their own land. Not much difference between the original *moos* and comparatively newly settled *moos* are marked regarding the management of land in Pochaok.

Land management among all the *moos* in the study area reveals the followings:

1. Number of households belonging to the original *moos* in each study village is more as compared to those who settled lately in the village.
2. Self-cultivation is the basic pattern of land management among the Lepchas in all the villages. As high as 82.35 per cent lands are managed by the owners themselves.

Table 3.3: Land Management by Different Moo

Sl. No.	Name of *Moo*	Non-Cultivator	Non-cultivating land owner: Absentees	Non-cultivating land owner: Non-cultivator	Owner Cultivator	Owner cultivator cum share cropper	Share cropper	Share cum Agr. Labour	Agr. Labour	Total
1	2	3	4	5	6	7	8	9	10	11
	A. Village: Mani Gumpa									
1	*Holoongmoo*				3 (42.86)	3 (42.86)			1 (14.28)	7 (100.00)
2	*Gauloogmoo*			1 (100.00)	4 (57.14)	2 (28.57)				7 (100.00)
3	*Pheyonglamoo*					2 (100.00)				2 (100.00)
4	*Liangmoo*									1 (100.00)
5	*Namchumoo*	2 (100.00)								2 (100.00)
6	*Nanimoo*									1 (100.00)
7	N.A.	1 (50.00)						1 (50.00)		2 (100.00)
	Total	2 (0.09)	1 (4.54)	2 (9.00)	8 (36.37)	7 (31.83)	-	1 (4.54)	1 (4.54)	22 (100.00)
	B: Village: 5th Mile Lepcha Goan									
1	*Sadamoo*	1 (12.50)			6 (75.00)	1 (12.50)				8 (100.00)
2	*Singthimoo*				3 (75.00)				1 (25.00)	4 (100.00)
3	*Tingmoo*				1 (50.00)				1 (50.00)	2 (100.00)
4	*Tukutsomoo*				2 (100.00)					2 (100.00)
5	*Karthakmoo*				2 (100.00)					2 (100.00)
6	*Torongmoo*				1 (100.00)					1 (100.00)

7	*Ethanmoo*				1 (100.00)					1 (100.00)
8	*Namchumoo*				1 (100.00)					1 (100.00)
	Total	1 (4.76)			17 (80.95)	1 (4.76)			2 (9.53)	21 (100.00)
					C : Village : Pochaok					
1	*Sangmamoo*				22 (100.00)				22 (100.00)	
2	*Gangtokmoo*				8 (100.00)					8 (100.00)
3	*Fudungmoo*				10 (100.00)				10 (100.00)	
4	*Gauloogmoo*				6 (100.00)					6 (100.00)
5	*Tamblayangmoo*				7 (100.00)					7 (100.00)
6	*Sambarmoo*				3 (100.00)	1 (25.00)				4 (100.00)
7	*Kabimoo*				4 (100.00)					4 (100.00)
8	*Mulummoo*				4 (100.00)					4 (100.00)
9	*Mulumyak Chiboomoo*				1 (100.00)					1 (100.00)
10	*Karvomoo*				2 (100.00)					2 (100.00)
11	*Adenmoo*				1 (100.00)					1 (100.00)
12	*Tihilongmoo*				2 (100.00)					2 (100.00)
13	*Numfrichingsmoo*				1 (100.00)					1 (100.00)
14	*Fudunglaghamoo*				1 (100.00)					1 (100.00)
15	*Sokomoo*									11 (100.00)
16	*Yanchungmoo*				-			1(100.00)		1 (100.00)
17	*Pachisingamoo*				-				1 (100.00)	1 (100.00)
	Total				73 (96.04)	1 (1.32)		1 (1.32)	1 (1.327)	6 (100.00)
	Grand Total	**3**	**1**	**2**	**98 (82.35)**	**9 (7.75)**	-	**2 (1.68)**	**4 (3.36)**	**119 (100.00)**

3. Except Mani Gumpa, the category of owner cultivator cum sharecropper has recently emerged as a partial change in the land management system.
4. Share cropping, as a regular mode of land management does not figure at all in any village. Lepchas irrespective of *moo* prefer to manage land by themselves. Their second preference is leasing land for share-cropping. Normally, the landless households do not get land for share-cropping.
5. Number of agricultural labour (*milaok*), though negligible are found more among the late settlers or among those adopted children soul (*Ta Gri Kup Tsaop*) who got the *moo* from their pater and land for habitation. Lepchas in general do not work as agricultural labour.
6. Out of 119 households, there are only three (2.52 per cent) non-agriculturists. They have no cultivable land or in any way attached with agriculture. They are the service holders and belong to newly settled *moos* of the villages. This supports the age-old proverb 'Landless Lepcha is a myth'.
7. The non-cultivating landowners comprising of both absentee and resident non-cultivating owners are found only in Mani Gumpa. They mostly belonged to the newly settled *moos*. The low percentage (2.25) of non-cultivating landowners indicates Lepchas' adherence to self-cultivation.

In a word, the Lepcha owner cultivators largely manage land in the study area. Lepchas are basically agriculturists and consider cultivation as their way of life. It is truer in the case of Pochaok (96.04 per cent) which is situated far away from the town and where alternative employments are almost absent. Village-wise land management by the different *moos* in the study area is shown in Table 3.3.

Terms and Conditions of Share Cropping

Sharecropper, which Lepchas call *Pachure*, is another important agrarian category among the Lepchas. Share cropping as an absolute mode of land management does not emerge at all in the study area (table 3.1). No household depends solely on share-cropping as its means of livelihood. In other words, no land-owners (*Lyaang drok*) can rely on the landless households for the cultivation of their land on share-cropping. Some amount of share-cropping is however recorded with the category of owner cultivator cum share-cropper. In identifying the causes behind leasing out of land for share-cropping it has been observed that the rent free institutional (*Gumpa)* land of Mani Gumpa is the main land available for share cultivation. A small fraction of land has also been leased out (*Shyao*) for share-cropping due to non-availability of family labour by the owner and by the absentee landowners.

Either parties maintain no written documents regarding the terms and conditions involved in share-cropping. Although everything is verbally decided, but no conflict whatsoever is reported between the owner and share-cropper. The system is maintained over generations, and only in one case it has been carried out for last three years in Mani Gumpa village. Sharecropping can be categorised in two broad types: traditional and contractual.[2] There is a certain demand in getting land for sharecropping than the supply (letting out), which is almost negligible. In recent years, landowners prefer to keep their land unused rather than leasing it out for sharecropping thus avoid and falling under the trap of tenancy law, which is mostly designed in favour of the share-croppers. Choden Lepcha of Mani Gumpa informed, "This year I had to take lease a portion of land from late ex-MLA Gajendra Gurung which is just bordering our village. I requested but failed to get land from our village landowners. Thus I had to opt from the neighbouring village as I am badly in need of new land for gladioli cultivation."

Lands under the traditional share-croppers are used for the cultivation of age-old crops like paddy, maize and millet whereas the contractual share-croppers prefer to produce modern cash crops like gladioli in such lands. After harvest the traditional crops are normally shared equally (50:50) between the landowner and share-cropper. But there are some exceptions also. In 5th Mile Lepcha Gaon the lone landowner gets only half of the produce in case of paddy while the other crops, like maize and vegetables are enjoyed absolutely by the share-cropper. But as a good gesture, many a times, a share-cropper sends a minor fraction of his produce to the owners' house. Subash Lepcha informed "this year I received 5.5 *tungfri-khaa-kaat* (nearly 80 kg.) of paddy as my share. For maize I need not pay anything to the landowner as I have already paid 1 *tungfri-khaa-kaat* of paddy in advance during the harvest of paddy in lieu of whatever maize I can produce in the field." In Pochoak along with fifty per cent paddy the share-cropper used to give extra ¼ amount of paddy as his share for the other crops to be produced in the remaining part of the year. The landowners thus get ¾ proportion of paddy produced in their land immediately after harvesting. On the other hand the share-croppers get ¼ of paddy and the entire amount of other products cultivated during the whole year.

The terms of share in case of contractual share-cropping are different from the traditional one. The lands in such cases are used for producing cash crops and which need greater investment than usually required for food crops like paddy. Land is normally leased-out for three years and in each year a lessee needs to pay a fixed amount of money or preferably paddy in lieu of other crops. The share-cropper may not produće paddy at all but needs to meet the agreement by purchasing paddy or managing paddy from other sources. In most cases the amount of paddy to be given to the lessor is decided on the basis of average productivity of the land. Mingma Tshering Lepcha informed that this year his brother has taken a plot of land on contract basis and "he has to pay 3 *tungfri-khaa-kaat* of paddy against the leased-in land whose productivity is 7-8 *tungfri-khaa-kaat* per year. My brother has taken a risk because cultivation of modern crops is very uncertain and many could not recover the invested amount in the previous years." The landholders in such cases are risk free and receive the contracted amount irrespective of the volume of product. As agriculture is nature based, there is fluctuation in crop productivity. In some cases the harvesting period of certain modern crop differs from traditional ones. But it is customary on the part of the leaseholder to pay his rent/share during the harvest of paddy, which often appears somewhat burdensome on the part of the lessee.

The landowner's contribution to cultivation limits mainly to supply of land to the share-cropper. Sometimes the share-cropper does supply non-land agricultural inputs like seed, fertiliaer, but their supply is neither uniform nor regular. After harvest while receiving their share of paddy, landowners deduct the amount of paddy used as seed. Some argue that beside paddy they do not receive anything so that share-cropper should provide with seed. Some are of the opinion that seed (*be*) and cow dung manure (*biyet*) can easily be purchased by the sale money of byproducts of paddy like the straw or hay of paddy. Lepchas mostly use cow dung available domestically for cultivation. It means Lepchas hardly invest anything on purchasing fertiliser. Hence, the sharing of cost on fertiliser by the landowner is not much relevant while selling the straw of paddy can easily purchase seeds. The shareholder without any cattle cannot get domestic manure. The local price of one *tung-jyaang* (12-15 kg) of cow dung manure is Rs.10/-, which can be recovered by selling the straw at the rate of Rs.40/- per bundle (30-35 kg. approx).

The management of leased-in land lies entirely in the hands of share-croppers. Sometimes they do consult with the owners but in most cases it is solely controlled and managed by the tenants. Decision regarding types of crops, use of labour, capital, fertilizer, pesticides, is the prerogative of the lessee. The landowners may not even visit the land or supervise it. Their control on land limits on payment of land rent only. Beside the revenue and legal part, practically all controls are vested to the share-croppers.

In addition to giving land for cultivation, the landowners who are comparatively richer often help the tenants in a number of occasions. In Mani Gumpa, the land belongs to *Gumpa* and this institution extends spiritual and financial support to the tenants. All these share-croppers are actively involved in different types of ritual activities. They also provide physical and other services for the construction and management of the *Gumpa*. These share-croppers are the portfolio holders of the *Gumpa* and actively take part in all decision-making. In needs the tenants also take loan (both in cash and kind) from the *Gumpa* without interest. Such tenants hardly make any difference between their own land and lease in land. They consider it to be their duty to look after both the *Gumpa* and its land. A sort of deep mutual involvements and relations exist between the two parties. But the situation is not the same in other two villages where the landowner happens to be the individual. Although no complain from either the party is reported but the sort of oneness like that of the Mani Gumpa is missing for obvious reason. Regarding other types of help Budha Sing Lepcha of Pochaok remarks, "I never seek any sort of financial or other types of help from my landowner. Why shall I do so? He has helped me a lot by leasing his land to me. What else can I expect from him? He is a family man having so many problems of his own and I do not like to burden him any more." Same is the opinion of Subhash Lepcha of 5th Mile Lepcha Gaon.

Recently in share-cropping, a new type of arrangement has emerged in Pochaok. After sowing and nursing, the landowners lease out the ginger field just before the harvest. The lessee takes the responsibility for harvesting and marketing of ginger. Some young Lepchas of the village have formed a sort of co-operative and shoulder the remaining work of the crop i.e. harvesting and marketing either by their own or employing wage labour. In such an arrangement the landowners keep themselves free from organising the labour and bearing risk of any damage caused by insects. The youngs, on the other hand, take some risks and in many cases within very short period make a good profit. This is an emergent phenomenon and is yet to get a sound footing.

OWNERSHIP OF LAND

Lepchas in the contemporary period have settled in the terraced based cultivation. Over decades the individuals have basically owned land in the Lepcha society, like those of neighbouring communities. The ownership patterns of land are relevant for the identification of the type of society or social formation of any community. Some of the aspects of landownership pattern as prevalent among the Lepchas are discussed in the following sections.

Gender and Land Ownership

Pattas of land among the Lepchas are in the names of the heads of family who are generally the male members. In Lepcha society, girl child is welcomed and occupies prestigious position. In context to sharing of wealth among son and daughter, L.S. Tamsang informed "in our society boys receive father's property while girls enjoy right over mother's property. In contemporary period this is limited to movable property like jewellery while lands are in the hands of males and are distributed among sons." It has been observed that in few cases the married girls are gifted with small plot of land for residential purposes only. In those cases where the family got no male child, the girls inherit the landed properties. But if the household got male offspring, girls are denied any cultivable land.

While distributing lands, no uniform criteria are being maintained but usually the eldest male member of the family as per requirements distribute and demarcate land areas among the direct descendants. The different types of land e.g. wet land; dry land, stony land etc. are distributed among the heirs as per family size and other sources of income. Normally the landscape, rivulet, hill top or other specific natural objects are used for demarcating the boundary of land and no water tight division of land is followed. Normally the house and its adjoining areas are given to the eldest son and the rest of the land is distributed almost equally among other sons. A Lepcha family without male offspring occasionally gifts land to the girl child and invites the son-in-law to reside with his bride who inherits the parent's property. Families either without any male offspring or without any issue adopt child (*Ta-gri-kup-tsaop*) and with the permission of the *Keyong Sezong*, the village level organisation accepts the child and allows inheriting all types of property. The non-Lepcha child is also adopted and assimilated into the society by giving Lepcha *moo* or even ST certificate. Appendix-I shows the list of adopted child. Appendix-II shows that two adopted boys and five girls after their marriage received land from their grandfather for dwelling purposes only. The table reveals that girls after marriage are awarded with small plot of land for residential purposes while the adopted son in absence of any issue of the family receives entire landed property.

Lands are enjoyed by the members of present generations, but *pattas* , in many cases, are in the name of their late grand or great grand father. Samudra Prasad, the Bhumi Sahayak of Sindipong *Khasmahal* informed "the individual against whose name the plot number of any specific land is recorded as per settlement record do not conform with the individual who is actually possessing and using the land. For generations together lands have not been transferred to next heirs although the record holder expired long back. Lepcha names are so common that it may often mislead if proper care regarding father's name are not taken care of alongwith the opinion and consultation of the concern village headman." Run Tshering Lepcha and John Tshering Lepcha of 5th Mile Lepcha Gaon are enjoying the proprietary right over the land which is still in the name of their grand mother who passed away long back. Many a cases land taxes are often paid by one household member particularly by the elderly brother (*Ta-do-num*). He usually preserves the land records in his custody while the brothers or even the descendants individually own land in practice.

Land Ownership and Genealogy

Customarily, lands in Lepcha society pass on directly to their male descendants. It has also been observed from field survey that no part of land has been sold or purchased during the last three decades. In 1982, one Lepcha household however, purchased 8 decimal of land from another Lepcha at the cost of Rs.60 thousand in 5th Mile Lepcha Gaon. Over generations, the male child inherits the land. At present each household owns very small amount of land. In Lepcha society the proprietorship over land may change but within the limit of one's own clan (*Ta-do-git*) and more particularly within one's own consanguine (*Ta-do-aagyit athaong*).

Table 3.4 shows distribution of Lepcha *moo* by households, population and land holding for three study villages. The table reveals a skewed distribution of land ownership among the moos. Those *moos* that are the original inhabitants of the village normally possess more land than the new comers.

The village Mani Gumpa is the smallest one in terms of its population and land holding. It is dominated by three *moos* – *Holoongmoo, Gouloogmoo* and *Pheyonglamoo*. The first two *moos* have greater share to population, household and land while *Pheyonglamoo* has the rent free *Gumpa* land in its possession. Proportionately, *Holoongmoo* and *Gauloogmoo* who collectively constitute 63.64 per cent of households and 66.67 per cent of total population, own 49.19 per cent of land in the village. Villagers cannot recall which one of these two *moos* came first to settle in the village but they considered both of them as the original inhabitants of the village. During British rule, one Passang Sherpa, the great grand father of *Holoongmoo* decedents came to marry Rinji Pemo, a Lepcha girl of the village and settled in the village. The 4th and 5th descendants of Passang Sherpa are at present the *Holoongmoo.* It ranks first in terms of households, population and land holding in the village. But after distributing land per head land become the lowest for the *moo.*

Table 3.4: Household, population and land holding as per *Moo*

Sl. No.	Name of Moo	No. of Household	No. of Population	Landholding (in acre)
	A. Village : Mani Gumpa			
1	*Holoongmoo*	7 (31.82)	43 (35.83)	6.12 (27.57)
2	*Gauloogmoo*	7 (31.82)	37 (30.84)	4.8 (21.62)
3	*Pheyonglamoo*	2 (9.09)	16 (13.34)	5.96 (26.85)
4	*Liangmoo*	1 (4.55)	7 (5.83)	3.2 (14.41)
5	*Namchumoo*	2 (9.09)	7 (5.83)	0.25 (1.13)
6	*Nanimoo*	1 (4.55)	3 (2.5)	0.18 (0.81)
7	N.A.	2 (9.09)	7 (5.83)	1.69 (7.61)
	Total	22 (100.00)	120 (100.00)	22.2 (100.00)
	B. Village : 5th Mile Lepcha Gaon			
1	*Sadamoo*	8 (38.09)	52 (39.69)	7.70 (18.75)
2	*Singthimoo*	4 (19.07)	27 (20.62)	3.84 (9.35)
3	*Tingmoo*	2 (9.52)	10 (6.37)	1.66 (4.04)
4	*Tukutsomoo*	2 (9.52)	9 (6.87)	13.72 (33.41)
5	*Karthakmoo*	2 (9.52)	9 (6.87)	4.40 (10.96)
6	*Torongmoo*	1 (4 76)	5 (3.82)	7.33 (17.85)
7	*Ethanmoo*	1 (4.76)	4 (3.05)	0.59 (1.43)
8	*Namchumoo*	1 (4.76)	15 (11.45)	1.73 (4.21)
	Total	21 (100.00)	131 (100.00)	41.07 (100.00)

(contd. . .)

Table 3.4: (Contd.)

Sl. No.	Name of Moo	No. of Household	No. of Population	Landholding (in acre)
	C. Village : Pochaok			
1	*Sangmamoo*	22	122	82.00
		(28.95)	(27.35)	(24.85)
2	*Gangtokmoo*	8	62	39.00
		(10.53)	(13.9)	(11.82)
3	*Fudungmoo*	10	51	45.20
		(13.16)	(11.43)	(13.69)
4	*Gauloogmoo*	6	37	32.50
		97.890	(8.29)	(9.85)
5	*Tamblayangmoo*	7	27	30.90
		(9.23)	(6.06)	(9.37)
6	*Sambarmoo*	4	27	17.25
		(5.27)	(6.06)	(5.23)
7	*Kabimoo*	4	17	12.60
		(5.27)	(3.82)	(3.82)
8	*Mulummoo*	4	16	6.00
		(5.27)	(3.59)	(1.82)
9	*Mulumyak Chiboomoo*	1	16	9.00
		(1.31)	(3.59)	(2.72)
10	*Karvomoo*	2	13	12.00
		(2.63)	(2.91)	(3.64)
11	*Adeumoo*	1	13	2.00
		(1.31)	(2.91)	(0.61)
12	*Tihilongmoo*	2	13	17.00
		(2.63)	(2.91)	(5.15)
13	*Numfrichingsmoo*	1	9	5.51
		(1.31)	(2.02)	(1.67)
14	*Fudunglaghamoo*	1	7	14.00
		(1.31)	(1.57)	(4.24)
15	*Sokomoo*	1	7	5.00
		(1.31)	(1.57)	(1.52)
16	*Yanchungmoo*	1	5	-
		(1.31)	(1.12)	-
17	*Pachisingamoo*	1	4	-
		(1.31)	(0.9)	-
	Total	76	446	329.96
		(100.00)	(100.00)	(100.00)

5th Mile Lepcha Gaon, the second largest village is inhabited by eight *moos*. Of them *Sadamoo* and *Singthimoo* respectively ranks first and second by numerical strength while *Sadamoo* and *Tukutsomoo* in terms of land holding. These three *moos* jointly owned 62 per cent of the total land and 67 per cent of population in the village. It has been reported that five traditional Lepcha houses, *Dokeymoolees* or in short *Ranglees*, belong to four different moos. They are: *Sadamoo, Singthimoo, Karthakmoo* and *Ethanmoo*. These *Ronglees* were:

i) *Cholongbong,* means orange place, belonged to *Sadamoo.*

ii) *Ding,* means flat land to stand for a while, belonged to *Sadamoo.*

iii) *Siking,* means upper ridge, belonged to *Singthimoo.*

iv) *Kakibong,* means a variety of tree, belonged to *Ethanmoo.*

v) *Salbong,* indicate a variety of tree, belonged to *Karthakmoo.*

Lepchas consider *Ranglee* as a symbol of their culture and an excellent specimen of their engineering work. Lepchas proudly refer to those villages where there were *Ronglee* or presence of *Ranglee* at the present day. Existence of *Ranglee* can be considered as an important marker of Lepcha habitation in any hilly areas. It can be further inferred that those who had *Ronglee* are the original inhabitants of the village. All other *moos* settled in the village either by purchasing land or getting gifts from in-laws etc., as adopted child.

Among the study villages, Pochaok is the largest one. In this village, among the 17 *moos, Sangmamoo* alone has a share of 22.35 per cent to total population and 24.85 per cent to land. The other leading *moos* are *Gangtokmoo, Fudungmoo, Gauloogmoo* and *Tamblayangmoo*. All of them are the traditional or original *moos* of Pochaok. *Gauloogmoo* is the only common *moo* found in Mani Gumpa; all the other *moos* are different from the other two villages. *Fudungmoo* occupies second position in terms of its land holding and third by population size. Existence of two *Dookymoolees* indicates the original household of the village belongs to *Fudungmoo. Gangtokmoo* ranks second in terms of population while third in terms of household and land holding. *Gauloogmoo* and *Tamblayangmoo* respectively rank 4th and 5th in terms of all the three criteria. The average landholding per household in Pochaok is much higher (4.34 per cent) than in Mani

Gumpa (1.01 per cent) and 5th Mile Lepcha Gaon (1.96 per cent). It has been noticed that Lepchas in the later two villages reported their land possession in terms of decimal while for Pochaok they replied in terms of acre. It is evident from the Table 3.4 that the amount of land which a single household in Pochaok is holding many a times more than the total amount of land in the possession of entire *moo* in the other two villages. In Pochaok, which is located in a far-flung area, all the households own relatively large sized landed property for agricultural purposes.

The genealogical study reveals that out of 31 *moos* only 11 *moos* are original *moos* of the three villages (2 in Mani Gumpa, 4 in 5th Mile Lepcha Gaon and 5 in Pochaok). The other *moos* have settled at least before three decades and whose details are not available.

It has been noted in the introductory chapter, the ownership right of land can be viewed from two angles – a) the right of transfer and b) the right of use. Let us now discuss these two components of ownership right in the case to the Lepcha society.

Land Transfer

There are two types of land transfer: (a) permanent transfer by sale or partitioning over succession, and (b) temporary transfer in the form of share-cropping or allowing others to reside on land temporarily without conferring any legal right of ownership.

Lepchas now-a-days hardly sell any land. The last case of land purchase in 5th Mile Lepcha Gaon dates back to the year 1982. Lepchas of Mani Gumpa and Pochaok could not recall any incident of land selling in their own villages. They do not know the price of their land and when asked referred only to the price to the neighbouring villages. On sympathetic or some other considerations Lepchas often allow temporary transfer of land for residential use or share-cropping. The same moo and the genealogical table thus permanently occupy lands 3.4 shows that majority of land are still occupied by the original *moos*.

Two contradictory concepts i.e., 'landless Lepcha is a myth' and 'land alienation is a century old problem among the Lepchas' can be understood from historical perspective.

During the Tibetan rule, the ownership right of land, excluding the lands owned by Kazis and Lamas, by the lower strata of people had never been recognised. Ultimate ownership right of land lied in the hands of Chogyal. In case of giving ownership right and withholding right the will of the Chogyal was final. Common Lepchas could live and cultivate free land but in the process of land use they cannot enjoy any right to transfer with out the royal permission. In the case of terrace cultivation the matter differs a little. In this case, the Lepchas enjoyed the right to transfer only the 'land-use right' of terrace land but not the ownership right of the land. Hence, Lepchas finally became landless in true sense though they are the aboriginals of the land.

The system was different during the British rule. After the first survey and settlement of Kalimpong tract in 1882, the *raiyats* received *patta* for their holdings and thus established their right on land (Bell, 1905: 12). But land alienation became a problem and also realised by the Britishers during the first quarter of 20th century. "One of the main considerations in the management of the estate has been the protection, so far as was possible, of Lepchas and Bhutia population, especially the former, from the consequences of their own extravagance, and to prevent them from being displaced by their thriftier Nepali neighbours. Ordinarily no sales of land held by Lepchas or Bhutias are permitted except to a Lepcha or a Bhutia." [Philpot, 1925: 8].

The system of protection and reservation of Lepcha land continues even after independence. The West Bengal Land Reform (Amendment) Act of 1965 imposes restrictions on alienation of land by the Scheduled Tribes.

"Any transfer by a *raiyat* belonging to a Scheduled Tribe of his holding or part thereof shall be void." Regarding mode of transfer of land it says, A *raiyat* belonging to a Scheduled Tribe may transfer his holding or part thereof in any one of the following ways: namely (a) by a complete usufructuary mortgage entered into with a person belonging [to a Scheduled Tribe] for a period not exceeding seven years, (b) by sale or gift to the Government for a public or charitable purpose, (c) by simple mortgage to the government or to a co-operative societies.' [Mallick, 1995: 264]

The Tribal sub plan of West Bengal 1978, acknowledges the alienation of Lepcha land by the more stronger non-tribal communities under different pretext and points out poverty as the root cause of such transgressions, and gives the mode of such transfer by fraud, benami transfers caused by defalcation in the payment of loans [Lepcha, 1979: 155]. It has also been reported that the non-tribals evaded the rule by marrying the Lepcha girls and buying the lands of the Lepchas in the name of their Lepchani wives. The son of the soil who once roam over the entire hill region freely, restricted to use only their small plot of lands for which *patta* was given and ultimately confined to very limited areas due to transfer either among other communities or among the heirs of the same community.

In the process of historical evolution, Lepchas from their roaming and shifting cultivation stage have settled down to terrace based settled cultivation. Land was once belonged to the society or community and each individual enjoyed equal right to use the land. During those periods both the questions of right of transfer and right of use were useless. Later on, during the different phases of alien rule, Lepchas were subject to different types of ownership right with variation in both right to transfer and right to use of their own land.

On the ground of protection and reservation of Lepcha land, the rulers of Colonial and independent India follow more or less same land transfer policy. Since British period, Lepchas are enjoying individual ownership right over land. But they are not free in the matter of right to transfer. They can sell land only among the scheduled tribes and not to any other community.

Recently the Lepcha Association has made a drive to sensitise the Lepchas regarding their aboriginality in the region. As a part of their awareness drive, the Association[3] puts a restriction on sale of land to any non-Lepchas inclusive other scheduled tribes. It urges upon the fellowmen not to sell their land and if required at all only to the Lepchas.

Now the Lepchas can sell land only to the Lepchas. Thus, the sale or transfer of land is confined legally within the community itself. In our study villages no sale of land has been recorded in recent past. But lands have been transferred over generations patrilineally and thus, remain in the possession of the same *moo* of the Lepchas.

Users of Land

Land is used by two groups of people (a) owners of land and (b) share-croppers and agricultural labourers. These two groups are quite heterogeneous in terms of social composition. It has been observed that the educated youths are guided more by the modern outlook and in many times are in conflict with the elderly persons of traditional outlook. Both the cropping patterns and process of production varies widely between the youths and the elderly persons. On the basis of primary occupation of Lepchas and their nature of involvement in actual operations they may be classified into following categories:

1) **Absentee non-cultivating landowners**: Such landowners mostly got their lands on hereditary basis but do not live in the village due to employment and other reasons. These Lepchas settled elsewhere however visit their land during harvesting to collect their shares. Such absentee landowners have nothing to do with actual operation and use of land.

2) **Resident but non-cultivating landowners**: Unlike the first group, these landowners stay in the village but do not cultivate the land on their own. They undertake the following methods in cultivating land:

    a) Depend entirely on village labour of permanent nature. It is the labours that generally bring their implements and tools. They employ hired ploughman with bullocks for ploughing and levelling the land on rent.

    b) Some owners cultivate the land by appointing share-croppers. Non-availability of family labour, possession of larger acres of land are the major contributing factor of giving land on share-cropping.

    c) Some owners who are principally engaged in other off-form occupations cannot work in the field. They usually undertake cultivation by supplying agricultural implements and tools to the hired labours and use ploughman and bullock on hire.

    d) The relatively large-sized landowners with less family labour cultivate their land with the help of village labour in exchange of crops and other social agential services. These land owners occupy a prestigious position in the society like mandals and extend various agential services to the village. They act as agent between the government and the illiterate and ignorant villagers.

3) **Owner cultivator**: The landowners who cultivate land on their own belong to following categories:

a) The small and middle landowners undertake all agricultural operations with their family labour. They usually hire ploughman for land tilling and levelling but other operations are entirely done by household labour.

b) The middle and large landowners operate their land with family labour and mutual exchange of labour. They work on their own land as well of others. They also exchange their ploughman and bullock with others in lieu of labour.

c) Landowners in some cases receive both human and animal labour against cash or crops. Lack of family labour compels them to purchase outside labour by paying them in crops. Those outside labours normally do not possess any land and they may not need labour in exchange. So the landowner pays them in paddy.

d) Lepchas with large sized lands cultivate a part of their land with their household labour and leased out the remaining part to others for share-cropping.

e) Owner cultivators are also partly share-croppers. They cultivate their own land and leased in land with the help of their household labour.

4) **Share cropping:** In Lepcha society share-cropping is very rare and is operated mainly with the institutional lands (e.g. *Gumpa* land). The small landowners and landless Lepchas undertake share-cropping by using their household labour. In addition to hired or exchanged labour at times of requirement, they also deploy ploughman and bullocks

on rent. Small landowners with bullocks prefer to get some land on lease so that they could make a viable use of bullocks for agricultural operations. Share cropping is normally found in the case of traditional crops like paddy, maize and millet and where the produce is shared on 50:50 bases.

5) **Contractual lease**: Beside conventional pattern of share-cropping, lands are also leased out on contract basis. These lands are used mainly for the cultivation of commercial crops like gladioli. But the payments are made on the basis of average production of major traditional crops like paddy, millet and maize and are being fixed on the basis of mutual negotiation and agreement. The risks of production are borne by the tenants and the landowners receive a fixed amount of crop. Lands are normally leased out on such contract initially for three years. After wards it could be renewed on the basis of new terms and conditions. In Mani Gumpa, there is one Choden Lepcha who has gone for such a lease contract to cultivate gladioli. Recently, another form of contractual lease has been noticed in Pochaok where contract is being made only for harvesting and marketing of ginger.

6) **Agricultural labour**: Landless agricultural labour work on others field against daily wage, meal. They also work against payment in crop after harvest. But they however get food when they are at work. Labours, thus, meet their present consumption requirement by taking food daily during work and store agricultural products for future consumption. They offer labour to the land owners during agricultural operations in conditions of getting it back as and when asked for in other purposes like construction of house, cowshed, and fencing. Small and medium landowners sell their excess labour on wage basis to augment their family income. They also mutually exchange their family labour with others in order to get back it in terms of plough and bullock at times of their own cultivation.

SOME RELEVANT ASPECT OF LAND

Ownership and management of land are the two key components of social formation in the context of any society. Beside these, knowledge of some other aspects of land can also substantiate to identify the type of the society. Followings are some such relevant aspects connected with Lepcha land in our study area:

Pattern of Land-holding

It has been observed that 94.96 per cent households of the study area are involved in agricultural operation while 66.85 per cent of population accepts agriculture either as their principal or subsidiary occupation. The economic condition of the Lepchas can better be understood from their access to land and distribution into size-classes.

It is evident from Table 3.5 that the proportion of landless households is highest in 5th Mile Lepcha Gaon (9.52%) followed by Mani Gumpa (9.09%) and Pochaok (2.63%). In most of such landless cases the married girl got a small plot of land from her consanguine for dwelling purposes.

Table 3.5: Village-wise Land-holding Pattern

Name of Village	Landless	Below 1 acre	Between 1-3 acre	Between 3-5 acre	Between 5-8 acre	Above 8 acre	Total
	2	3	4	5	6	7	8
Mani Gumpa	2 (9.09)	12 (54.55)	7 (31.82)	1 (4.54)	- -	- -	22 (100)
5th Mile Lepcha Gaon	2 (9.52)	7 (3.33)	7 (33.33)	4 (19.05)	1 (4.77)	- -	21 (100)
Pochok	2 (2.63)	- -	22 (28.95)	18 (23.69)	25 (32.89)	9 (11.84)	76 (100)
Total	6 (5.04)	19 (15.97)	36 (30.25)	23 (19.33)	26 (21.85)	9 (7.56)	119 (100)

Note: Figures in the parentheses indicate percentages.

Mani Gumpa is inhabited by small landholders whose percentage is lowest for Pochaok but large for 5th Mile Lepcha Gaon. There are negligible medium landholders in Mani Gumpa; same is the number in 5th Mile Lepcha Gaon while moderate for Pochoak. Large landholders are present only in Pochaok while both Mani Gumpa and 5th Mile Lepcha Gaon such category of landholders is absent totally. The land holding pattern is inversely related with the distance from road and town areas. Medium and large landholders are present only in Pochaok, which is far away from town, market and road. Distribution of lands among large number of consanguine has further limited the size of holding. This is more so with the original inhabitants where lands have been distributed over generations. Table 3.4 also shows lower average holding of land for the original *moos* inspite of their larger total land holding per *moo*.

Intensity of Land-use

Table 3.6 shows the intensity of land use pattern. In general Lepchas could not spare their lands for mono crop cultivation. Mono cropping is the luxury for the small landholders or those who depend solely on agriculture. As the rate of production is low and the lands are scarce in relation to demand and availability of labour, they cannot go for mono crop and keep their land fallow. Even at times of distress if the family labour are not available, the villages take special initiative to complete the agricultural operations without expecting anything in return.

Table 3.6: Intensity of Land-use

Village	Total household	Non cultivator	Agricultural labour	Mono crop	Bi-Crop	Multi-crop
Mani Gumpa	22 (100.00)	2 (9.09)	1 (4.54)	-	3 (13.64)	16 (72.73)
5th Mile Lepcha Gaon	21 (100.00)	1 (4.76)	3 (14.29)	-	1 (4.76)	16 (76.19)
Pochoak	76 (100.00)	1 (1.31)	-	1 (1.31)	31 (40.79)	43 (56.59)
Total	119 (100.00)	4 (3.36)	4 (3.36)	1 (0.84)	35 (29.41)	75 (63.03)

Note: Figures in the parentheses show percentages.

The percentage of households using the land for raising double crop is highest in Pochaok (40.79) followed by Mani Gumpa (13.64) and 5th Mile Lepcha Gaon (4.76). The data reveal that households in this category are cultivating mostly paddy and maize, the two traditional crops of the region. These households are more guided by their traditional orientation and outlook. They do not like to undertake the risk of modern farming and which also requires larger investment. These Lepchas are mostly illiterate, belong to older generation and quite accustomed to smooth and easy way of life. In few cases, the location and physical condition of the soil also do not permit them to undertake multi-cropping. They use their agricultural land mainly to raise staple food, kitchen garden for vegetable and sell their physical labour on daily wage basis to augment their family income.

The small landholders are using their land intensively. The percentage of landowners engaged in multi-cropping is highest in 5th Mile Lepcha Gaon (76.19) followed by Mani Gumpa (72.73) and Pochaok (56.59). Lepchas rotate crops in such a way that from the same plot of land they can produce all those crops, which are needed for their daily consumption. It has been observed that one plot of land can grow as much as nine varieties of crops in a year. A calendar year can be divided into three cropping seasons – each one has further been used for producing 2-4 crops simultaneously. Paddy field is used for cultivating dal, soyabean and *bhatamas* simultaneously. Similarly, maize fields are used for producing bean, *karela*, and sweet pumpkin. Potato fields are also used for the cultivation of maize. Land is used in its best possible manner very intensively. It has been observed that educated youths engaged in agriculture have changed the cropping pattern and like to go for modern cultivation.

Land Rent

The existing literature shows that during the first half of twentieth century, Lepchas of Sikkim had to pay negligible tax to the then Choygel ruler. "As they had not much call on them for free labour contribution nor much of tax to pay, they were very happy." [Maharaja and Maharani of Sikkim; Nakane, 1966: 216] Stocks noted: "Taxes are very low, though they are on an average to what a peasant earns, amounting roughly to Rs. Thirteen eight annas per annum (about one

English Pound), which includes Rupees three from every basti claiming exemption from coolie work" [1925: 476]. During the first phase of Choygel period in the absence of coins a 'basket of corn' was given to royal treasury as revenue. Dharani Dhar Dahal [1984] mentioned that the system of land revenue started in Sikkim during the reign of Phuntso Namgyal II when one Rabden Sherpa visited Sikkim from Tibet.

No information regarding systematic tax rate during the Bhutan reign over Kalimpong area is available except some sporadic mention about plundering both women and wealth from the Lepchas. "These dreaded people would go berserk and rampage, burn, plunder and loot the whole area they happened to pass through." [Fonning, 1987: 12].

Philpot submitted his report on survey and settlement of Kalimpong estate in 1925. Table 3.7 compiled by him shows the existing rate as proposed by C.A. Bell's report (1901-03) (shown in Col.a), the rate proposed by Philpot (Col.b) and the rate ultimately sanctioned (Col.C). Kam Dorjee Lepcha informed "the land revenue was increased from Rs.1.25 per acre during British period to Rs. 2/- by the present West Bengal Government. But Britishers were very particular in collecting the revenue through village Mandals, while the present Bhumi Sahayak rarely visits our village and we need to go to his residence for paying rent."

The rate of rent in the contemporary period is as follows:

No tax is levied up to (i) 4 acre of wetland, (ii) 6 acre of dry land, and (iii) 4 acre of wetland and 2 acre of dry land. The earlier system of dry land and wetland still prevails. Samudra Prasad, Bhumi Sahayak of Sindipong *Khasmahal* informed that in Mani Gumpa the highest amount of rent (Rs.5.89) is paid by Ongu Tshering Lepcha for his 3.20 acre of land while the minimum (Rs.0.81) is paid by Aghi Tshering Lepcha for his 0.18 acre of land. In addition to land tax, rent for each household consists of road-cess (12 per cent), PWD – cess (25 per cent), education – cess (10 per cent) and rural employment-cess (30 per cent). Households of Mani Gumpa on the average pay Rs.1.50 as rent. Inspite of the negligible amount, the Lepchas are reluctant in paying their rent regularly.

Table 3.7: Land Rent during 1901 – 1903 and 1925

Group	Wet land						Dry land						Waste land					
	a		b		c		a		b		c		a		b		c	
	Rs.	A	Rs.	A	Rs.	A	Rs.	A	Rs.	A	Rs.	A	Rs.	A	Rs.	A	Rs.	A
Group I	1	4	1	14	1	10	0	15	1	10	1	8	0	3	0	4	0	4
Group II	1	0	1	8	1	5	0	12	1	5	1	3	0	3	0	4	0	4
Group III	0	11	1	0	0	14	0	8	0	14	0	13	0	2	0	3	0	4
			1	3					1	0								
Group IV	0	9	0	14	0	12	0	7	0	12	0	11	0	2	0	3	0	3
Group V	0	8	0	12	0	10	0	6	0	9	0	9	0	2	0	3	0	3

Source: H.C.V Philpot, ICS Settlement Officer, Final Report on the Survey and Settlement of Kalimpong Government Estate 1919-21. p.34.

Note: Col a, b and c stand for rates before 1925, rate proposed by Philpot in 1919-21, and rate sanctioned actually.

Rent-free Land

Since the Tibetan and British rule the lands particularly used for religious purposes like, construction of Church, *Gumpa* etc., are kept as rent free land. For maintenance of these religious institutions some cultivable lands in the surrounding areas are also kept rent free. The first survey and settlement of Kalimpong was conducted by Mr. Marindin in 1882 also identified rent free land for Buddhist Monasteries and Hermitages and for that matter sanction was conveyed in the Government of Bengal's order No.2872 – 1159 LR dt 28th Dec. 1881. Out of nine such *Gumpas* mentioned by Philpot in his survey 1919-21 which were enjoying rent free land since 1882, Mani Gumpa of Sindipong under the present study area is one of them. The area under Mani Gumpa remained the same 6 acres during 1882 and 1902 while it increased to 7 acre during 1920. (Philpot, 1925: 19).

The great grandson of the head lama not only occupies the residential house of the *Gumpa* but also hereditarily cultivates the rent-free *Gumpa* land. The Lepchas of the village on share-cropping also cultivate some rent free lands of the Gumpa. They need to pay fifty per cent of the produce to the *Gumpa.* Although a part of the agricultural produce is used for the maintenance of the *Gumpa* and organising different religious activities but the present descendants of head lama are using most of the land as their family property.

Measurement and Record of Land

Lands in the hilly region of Darjeeling are measured in the standard modern measurement units like acre and decimal. During the British rule, the different surveys of Kalimpong Estate were carried out by Marindin (1882), C.A. Bell (1901-03), H.C.V. Philpot (1919-21) in the modern English scale of land measurement. It may be inferred that since the British period the authorities are using the standard measurement of land. But Lepchas usually use some natural objects particularly tree, rivulet etc., as identification mark of land under their possession.

The standard unit of measurement is used for all official purposes like transfer of land, paying land rent. The area has been surveyed by the government of West Bengal and specific plot number and *Khatian* number have been allotted in terms of the modern unit of measurement of decimal and acre (100 dec. = 1 acre). A copy of one *Khatian* of 5th Mile Lepcha Gaon is attached herewith in the Appendix III. For all practical purposes Lepchas do not know either the total land under their possession or the land for specific agricultural use. In the case of cultivated land, they just count the number of terrace steps whose length and breadth varies widely depending upon the availability of the slope of the land. Another way of local measurement is the quantity of seed used or the quantity of agricultural products they receive after harvest. For measuring the areas of wetland, Lepchas mention about how many *Tungri*, (a container having approximately 4 kg of paddy) of seed they use for the field. Some Lepchas also refer to the stock of hay whose volume gives some idea about the production of paddy and hence the area under its cultivation.

Dry land is measured in terms of *Tunjiang* (a container made of bamboo) of maize they receive from the field. Gunny bags of ginger or cardamom are also some other indigenous ways by which land is also measured.

Lepchas, thus, use two different units of measuring land (i) official unit of measurement in terms of acre and decimal and (ii) indigenous unit of measurement in the form of seed used in terms of *Tungri*, production of paddy in terms of *Tungfri-Khaa-kaat*, *Tunjiang* of maize, stock of hay.

Classification of Land

Philpot [1925:29] classified land in Kalimpong Estate into nine categories: (1) cardamom land, (2) terraced land, (3) unterraced land, (4) orchard, (5) homesteads, (6) new fallow (i.e. fallow of three years or less), (7) old fallow (i.e. fallow of more than three years), (8) other cultivable land and (9) uncultivable land.

In our study area, we identified seven categories of land. They are: (1) Cardamom field (*Tambrak-nyaot*), (2) Water logged or wet land (*Zo-nyaot*), (3) Dry land (*Moong-nyaot*), (4) Kitchen garden (*Sing*), (5) Bamboo field (*Maat lobong*), (6) Lands enjoy continuous flow of water (*Sim*), and (7) Stony and uncultivable land.

i) Cardamom field (Tambrak-nyaot)

Cardamom grows in comparatively cold region, as the plant cannot bear much heat. In the entire moist region where either tree shades rich soil or hillocks and streamlets wet the land throughout the year, cardamom can be planted. It is said: cardamom needs shed, moderate warmth, a good supply of irrigated water and a rich soil. Both the wet and dry land can be used for plantation. But good irrigation alongwith some warm climate is necessary for cardamom. Lepchas do produce cardamom in both terraced and unterraced land. In the natural slope of the undulating hill or even without hampering forest, cardamom can be planted. O'Malley noted, "Lepchas mostly cultivate at the lower level, and are particularly found of cardamom cultivation at the bottom of the valley." [1907: 65]. In our study area there is cardamom cultivation only in Pochaok where the upper part of the village is used for this cultivation.

*ii) Wet land (***Zo-nyaot***)*

Lands at comparatively lower part of the village in the valley areas or lands near the stream or rivulet are suitable for making wetland. In hilly slope where the terrace comprises of small patch of land there is a need to raise a boundary at the opposite side of the hills. In a comparatively valley areas lands are separated by raising earthen boundary on all the four sides. The boundary helps in retaining water inside the field and thus makes it suitable for transplanting paddy seedlings. The black soil is found quite suitable for paddy cultivation.

*iii) Dry land (***Moong-nyaot***)*

In such land water is not available and they are located away from stream and rivulet. The terrace land without any earthen boundary at the end of terrace is known as dry land. Here instead of raising earthen boundary, lands at the outer edge are kept slightly lower so as to pass water out of the field. Crops like millet and maize, which require less water, are cultivated in dry land.

Wetland can be converted into dry land by removing the boundary. In the same way by raising earthen boundary dry land can be converted into wetland. Tshering Lepcha of Mani Gumpa gives the following reasons for converting his wet land into dry land: "Lands located just below my dwelling house have been converted into dry land by destroying the boundaries. Wetland stores water for longer period turning the land of upper areas quite susceptible to land slide particularly during the rainy season. Beside that, I have started cultivating gladioli, which require less logged water. So there is no need to keep the boundaries. Moreover, the amount of land used for boundary, whatever small that may be, is just a wastage of scarce resource. Thus simply by removing the boundary the entire land could be brought under cultivation."

iv) Kitchen garden (Sing)

The Lepchas often use a part of homestead land as kitchen garden where they produce vegetables for domestic consumption. The roof of the dwelling house is used for some cripper vegetables. Normally Lepchas produce pumpkin, squash, green chilli, tomato, *raisak*, cauliflower, cabbage in their kitchen garden. All such produces are solely used for domestic consumption and sometimes distributed among the neighbours or relatives as gift. No part is used for the market.

***v) Bamboo field* (Maatlobong)**

Lands located in steep zone or rocky areas, are usually chosen for bamboo plantation. Sometimes, lands around the dwelling houses are also used for the same. Normally lands used for bamboo are found unsuitable for other crops. Kam Dorjee Lepcha, a 77 years oldman, of Mani Gumpa said:

"Bamboo is quite useful for us but very harmful for other crops. The underground roots of bamboo spread over widely and extract fertility so much that no other crops can grow in the areas. The shadow of bamboo groves affects badly the growth of other crops. Bamboo does not give much return in monetary terms; often we freely distribute bamboo among our neighbours and relatives. No outsiders visit our village to purchase bamboo. We can not destroy bamboo altogether because we still believe in that proverb – Lepchas will not die so long as bamboo is there in our *Mayal Lyaang*."

vi) Continuous flow of water (Sim)

Sim might have derived from the English word 'slime' means slippery or gluey mud. Quite a small area in the study villages comes under the category of *sim*. The lands, which suffer from continuous flow of water round the year, are so marshy that one cannot do any cultivation there. Sangdil Lepcha humorously told "throughout the year our land provides sufficient water to all the households located below it but we are the most unfortunate because we can not use the *sim* land for productive purposes."

*vii) Stony land (***Farjar***)*

This type of land is kept as permanent fallow and nothing can be grown there. Such terrain is totally unfit for cultivation and any other purposes. In our study area not much area comes under the stony land. Major portion of it belongs to Pochaok.

The Landscape

The landscape and its location often considered as an important factor in determining the cropping pattern in this hilly region. Besides cropping pattern, while constructing their houses, Lepchas seek the advice of the elderly persons like *Bongthing* on which direction their house should face. The eminent botanists of the region also hinted upon the association between the face of the landscape and the type of vegetation. Farmers from their experience also identified the following crops as suitable in the different landscape:

i) East facing land: Rice, orange, ginger, maize, millet, dal, *and bhatamas.*

ii) West facing land: Maize, millet.

iii) North facing Land: Cardamom, orchids, moss, ferns etc.

iv) South facing land: Rice, dal, *and bhatamas.*

It has been observed that lands facing different directions in the hilly terrain encounter with the nature diversely. Maximum sun rays are enjoyed by lands facing the east; while rainfall is the highest for those lands facing the south; where as north facing lands receive more cold, wind, mist and are comparatively swampy and dumpy.

NOTES

1. Moo or clan plays a vital role from birth to death among the Lepchas particularly among the Buddhists. In Lepcha society male moos are different from those of females.' Male child receives father's moo while

girl child inherits mother's moo. Recently Lepchas started using moo as their title name (e.g. Simikmoo, Namchumoo etc.)

2. In traditional share-cropping, no documents are ever maintained by either party. The system is followed customarily without even going through dialogue on condition between the two parties. Each share half of the harvested crop. More importantly, no specific period of sharing land is maintained. Contractual share-cropping is a modern concept. Lepchas lease land on the basis of written terms and conditions for very short period of time. Sharing is mostly in terms of cash irrespective of type and quantity of crops grown.
3. Recognising the demand of the Lepcha Association, H.Q. Kalimpong, the Akhil Bharatiya Adivasi Vikas Parishad, West Bengal Branch, in their 19 Annual Conference at Ambika, Kalna, Burdwan on 23 and 24 March 2002 has resolved . . . 'the Lepcha land/properties forcibly occupied by non-tribals must be restored to the Lepchas strictly implementing the protective provisions of the West Bengal Land Regulations Act, 1955 and SC and ST (Prevention of Atrocities) Act 1989.' [Aachuley, Vol 6, No.2, July 2002: 14-15].

CHAPTER FOUR

SOURCE AND TYPE OF LABOUR

Social formation depends on the social existence form of labour and more explicitly by the type of labour used, source of supply of labour, nature of division of labour, type of payment. In tribal society, labour is supplied mainly by the family or community in reciprocal terms and for which no wage is paid. Some works are carried out jointly by the kinsmen or the community in non-remunerative terms. Work in agriculture is considered as family work and all members irrespective of age and sex do participate in it as per requirement and their capacity.

Division of labour is a capitalistic concept and so it is not the characteristic feature of a tribal society. Under capitalism works in all sectors including in agriculture are divided where trained and efficient workers get maximum return. No such division of labour is there in tribal economy and irrespective of age and sex they do all types of work. Ideally speaking, division of labour, in true sense, is supposed to be absent in tribal society.

In this chapter the different components of labour among the Lepchas have been examined from three broad premises: source of labour, type of labour, and classification of work.

SOURCE OF LABOUR

In a Lepcha village one gets labour exclusively from within the village and inter-village movement of labour is almost negligible. Labour in Lepcha society is basically means the household labour.

Households in our study area consist of members related either through blood or marriage or adoptation. The villagers do not make any difference among these categories of kinsmen living under a common roof, that is, the household. A household is normally composed of a group of persons who commonly live together and take their meals from a common kitchen unless the exigencies of work prevent any of them from doing so. There may be a household of related persons by blood or a household of unrelated persons or having a mix of both. There is not much difference between a family and a household in Lepcha society.

Household among the Lepchas confined to purely biological concept of married couple, living together within their descendants and in some cases members of older generations. Two peculiarities have been noticed in the said composition of Lepcha household: (i) presence of good number of unmarried persons (both male and female) and (ii) the adopted children. As household labour both of them play important role in Lepcha society. Let us look into the said composition of the Lepcha households.

Age and Sex Composition of Household

Household size by their age and sex composition has an important bearing with the supply of labour. Table 4.1 shows the aggregate distribution of households by size, age and sex. The small household within 1-3 members mostly comprises of husband and wife and their unmarried children. After marriage the spouses generally settle in separate establishment.

The population have been divided in four age groups. The minor age group (0-6 years) cannot help in agriculture. The children belonging to the age group of 7-14 years do help in carrying out a number of agricultural operations. In addition to their principal activities of attending school, a good number of them are involved in agricultural works. The population in the age group of 15-60 years is the full-fledged working population and who mainly contribute their labour to agriculture. The smallest proportion of population belongs to the older age group (above 60 years) and whose role is restricted mainly to advice, co-ordinate and organise agriculture.

Table 4.1: Household size by age and sex of the three villages

Household size	No. of HH	Population			0-6 years			7 – 14 years			15 – 60 years			Above 60 years		
		M	F	T	M	F	T	M	F	T	M	F	T	M	F	T
1-3	17 (14.29)	25 (7.00)	21 (6.18)	46 (6.60)	3 (5.36)	1 (2.44)	4 (4.12)	-	1 (1.56)	1 (0.76)	19 (8.92)	19 (8.92)	38 (8.92)	3 (14.29)	-	3 (6.98)
4.10	91 (76.47)	275 (77.03)	241 (70.88)	516 (74.03)	37 (66.07)	29 (70.73)	66 (68.04)	61 (91.04)	43 (67.19)	104 (79.39)	162 (76.06)	151 (70.89)	313 (73.47)	16 (76.19)	17 (77.27)	33 (76.74)
Above 10	11 (9.24)	57 (15.97)	78 (22.94)	135 (19.37)	16 (28.57)	11 (26.83)	27 (27.84)	6 (8.96)	20 (31.25)	26 (19.85)	32 (15.02)	43 (20.19)	75 (17.61)	2 (9.52)	5 (22.73)	7 (16.28)
Total	119 (100.00)	357 (100.00)	340 (100.00)	697 (100.00)	56 (100.00)	41 (100.00)	97 (100.00)	67 (100.00)	64 (100.00)	131 (100.00)	213 (100.00)	213 (100.00)	426 (100.00)	21 (100.00)	22 (100.00)	43 (100.00)

Note: Figures in the parenthesis indicate their percentages to the total.
Note: M = Male; F = Feamle; T = Total.

As females do participate equally in agriculture their presence in different age groups help agriculture in different ways. It is evident from Table 4.1 that in each age group the females represent almost equally with the males. Hence, their labour and other contributions to agriculture remain more or less similar to that of their male counterpart.

In Mani Gumpa, the distribution of population over the different age groups reveals nearly the same characteristics to that of the total population. Table 4.2 reveals that largest percentage of population falls in the able bodied working age group of 15-60 years. So far as the household size is concerned, 75.95 per cent of population falls in the category of 4-10 members. It has been seen that the females in all categories contribute more than their male counterpart. It is evident that both the first two age groups are missing from the small sized household. It proves that in such nuclear households, the married couples are residing with their parents and all the members are supplying labour to agriculture jointly.

Table 4.3 shows distribution of population in 5th Mile Lepcha Gaon. Population, both male and female are concentrating more in the middle sized household and that too in the able bodied working age group of 15-60 years. Agriculture in this village like that of the other two villages, thus, has been carried out by this age group. The largest household size ranks second in supplying labour to agricultural operations.

Distribution of population in Pochaok is shown in Table 4.4. It is clear that 73.68 per cent of household and 70.85 per cent of population fall in the middle sized category. The highest proportion of population belongs to the age group of 15-60 years. The sex-wise distribution of population is the same to those of the two other villages.

The proportion of able bodied person in all the three villages is almost sufficient to meet the requirement of labour engaged in agriculture as principal and subsidiary occupation (66.85 per cent as per Table 2.13). It has been experienced that agriculture remained the main sector of engagement for the Lepchas. As almost all the households (94.06 per cent as per Table 3.5) possess agricultural land and as there is no alternative source of engagement, it can be inferred that Lepchas cultivate land mainly with their village labour. Beside the

Table 4.2: Household size by age and sex (Name of Village: Mani Gumpa)

Household size	No. of HH	Population			0-6 years			7–14 years			15–60 years			Above 60 years		
		M	F	T	M	F	T	M	F	T	M	F	T	M	F	T
1-3	4 (18.18)	4 (7.41)	5 (7.57)	9 (7.50)	-	-	-	-	-	-	3 (7.89)	5 (10.64)	8 (9.41)	1 (20.00)	-	1 (8.33)
4-10	16 (72.72)	41 (75.93)	46 (69.70)	87 (72.50)	1 (33.33)	-	1 (33.33)	8 (100.00)	9 (75.00)	17 (85.00)	28 (73.68)	31 (65.96)	59 (69.41)	4 (80.00)	6 (85.71)	10 (83.34)
Above 10	2	9 (9.09)	15 (16.66)	24 (22.73)	2 (20.00)	-	2 (66.67)	-	3 (66.67)	3 (25.00)	7 (15.00)	11 (18.42)	18 (23.40)	- (21.18)	1 (14.29)	1 (8.33)
Total	22 (100.00)	54 (100.00)	66 (100.00)	120 (100.00)	3 (100.00)	-	3 (100.00)	8 (100.00)	12 (100.00)	20 (100.00)	38 (100.00)	47 (100.00)	85 100.00)	5 (100.00)	7 (100.00)	12 (100.00)

Note: Figures in the parenthesis indicate their percentages to the total.

Table 4.3: Household size by age and sex (Name of Village: 5th Mile Lepcha Gaon)

Household size	No. of HH	Population			0-6 years			7 – 14 years			15 – 60 years			Above 60 years		
		M	F	T	M	F	T	M	F	T	M	F	T	M	F	T
1-3	1 (4.76)	1 (1.47)	2 (3.18)	3 (2.29)	-	-	-	-	1 (12.50)	1 (6.67)	1 (1.93)	1 (1.96)	2 (1.94)	-	-	-
4-10	19 (90.48)	59 (86.76)	54 (85.71)	113 (86.26)	1 (200.00)	1 (100.00)	2 (33.33)	7 (100.00)	5 (62.50)	12 (80.00)	48 (92.30)	46 (90.20)9	94 (91.26)	3 (75.00)	2 (66.67)	5 (71.43)
Above 10	1 (4.76)	8 (11.77)	7 (11.11)	15 (11.45)	4 (80.00)	-	4 (66.67)	-	2 (25.00)	2 (13.33)	3 (5.77)	4 (7.84)	7 (6.80)	1 (25.00)	1 (33.33)	2 (28.57)
Total	21 (100.00)	68 (100.00)	63 (100.00)	131 (100.00)	5 (100.00)	1 (100.00)	6 (100.00)	7 (100.00)	8 (100.00)	15 (100.00)	52 (100.00)	51 (100.00)	103 (100.00)	4 (100.00)	3 (100.00)	7 (100.00)

Note: Figures in the parenthesis indicate their percentages to the total.

Table 4.4: Household size by age and sex (Name of Village: Pochaok)

Household size	No. of HH	Population			0-6 years			7 – 14 years			15 – 60 years			Above 60 years		
		M	F	T	M	F	T	M	F	T	M	F	T	M	F	T
1-3	12 (15.79)	20 (8.51)	14 (6.64)	34 (7.62)	3 (6.25)	1 (2.50)	4 (4.55)	-	-	-	15 (12.19)	13 (11.30)	28 (11.76)	2 (16.67)	-	2 (8.33)
4-10	56 (73.68)	175 (74.47)	141 (66.82)	316 (70.85)	35 (72.92)	28 (70.00)	63 (71.59)	46 (88.46)	29 (65.91)	75 (78.13)	86 (69.92)	74 (64.35)	160 (67.23)	9 (75.00)	9 (75.00)	18 (75.00)
Above 10	8 (10.53)	40 (17.02)	56 (26.54)	96 (21.53)	10 (20.83)	11 (27.50)	21 (23.86)	6 (11.54)	15 (34.09)	21 (21.87)	22 (17.89)	28 (24.35)	50 (21.01)	1 (8.33)	3 (25.00)	4 (16.67)
Total	76 (100.00)	235 (100.00)	211 (100.00)	446 (100.00)	48 (100.00)	40 (100.00)	88 (100.00)	52 (100.00)	44 (100.00)	96 (100.00)	123 (100.00)	115 (100.00)	238 (100.00)	12 (100.00)	12 (100.00)	24 (100.00)

Note: Figures in the parenthesis indicate their percentages to the total.

able bodied age group, the other age groups do extend helping hand in agriculture. The picture is more or less same for each of the three villages individually also. The Lepcha villages are, thus, self-sufficient in supplying labour for agriculture.

Unmarried Members

The unmarried children particularly the girls are the key members in some of the Lepcha households. They take part in policy-making and economic activities including agricultural operations. The unmarried aged girls in few cases are also the heads of the household. As per Lepcha marriage (*bri*) system, the bridegroom is supposed to approach the bride's family and in this process the matchmaker (*peeboo*) plays an important role. Presence of good number of quite adult/aged unmarried Lepcha girls in the villages is something quite interesting. It is said that they are not approached by the groom for marriage. But the labour contribution of unmarried girls to agriculture might have been found responsible in not taking much initiative in arranging their marriage. It may be noted that average age of marriage among the Lepchas is about 20 years for both the sexes. Detail of unmarried persons belonging to the age group above 20 years is shown in Appendix IV.

Table 4.5 shows the involvement of both bachelor male and female of higher age in agricultural operations as their principal or subsidiary occupation.

It is evident that about 16 per cent people in the study area are unmarried where the percentages of male and female are 15.69 and 15.88 respectively. The proportion of unmarried adult is the highest in 5th Mile Lepcha Gaon (28.24 per cent) followed by Mani Gumpa (20.83 per cent) and Pochaok (10.76 per cent). Higher proportion of unmarried women is there in 5th Mile Lepcha Gaon (30.16 per cent) followed by Mani Gumpa (25.76 per cent) and Pochaok (8.53 per cent). The proportion of unmarried male (12.77 per cent) is more than the female (8.53 per cent) in Pochaok while in other two villages women are more than their male counterpart.

The involvement of unmarried adults in agricultural operation is shown in Table 4.5. Out of total labour engaged in agriculture as principal occupation, the contribution of unmarried persons is 29.21

Table 4.5: Involvement of Unmarried child above 20 years in agricultural operations.

Name of village	Sex	Population			Involvement in Agriculture as					
					Principal occupation			Subsidiary occupation		
		Total	Unmarried above 20 years	% of total	Total	Unmarried above 20 years	% of total	Total	Unmarried above 20 years	% of total
Mani Gumpa	Male	54	8	14.81	13	5	38.46	21	2	9.52
	Female	66	17	25.76	21	9	42.86	25	5	20.00
	Total	120	25	20.83	34	14	41.18	46	7	15.22
5th mile Lepcha Gaon	Male	68	18	26.47	20	9	45.00	22	2	9.09
	Female	63	19	30.16	15	2	13.33	23	9	39.13
	Total	131	37	28.24	35	11	31.43	45	11	24.44
Pochaok	Male	235	30	12.77	126	30	23.81	42	-	-
	Female	211	18	8.53	7	4	57.14	131	12	9.16
	Total	446	48	10.76	133	34	25.56	173	12	6.94
Total	Male	357	56	15.69	159	44	27.67	85	4	4.71
	Female	340	54	15.88	43	15	34.88	179	26	14.53
	Total	697	110	15.78	202	59	29.21	264	30	11.36

per cent. In this the contribution of female (34.88 per cent) is higher than male (27.67 per cent). In Mani Gumpa females contribute more (41.18 per cent) in agriculture than in 5th Mile Lepcha Gaon (31.43 per cent) and Pochaok (25.56 per cent).

The participation of unmarried adult in agriculture as subsidiary occupation is somewhat less. Out of a total population which accepted agriculture as subsidiary occupation the proportion of unmarried adult is 11.36 per cent. But the contribution of female is more (14.53 per cent) than males (4.71 per cent). Females contribute more labour than their male counterpart in all the three villages. It has been observed that the Lepcha women are principally engaged in household activities and do participate in agriculture subsidiarily, while for the majority of males agriculture is their principal occupation.

The need of household labour in agriculture might have restricted the aged female Lepchas not to get married and leave the house. This is possibly a contributing factor in limiting the growth of Lepcha population. The unmarried adults of any kinship category are the most welcomed members in the household and in most cases they shoulder the entire burden of agricultural operations.

Adopted Members

Another potential contributor of labour in Lepcha agriculture is adopted child (*Kup-trop*), particularly the male child. Details of adopted child are shown in Appendix-I. The adopted children are the most reliable source of household labour in agriculture and can comfortably substitute the wage or contractual labour. Instead of appointing agricultural labour on monthly or yearly wage basis, the Lepchas prefer adopted child. In the household an adopted child gets equal facilities as enjoyed by their own child except their ownership right on land. The adopted boy or girl has been conversed to Lepcha by embrassing the *moo* of his or her foster father (*jiut-be*) or foster mother (*jiut-mu*). They also enjoy the status of scheduled tribe (ST). In most cases they manage ST certificate from the concerned department and avail special facilities specified for STs in the school and in employment. The adopted children are involved in the activities of the household in such a way it is difficult to differentiate their separate existence. The adopted children are however, given only a small plot of land for habitation whereas the cultivated land is equally distributed exclusively among their own children. In case the parents are, without any issue their adopted children inherit the entire landed property. Let us discuss about the involvement of adopted children in agricultural operations.

Table 4.6 shows village-wise distribution of adopted children. It is evident that almost all the adopted children belong to 5th Mile Lepcha Gaon while only one to Mani Gumpa. In Pochaok there is no such child. Out of seven adopted children in 5th Mile Lepcha Gaon, six are male and one is female. All the adopted children are involved in agriculture. For five of them agriculture is their principal occupation while for the rest it is a subsidiary one.

Interestingly, all the adopted children are non-Lepchas.Three of them have settled in the village on the plot of land given to them by their foster father. Some aged bachelor adopted children live quite comfortably with other members of the household. It is perhaps the need of the labour in agriculture which prompted the households to adopt the male child. The households with larger agricultural lands are more inclined to adopt male child. They prefer to adopt child instead of going for appointing monthly or yearly contractual labour.

TYPE OF LABOUR

Labour in Lepcha society can be classified into three broad types: household labour, wage labour and exchange labour. But for all practical considerations they are not mutually exclusive categories. All types of labour employment remain confined within the village. It is the same person who at times participates in agriculture as household labour often works as wage labour, and exchange labour. Often in the same household when some members act as household labour some other functions as wage or exchange labour. In this section we have tried to put some light on the three types of labour in Lepcha society.

Household Labour

Lepchas prefer to cultivate their own and or leased land with the help of household labour. Column 5 and 6 of Table 3.2 show the pattern of land management by the owner cultivator and owner cultivator cum share-cropper. In both the cases the operations are done basically by

Table 4.6: Involvement of Adopted Child in Agricultural operations

Name of village	Sex	Population			Involvement in Agriculture as					
					Principal occupation			Subsidiary occupation		
		Total	Adopted child	% of total	Total	Adopted child	% of total	Total	Adopted child	% of total
Mani Gumpa	Male	54	1	1.85	13	1	7.69	21	-	-
	Female	66	-	-	21	-	-	25	-	-
	Total	120	1	0.83	34	1	2.94	46	-	-
5th mile Lepcha Gaon	Male	68	6	8.82	20	4	20.00	22	2	9.09
	Female	63	1	1.59	15	-	-	23	1	4.35
	Total	131	7	5.34	35	4	11.43	45	3	6.67
Pochaok	Male	235	-	-	126	-	-	42	-	-
	Female	211	-	-	7	-	-	131	-	-
	Total	446	-	-	133	-	-	173	-	-
Total	Male	357	7	1.96	159	5	3.14	85	2	2.35
	Female	340	1	0.29	43	-	-	179	1	0.56
	Total	697	8	1.15	202	5	2.48	264	3	1.14

the household labour. When it is not sufficiently available (due either because of small size of household or possession of large cultivable land), Lepchas go for either wage labour or exchange labour.

No direct payment is made to the household labour. As agriculture is the mainstay of livelihood of the Lepchas, they want to keep themselves engaged in the activities centering around it. In other words, it is basically the peasant farming where the potential household members supply labour and produce crops to meet the consumption need of the household. In this system all the members irrespective of their contribution to cultivation equally enjoy the return from agriculture. Household members by their sex and age participate in different agricultural operations. The young male members normally undertake comparatively arduous works like ploughing, carrying of crops, use of shovel or spade. The women, on the other hand, do less arduous works like plucking of seedlings, transplantation, weeding. The aged male members often advise and share their experience at different stages of agricultural operations. They according to their physical capacity do accompany the working force in the field either as additional helping hands or as companion who entertain and encourage others by telling stories, sharing experiences. The school going children also do participate in the cultivation of their field mainly during peak seasons. They normally involve in less laborious operations like weight during levelling, or in transplanting, weeding and plucking. From early morning to late evening as per requirement and availability of labour, the Lepchas keep themselves busy in their field operations.

The male members of each Lepcha household consider agriculture as their principal occupation while the females and children in most cases consider agriculture as subsidiary sector of engagement. Choden Lepcha of Mani Gumpa, who graduated in 1987 narrates: "I applied several times for government jobs but nobody considered my candidature. I have lost all the hopes for any job and at present have chosen agriculture as a profitable sector of engagement. Now I am not getting any free time from my gladioli field and I am happy that I could engage other in my farm on wage basis". It has been observed (Table 2.14) that only 12.91 per cent people are engaged in off-farm activities. Thus, agriculture remains as the principal sector of engagement and earnings and where most of the Lepchas cultivate their own land with the help of household labour.

Wage Labour

Mainly the landless Lepchas work as agricultural wage labour. The small and medium landowners with more household members normally sell their labour on wage basis. Lepchas enjoy wage labour mainly for cash crops like cardamom, gladioli and vegetable. Earlier the use of wage labour for food crops was almost absent. But recently some changes have been noticed in this regard. Lepchas (mainly large and medium landowners) with inadequate household labour cultivate their land with the help of wage labour. They deploy wage labour in the cultivation of both cash and food crops.

Unlike the other two types of labour, wage labour is employed even from outside the village and from other communities. During the peak agricultural season, the Lepchas usually invite other community labours from outside. For some special types of work, particularly for newer variety of crops, the outside labours are found to be more efficient. Introduction of newer variety of crops, like gladioli, vegetables has increased the rate of use of outside labours. The self-sufficiency among the Lepchas in terms of labour employment, thus, cannot simply sustain. The Lepcha economy has become a part of wider economic system along with the cultivation of cash crops and where they use good number of wage labour from outside.

Wages paid to the agricultural labours vary according to their age and sex. Works are classified and labours are employed on the basis of age and sex. Wage even for the same type of work may vary on the basis of age and sex of the labour. The usual wage paid to the different types of labour are as follows:

Types of labour	*Wage per man day*
Adult male labour	Rs. 30/-
Adult female labour	Rs. 25/-
Child labour of both sex	Rs. 20/-

Wage labour works for 8 hours in a day from 8.00 a.m. to 5.00 p.m. with an hour lunch break at noon (12.00 noon to 1.00 p.m.).

Some Lepchas who cultivate cash crops prefer wage labour than exchange labour. Labo Tshering Lepcha of Mani Gumpa considers "wage labour comparatively cheaper and more productive than exchange labour. Nobody takes exchange labour seriously and usually join and leave work according to their convenient time. The number of heads irrespective of age and sex are important than the productive capacity of the heads. All kinds of labour of all age and sex are weighted equally in exchange labour. Even one bullock can be used and exchanged equally with one human labour of any age and sex. Although we do not pay anything in terms of cash or kind but we need to entertain them with tiffin and lunch which altogether adds more than what we pay for the wage labour". It has been observed that Lepchas need to supply *chi* (indigenous drink) to such a labour which involves more cost. So, there is a tendency to move from exchange labour to wage labour even for food crops in Lepcha villages.

Beside payment in cash, in some cases particularly in paddy cultivation, wages are paid in kind. But here a labour requires to wait till the harvesting of paddy. For one days labour he/she is remunerated with one *tungfri* (four kg.) of paddy irrespective of age and sex. Landless labour or household with dry land generally prefers to work against payment in paddy. Households with surplus labour do not require exchanging labour while small sized households with large holding are not in a position to supply labour but they are in need of labour to run their cultivation. Exchange of labour for paddy, thus, benefits both the parties.

Introduction of wage labour in the cultivation of cash crops has taken the Lepchas away from their dependence on and arrangement of community labour offered on exchange basis. Recently, the Lepchas have started engaging casual labour from outside the community on daily wage basis. The shift from food to cash crop has possibly accelerated this process of new type of labour employment in Lepcha society.

Exchange Labour

The system of labour exchange is popularly known as *tyaolmaatheong* in Lepcha. It is a reciprocal method of labour supply in the study area. The term *tyaolmaath* means to help or to co-operate.

This is perhaps one of the traditional arrangements of mutual existence. A kind of communal understanding and mutual help among the Lepchas still have been maintained through mutual exchange of labour in agriculture. It is a part of their old culture and a sign of unity and integrity in the Lepcha society.

Labour is exchanged in the cultivation of traditional variety of crops like paddy, maize and millet. Labour of any age and sex is exchangeable. No records are maintained on equitable exchange of labour. On that aspect no dispute or disparity has ever been brought to our notice. In a number of cases, labours received for one crop have been exchanged with the co-partner at the time of next crop or next year. It is true that when a comparison between an adult male and a girl child labour cannot be made but in Lepcha society all of them are treated equally under labour exchange mode.

Labour exchange system is not all that is acceptable in the case of commercial crops like gladioli, cardamom and vegetables. Here the Lepchas prefer wage labour than exchange labour. The underlying reasons have been discussed in the section of wage labour. Even in the case of food crops some Lepchas prefer wage labour than exchange labour.

Lepchas often exchange human labour against the use of draught-animals from others. Details of animal labour have been discussed in chapter five. It has been observed that only a few households (3 out of 22 in Mani Gumpa, 3 out of 21 in 5th Mile Lepcha Gaon and 17 out of 76 in Pochaok) possess bullocks. Those who receive the service of bullock usually pay back it by extending their own labour. A person enjoys the labour day of a ploughman and a pair of bullocks in lieu of three human labour days. Usually the large and middle sized landowners who possess bullock go for such type of labour exchange. Such an exchange benefits both the parties who possess bullocks and who do not.

Among the Lepchas other non-agricultural works are also done by exchanging labour. The usual works involved in this category are: construction of houses, repairing and painting of houses, cutting down trees and hewing them for firewood etc.

Labour in these categories is not always mutually exchanged. The Lepchas generally extend their services to others as and when required without keeping any record of number of days or types of work done. Young male members are commonly used for these types of works and they are entertained with tiffin, tea and lunch. The aforesaid works are mostly carried out during off agricultural season and the Lepchas irrespective of *moo* or religious background do mutually extend labour to one another.

Matrices for reciprocal exchange of labour for agricultural and non-agricultural purposes for the two villages (Mani Gumpa and 5th Mile Lepcha Gaon) are shown in Appendices V, VI, VII and VIII respectively. The reciprocal exchange of labour for Pochaok could not be arrested in terms of such matrix because of its large number of households.

The matrices reveal that the system of reciprocal exchange of labour on the average for all the households are more (nearly double) for non-agricultural purposes than for agricultural ones. There are some households (six in Mani Gumpa and five in 5th Mile Lepcha Gaon) for which no such relations have been established for agricultural purposes but all the households in both the villages are related with others in terms of labour exchange for non-agricultural works. Some households do not possess any cultivable land and extend labour in agriculture on wage basis. But they always go for reciprocal labour exchange with some other for non-agricultural activities.

Considering the reciprocal exchange of labour for both the agricultural and non-agricultural purposes together we can identify the Lepcha villages as a compact unit of society where labour is exchanged without any social, political, religious or economic differences. Religion, *moo*, household size, economic solvency, educational standard do not stand any way to extend and receive labour services. Only in case of religious festivals and functions, labour is available from within the same religious denomination and faith. But religion does not stand in the way in exchanging labour for agricultural purposes.

CLASSIFICATION OF WORK

Division of labour is a modern capitalist concept where works are divided among the workers as per efficiency and productivity. In peasant economy, in general and in tribal peasant economy in particular, labours are not getting any training for becoming efficient for any particular job. This is more true in the case of agriculture where people learn the work through observation, involvement and experience. No arrangements are made for training the individual to become an agricultural labour.

Another peculiarity with agricultural labour is in respect of the types of work. Unlike the secondary or tertiary sector, labour in agricultural sector does not know only one particular type of work but they need to know all types of work associated with agricultural operation. The nature of work depends on the type of crop and the season. Some operations are common for all types of crop whereas a few others are peculiar to specific crop.

Different types of work are involved in agriculture. Among them some are undoubtedly arduous. Also there are comparatively soft and lighter works. Workers mostly spend the day in the open field where they encounter with different natural odds like sunshine, rain, cold. The work in the Lepcha agriculture can be classified in different categories. Different types of work are performed by different persons on the basis of their age, sex and experience.

Most of the adult male members of the Lepcha household contribute labour in their own land and agriculture. Almost all the households possess agricultural land and its male members accept agriculture as their way of life. A higher percentage of adult males among the Lepchas consider agriculture as their principal or subsidiary occupation.

The Lepcha women are also taking more or less equal part in various agricultural operations except some hard works like ploughing and levelling. Those who do not actively participate in the outdoor field operations also help indirectly by performing many indoor works related to agriculture and allied activities.

The child labour is a part and parcel of Lepcha agriculture. Although the Lepcha children participate in agriculture occasionally, but their contribution cannot be ignored altogether. During school holidays or off-time they keep themselves engaged in different agricultural activities. During the peak season some Lepcha students, instead of attending school do participate in agricultural activities. No hard works are normally carried out by the children. Works like carrying tea, tiffin to the field, keeping birds or cattle away from the field; caring cattle at the shed are often done by the children. They actively assist their parents in all types of lighter agricultural works like transplantation of seedlings, in weeding, plucking fruits etc.

Let us now discuss in brief how different agricultural operations for different crops are carried out by the Lepchas on the basis of age and sex.

Paddy (Zo)

Paddy is staple food for the Lepchas. Depending on the availability of wet land (*zo-nyaot*) with black soil (*farnuk*), Lepchas cultivate paddy (*zo*) in all the three study villages. The terrace fields (*thafaong*) which are near the rivulet (*ung-kyoong*) and comparatively flat (*taom*) are suitable for paddy. In Mani Gumpa the younger generation is in favour of cultivation of gladioli instead of paddy while the elders prefer to stick to paddy. Gladioli as a substitute to paddy has already entered in the village and the youngs are trying to earn more cash from this new crop. The entire lower Pochaok and greater part of 5th Mile Lepcha Gaon are used for paddy. Inspite of the introduction of new crops paddy remains the single largest crop in the study area.

The major works involved in paddy cultivation are shown in Table 4.7. The adult male labours participate in all the operations connected with paddy. The less labourious works are performed by the females and children. Men are found indispensible for paddy cultivation. Although in some cases like making ridges, transplanting, weeding, harvesting, threshing, weighting the males work along with the females but some works like cleaning, ploughing, levelling are exclusively done by the males. In transplanting and weeding the contribution of females is more important. Those operations can be done more patiently and carefully by the women. The work of children is must for levelling where two children of same weight are to sit on either sides of the pointed leveller so as to dig the pointed portion inside the earth. The labour contribution of children and females cannot be underestimated in paddy cultivation of Lepchas.

Table 4.7: Lepcha Agricultural operations and classification of work.
Name of Crop: Paddy (Zo)

Sl. No.	Name of Operations			Classification of work			
	English	Nepali	Lepcha	Bullock	Male	Female	Child
1	Cleaning	*Ali Tashnu*	*Pachu Plyaok Syaong*		√		
2	Ploughing	*Zotnu*	*Oang long maa syaong*	√	√		
3	Levelling	*Hilaunu*	*Fanoak Vo Syaong*		√		
4	Making ridge	*Ali Lagaunu*	*Pacha kaa Syaong*		√	√	
5	Levelling	*Dade*	*Tset Syaong*	√	√		√
6	Levelling	*Bause*	*Hormu*		√		
7	Transplanting	*Ropnu*	*Zo chaok Syaong*		√	√	√
8	Playing with mud	*Mato Chitaunu*	*Faazi Laam Syaong*		√	√	√
9	Weeding	*Gornu*	*Zo Buk/Sat Syaong*		√	√	√
10	Harvesting	*Katnu*	*Ek Syaong*		√	√	
11	Threshing	*Bita Jharnu*	*Buk Syaong*		√	√	
12	Weighting	*Napnu*	*Naop Syaong*		√		
13	Carrying	*Boknu*	*Boo Syaong*		√		
14	Stacking	*Paraldai Karnu*	*Tang Syaong*		√		
15	Storing	*Bhara ma Raknu*	*Zo Tho Syaong*			√	√

Soyabean (*Slyaang*), Dal (*Kla*) and *Morshem* (*Porbeng*)

Along with paddy, Lepchas cultivate the above three crops in the same field. On the terrace wall of the paddy field, Lepchas cultivate soyabean (*slyaang*) while on the ridges of the field dal (*kla*) and *morshem* (*porbeng*) are cultivated. These small places and patches were kept unused by the Lepchas in the earlier days. But the scarcity of land compels them to use land whereever it is available to them irrespective of its amount.

Lepchas broadcast seeds of dal nearly 10-15 days after the transplantation of paddy and harvest them one week before the harvest of paddy. No interculture is required for these crops. As the works of the aforesaid crops are performed during the off-season, the male members complete the necessary task during their leisure. The work of threshing and storing are carried out mainly by the females inside the house while the children extend their helping hands.

Maize (*Kun-Tsoong*)

Maize (*kun-tsoong*) is the second popular staple food for the rural Lepchas. It is cheaper than rice, contains high calories and is used in variety of food preparations. Beside staple food, maize is used as fodder for cattle (cow, pig, hen, goat). By removing the soft skin around the maize with the help of wooden grinder (*tuk-tsoam*) – pestle (*talling*) and stone grinder (*tukvaar*), Lepchas prepare a paste like cake which they use for rituals and daily consumption.

Table 4.8 shows the works performed by male, female and child in maize cultivation. Works like ploughing, pulverising, levelling are done absolutely by the males. Females along with the males do the works like broadcasting, furrowing, sowing, weeding and storing. Children along with males help in levelling and assist female workers in plucking.

Millet (*Maong*)

Millet (*maong*) is a traditional crop of the Lepchas. It is a crop of dry land. Millet is used for preparing *chi* (local liquor) which Lepchas consume in all social, religious and even in daily consumption. Traditionally, the dry lands were used only for millet cultivation.

**Table 4.8: Agricultural operations and classification of work.
Name of Crop: Maize (*Kun-tsoong*)**

Sl. No.	Name of Operations			Classification of work			
	English	Nepali	Lepcha	Bullock	Male	Female	Child
1	Ploughing	*Zotnu*	*Long-maa-syaong*	√	√		
2	Pulverising	*Dalla Thoknu*	*Paang Koang Buk/Fanoak Vo Syaong*		√		
3	Levelling	*Dade*	*Tset Syaong*	√	√		√
4	Broadcasting	*Makai Charaunu*	*Kun-tsoong Lee Syaong*		√	√	
5	Furrowing	*Line Banaunu*	*Faat Thaap Syaong*		√	√	
6	Sowing	*Ropnu*	*Chaok Syaong*		√	√	
7	Weeding	*Gornu*	*Sat/BukSyaong*		√	√	√
8	Ridge Making	*Matolagaunu*	*Faat/Thaap Syaong*		√	√	
9	Plucking	*Tipnu*	*Oat Syaong*			√	√
10	Storing	*Than karnu*	*Tho Syaong*		√	√	

Although the land under the coverage of millet has decreased drastically, but still a good number of Lepchas cultivate it.

Comparatively less number of operations are required in the millet cultivation (see Table 4.9). Works in millet cultivation are performed equally by the male, female and child. Beside works like ploughing, levelling and transplanting all other works are done by the female and child labours. The contribution of females and children are more significant in the cultivation of millet than that of other crops. Male workers complete the first phase of operation while all remaining works in the later phase are performed jointly by the female and child labours.

Ginger (*Heng*)

Ginger (*heng*) is one of the important cash crops of the region. This is the crop from which the Lepchas fetch the return twice – once by selling the mother seed and then by selling the final crop. Inspite of the double return, Lepchas in recent days have reduced the cultivation of ginger due to its diseases. Lepchas of Pochaok are cultivating ginger while it is nil in the other two villages.

It can be said (Table 4.10) in ginger cultivation the males are weighted heavily and all works are assigned to them. Few works of less importance are done by the female and child workers.

Cardamom (*Tambrak*)

It is the most important plantation crop among the Lepchas of Pochaok. The black soil along with shade, moderate warmth, and sufficient water is necessary conditions for the cultivation of cardamom. It is reported by some [Gowloog, 1995: 40] that there is no Lepcha name for cardamom and they use the term *alaichi* (Nepali term) which indicates that this is not an indigenous crop of the Lepchas. But the Lepchas of Pochaok where cardamom is cultivated in abundance termed it *tambrak*. Villagers do not know from where it is imported, but they say that they have been cultivating it since time immemorial.

All works involved in cardamom cultivation except drying are done by the male workers while females and children perfom less important works as a helping hand.

Table 4.9: Agricultural operations and classification of work.
Name of Crop: Millet (*Maong*)

Sl. No.	Name of Operations			Classification of work			
	English	Nepali	Lepcha	Bullock	Male	Female	Child
1	Ploughing	*Zotnu*	*Long-maa-syaong*	√	√		
2	Pulverising	*Dalla Thoknu*	*Paang Koang Buk/Fanoak Vo Syaong*		√	√	
3	Levelling	*Dade*	*Tset Syaong*	√	√		√
4	Transplanting	*Ropnu*	*Chaok Syaong*		√	√	√
5	Harvesting	*Katnu*	*Ek Syaong*			√	√
6	Threshing	*Pitnu*	*Maong Buk Syaong*			√	√
7	Storing	*Thankarnu*	*Maong Tho Syaong*			√	√

Table 4.10: Agricultural operations and classification of work.
Name of Crop: Ginger (*Heng*)

Sl. No.	Name of Operations			Classification of work			
	English	Nepali	Lepcha	Bullock	Male	Female	Child
1	Ploughing	*Zotnu*	*Long-maa-syaong*	√	√		
2	Pulverising	*Dalla Thoknu*	*Paang Koang Buk/Fanoak Vo Syaong*		√		
3	Levelling	*Dade*	*Tset Syaong*	√	√		√
4	Sowing	*Ropnu*	*Chaok Syaong*		√		
5	Weeding	*Gornu*	*Sat/Buk Syaong*		√	√	√
6	Collecting mother	*Mau-Nikalnu*	*Aamoo heng Do Syaong*		√		
7	Row making	*Mato Lagaunu*	*Faat/Thaap Sydong*		√	√	
8	Harvesting	*Bachha Khanaunu*	*Aa Kup Do Syaong*		√		
9	Seed storing	*Bue Raknu*	*Le Lap Syaong*		√		

Table 4.11: Agricultural operations and classification of work. Name of Crop : Cardamom (*Tan brak*)

Sl. No.	Name of Operations			Classification of work			
	English	Nepali	Lepcha	Bullock	Male	Female	Child
1	Cleaning	*Safa kurnu*	*Sat Syaong*		√		
2	Ploughing	*Zotnu*	*Long-maa-Syaong*	√	√		
3	Levelling	*Dade*	*Tset Syaong*	√	√		√
4	Transplanting	*Ropnu*	*Chaok Syaong*		√		
5	Cleaning	*Farnu*	*Prek/Ek Syaong*		√	√	
6	Plucking	*Tipnu*	*Oat Syaong*		√	√	
7	Cleaning	*Farnu*	*Prek/Ek Syaong*		√	√	
8	Drying	*Surkaunu*	*Phak Syet Syaong*			√	√

GLADIOLI

Like cardamom in Pochaok and vegetables in 5th Mile Lepcha Gaon, the Lepchas of Mani Gumpa have started considering gladioli as their main cash crop. The elderly people are still guided by their traditional outlook and deny shifting to gladioli leaving traditional crops like paddy, maize and millet. At present, there are eleven households who consider it as a most important profitable cash crop. Over the years more lands are coming under gladioli cultivation. Gladioli gives monetary returns twice – (i) by selling the sticks bearing flower and (ii) by selling the globular base of the stem known as bulb *(aapaam)* which is used as seed for next year.

Table 4.12 shows different operations of gladioli cultivation as performed by male, female and child labour. It is well evident that males take active part in all types of operations while females and children are involved in less important and less labourious works. Involvement of the children are limited in levelling the field along with bullocks and ploughmen.

Vegetables *(Bifong)*

Lepchas of 5th Mile Lepcha Gaon consider vegetables (*bifong*) as their main cash crop. They mainly produce potato (*alubuk*), cucumber (*saret*), cabbage (*kagibi*), cauliflower (*riburn*), tomato (*birupaot*), radish (*laa-pup*), chilli (*sang kaar*), bean (*tuk-bit*), squash (*su-koos*), sweet pumpkin (*tangut*) and mustard leaves (*pachebi*).

In vegetable cultivation (Table 4.13) all types of work except plucking of fruits are done by the male workers while females and children are involved in a number of soft operations. Vegetables need constant nursing where females and children, particularly household members are found to be most suitable.

Lepchas cultivate both food and cash crops. The common crops in all the three villages are paddy, maize and millet. But the three villages differ in terms of their cultivation of cash crops. Cardamom and ginger are the two main cash crops in Pochaok while it is vegetable and gladioli for 5th Mile Lepcha Gaon and Mani Gumpa respectively. The different crops demand different types of operations and participation by age and sex.

Table 4.12: Agricultural operations and classification of work.
Name of Crop: Gladioli

Sl. No.	Name of Operations			Classification of work			
	English	Nepali	Lepcha	Bullock	Male	Female	Child
1	Ploughing	*Zotnu*	*Long-maa Syaong*	√	√		
2	Pulverising	*Dalla Thoknu*	*Paang Koang Buk/Fanoak Va Syaong*		√	√	
3	Levelling	*Dade*	*Tset Syaong*	√	√		√
4	Making Row	*Line Bananu*	*Faat/Thaap Syaong*		√	√	
5	Planting Bulb	*Ropnu*	*AapaamChaok Syaong*		√		
6	Weeding	*Gornu*	*Buk/Sat Syaong*		√	√	
7	Irrigating	*Pani Lagaunu*	*Oang Thaap Syaong*		√		
8	Cutting stick	*Phul Katnu*	*Ek Syaong*		√		
9	Extracting bulb	*Bulb Uthaunu*	*Aapaam Plya Syaong*		√		
10	Storing	*Bue Raknu*	*Aapaam Tho Syong*		√		

Table 4.13: Agricultural operations and classification of work.
Name of Crop: Vegetables (*Bifong*)

Sl. No.	Name of Operations			Classification of work			
	English	Nepali	Lepcha	Bullock	Male	Female	Child
1	Ploughing	*Zotnu*	*Long-maa Syaong*	√	√		
2	Pulverising	*Dalla Thoknu*	*Paang Koang Buk/Fanoak Va Syaong*		√	√	
3	Levelling	*Dade*	*Tset Syaong*	√	√		√
4	Broadcasting seed	*Bijan Charaunu*	*Le Paat Syaong*		√	√	
5	Irrigating	*Pani Lagaunu*	*Oang Thaap Syaong*		√	√	
6	Weeding	*Gornu*	*Buk/Sat Syaong*		√	√	√
7	Row making	*Mato Lagaunu*	*Faat Thaap Syaong*		√	√	√
8	Irrigating	*Pani Lagaunu*	*Oang Thaap Syaong*		√	√	
9	Pluck/Harvesting	*Katnu/Tipnu*	*Oat/Ek Syaong*			√	√

In general, all works with bullocks are performed by the adult male members. The children help in levelling the field as weight on both sides of the ladder (pointed for wet land and plain for dry land). No such works are performed by the females. There are several works which can be done absolutely by the males. Some works are performed solely by the females. It has been noted that comparatively more works are performed by the male members in cultivating cash crops while the role of females and children are more in case of food crops. The work of males often considered as principal type of involvement while for the females it is of subsidiary nature. Works of children are accepted as assistance and by their involvement, they get training in agricultural operations.

AGRICULTURAL HOLIDAYS

"We are not employees so as to enjoy holidays or vacation like you. We work in the field and have to attend the crop as per its requirements. Work at proper time is very important for agriculture. We cannot wait even for a single day in case of some agricultural operations. We need to meet the demands of the crop at proper time and quantity. Agriculture is our way of life and we engage ourselves in cultivation throughout the year without any rest whatsoever. But as you know, agriculture is seasonal, we do enjoy leisure. We cannot take leave as you can according to your personal need". It was a logical statement by Pascal Lepcha of Pochaok while enquiring about agricultural holidays.

It is true that Lepchas need to attend the crop as per its requirements but cross section data in the study area reveal that they do enjoy holidays in agriculture. Guided by the tradition, convention and religious beliefs, Lepchas and their bullocks remain off the field. Lepchas are sharply divided in two religious faiths – Buddhism and Christianity. The list of agricultural holidays is more clear among the Christian Lepchas than among the Buddhists. All the Lepchas of 5th Mile Lepcha Gaon and 68.38 per cent of Pochaok are Christians. Their list of holidays is shown in Table 4.14.

Almost all the Lepchas of Mani Gumpa (95.00 per cent) and 31.61 per cent of Pochaok are Buddhists. Their list of holidays in agricultural operations is shown in Table 4.15.

Table 4.14: Agricultural Holiday (for Christians)

Sl. No.	Occasions	Days and date	No. of days
1	Sunday	All	52 days
2	Good Friday	April	3 days
3	Christmas and New Years	December 20 – January 5	12 days
4	Church Activities	-	15 days
Total			82 days

Table 4.15: Agricultural Holiday (for Buddhists)

Sl. No.	Occasions	Months and Days	No. of Days
1	*Lirun Faat*	April – May	3 days
2	*Sekeor Rum Faat*	April – May	1 day
3	*Sekeor Rum Faat*	November – Dec.	1 day
4	*Gaeboo Achyok's Birthday*	20 Dec.	1 day
5	*Nambun*	December	10 days
6	*Rong Dung git*	Jan, 26	1 day
7	*Intensurup*	May	1 day
8	*Buddha Purnima*	May, Dec.	2 days
9	*Mane*	May, Dec.	2 days
10	*Chu chu*	May, Dec.	2 days
11	*Muk Zik Ding Rum Faat*	21 Feb	1 day
12	*Tendong Lho-Rum Faat*	8 Aug.	1 day
13	First day after hail storm	-	1 day
14	*Lyaang Rum Faat*	1 April	2 days
15	*Sugi*	-	1 day
	Total		30 days

In addition to the above list, both the Buddhists and Christians remain off the field in the event of:

a) Any death in the village

b) Any birth of new baby in the village

c) Unfavourable natural conditions

d) Diseases at home (individual)

e) Unforseen uncertainities

It is clear that Christian Lepchas enjoy more agricultural holidays and engaged in religious activities than their Buddhist counterpart.

CHAPTER FIVE

FINANCE, TOOLS AND TECHNIQUES

In peasant economy the role of capital is not at all significant. Capital can never emerge as a distinct pre-condition of production in tribal economy and where the need of capital is found somewhat negligible and supplied mainly by the land owner. Tribes commonly use their indigenous tools and techniques in production in general and in agriculture in particular. They do not like to deviate much from their traditional techniques and method of production.

Instead of presenting capital as a means of production, which is not possible in any tribal,economy, the present chapter deals with the state of finance and some relevant aspects associated with it. They are - source of supply of finance, variety of tools and techniques, manure and fertiliser, source of water, management of animal labour, exchange of animal labour and change in cultivation.

SOURCE OF FINANCE

The requirement of finance in Lepcha agriculture is minimum. Agriculture among the Lepchas is basically household based. They use either houschold or exchange labour. Particularly for traditional crops like paddy, maize and millet. Lepchas use domestic seeds which they usually keep separately after harvest. They use cow-dung as manure which is also .available domestically. Although, few Lepchas have bullocks, but most of them rear milch cow, goat, pig. Their wastages are used as manure in the fields.

Lepchas mostly meet their requirements of finance in agriculture from their own sources. They on their own manage the small amount of fund required for the traditional crops, but often face problem in the case of modern cash crops. Lack of institutional source of credit compels them to manage cash from local personal sources. The share-croppers only get the paddy seeds for next cultivation from their land owners at the time of harvest.

In case of any shortage of paddy or millet seedlings of small quantity, it is available in mutual terms from the neighbours without involving any cost or others in return. The neighbours however, supply cow-dung manure in exchange of either straw or cash. In Mani Gumpa some exchange gladioli bulb for cormlets. In Pochaok few farmers take ginger seed from the shopkeepers on the condition that they will sell their produce to them. Sometimes local grocers allow the Lepchas to take their daily necessities throughout the year and ask to repay the entire amount by selling the crops to them. The grocers thus play the role of middlemen and also purchase the agricultural crops. Some Lepchas supply to them milk daily and in exchange receive daily necessities. Some shopkeepers of Bihar origin in Pochaok are well versed in Lepcha language and can attract the innocent Lepchas as their customers. The same practice is also observed in other two villages where the shopkeepers are not the purchaser of crops but allow the Lepchas to receive the grocery articles throughout the year.

Lepchas of Mani Gumpa are facing difficulty in selling gladioli which is a perishable commodity. They cannot even wait for two days with the gladioli sticks. Two individuals are the main purchasers of gladioli — one individual Dhan Narayan Chettri and the other is a sort of co-operative run by its members. The payment and standardisation are better in case of the cooperative (run by Sirbandi club) than that of the private one. Unlike Pochaok, the Lepchas of Mani Gumpa face problems of getting any financial support as and when it requires for agricultural operation. Although the middlemen belonging to the business community exploit the Lepchas by paying low price, low grade or weight but do supply cash or other requirement at times of need. The Lepchas found them essential in the absence of any alternative institutional sources of finance.

Beside the above noted negligible and irregular kind of non-institutional financial support, the Lepchas sometime received the meager amount of institutional credit as may be illustrated in the following cases:

In Mani Gumpa, two households received loan for poultry farm from State Bank of India in early 80's. In 2000 another two households received subsidised fishery loan of Rs.5000/- each. It was sanctioned by the Department of Fishery, Governmen of West Bengal and was disbursed through the Union Bank of India, Kalimpong Branch. But the recipients complain that they are yet to receive the last instalment of the loan. Once all the villagers about 20 years back received HYV maize seed and some fertiliser from the Comprehensive Area Development Project, a Government of West Bengal organisation. But there was no follow up of the scheme and the villagers had to rely on their less productive traditional variety.

Bidhan Chandra Krishi Vishwavidyalaya (presently renamed as Uttar Banga Krishi Vishwavidyalaya, U.B.K.V.) has selected the 5th Mile Lepcha Gaon for their experiment and research for adoption of different high yielding variety crops. They periodically supply different varieties of seeds or seedlings at free of cost to the villagers and find the effect on their soil. But this is a short-term benefit extended by the university for their experiment purpose only without any follow up for the long-term. Recently, three young Lepchas of the village visited the university centre at Kalyani for agricultural training. "But as far as our agricultural pattern is concerned, we are not getting any practical benefit from such training", said Subhas Lepcha, a trainee.

Lepchas of Pochaok received some credit from the banks located at Budhabare. With the subsidised loan some purchased milch cow, goat but most of them could not repay the amount due to inappropriate use of the money. These defaulters cannot approach the bank for further loan nor does the bank take the risk of advancing fresh loan to them.

For institutional finance, the role of two non-governmental agencies is important to note:

GUMPA

The monastery in Mani Gumpa village is an important source of credit for the Lepchas at the time of their emergency. All the member households (near 68 households including from those of the neighbouring villages) received loan from the Gumpa in the initial period of establishment of the village. The present Lepchas have no idea about how much money they received but all are paying Rs.5/- as a sort of interest twice a year during chu-chu functions in the Gumpa. It is a non-refundable type of loan where the households need not to pay the principal amount but are liable to clear the interest.

Fertile and comparatively flat land of the village is in the possession of the Gumpa. All the lands are rent free. It helps the Lepchas by leasing them out on share cropping. The highest percentage (31.81) of share-cropping are recorded in Mani Gumpa because of availability of Gumpa land.

At times of requirement, particularly during bad harvest, Gumpa came forward to help uniformly to all its members as per requirement. Many Lepchas take crops particularly paddy and maize as loan during off harvest period to meet up their daily consumption needs from the Gumpa and return the same after harvest. No interest is charged against such crop loan. Gumpa also extends loan to meet some urgent requirements like medical or educational purposes.

WORLD VISION

World vision, a USA based NGO helped nine Lepchas by sanctioning loans for animal husbandry particularly in purchasing pig, goat, hen or cow. No interest is charged on the loan but the debtor needs to return the principal amount to the village level committee and the recovered money thus accumulated may create a self-supporting fund for the village.

Very recently, World Vision constructed eleven water tanks of 2000 litre capacity and connected them with the uphill stream by iron pipe. This water is mainly used for agricultural purposes and every household in the village are benefitted by the system. This has changed the dimension of agriculture in the village and the Lepchas now-a-days are showing more interest in cultivating vegetables which need comparatively more water.

It is, thus, clear that in the case of Lepchas the household fund like household labour remains as the main source of capital for the agricultural use. The little bit of support which the Lepchas received at different times from different institutions are neither sufficient nor stable. For all practical purposes no Lepcha depends on outside financial help for agriculture. The amount of money required is also low and the Lepcha agriculture remains as traditional one. Their higher dependence on rain water, traditional seed, household labour, village bullocks, plough, indigenous manure possibly do not compel the Lepchas to go beyond their household finance for agriculture. In the cultivation of cash crops like gladioli, vegetables, ginger, potato the picture is slightly different but still the Lepchas manage the required capital either from household or other sources available within the village.

TYPES OF IMPLEMENTS AND TOOLS

Agriculture of the Lepchas requires small number of implements and tools. The implements are normally owned personally by the users and wherever they go for work, they carry those along with them. The owners of bullock usually possess implements of ploughing and levelling. Modern tools like sprayer machines are possessed by fifteen households. But they are extensively used by all other Lepchas with or without paying anything to their owners.

The traditional Lepcha cultivation is known as *zomaal* which means sowing of paddy in the dry land. In this cultivation, the males generally dig the earth with pointed bamboo rods while the females follow them by pushing some seeds inside the holes or loosed earth. In early days, the Lepchas had no plough and the implements used by them were mainly meant for scraping and softening the soil for reception of seeds. The traditional implement used for loosening the earth and cleaning of seeds was the hoe. In addition there were two or three types of pronged hoes used for loosening the earth and removing the weeds. But now-a-days the implements used by the Lepchas are of the similar type as used by the others in the region. The following implements are used by the Lepchas in different agricultural operations.

Ploughing Implements

Plough (*longkung or halkung*) is used by the Lepchas for tilling the land. Ploughing is not suitable for small patch of land and which is cultivated by the Lepchas with the help of spade (*tackchoo*). Before ploughing with bullocks, spade is extensively used for cutting the earth on the ridge side of the terrace or rebuilding the boundaries with new earth for the field.

The plough used in the hills is heavier (nearly 20 to 25 kg. along with the plough share) than that of the plains. Lepchas use two types of plough – heavier one for the dry field and comparatively lighter one for the wet field. The height of the plough depends on the height of the ploughman.

A plough [Figure 5.1(a)] consists of different parts and is identified with particular Lepcha names. The horn shaped piece of wood (*kung*) with a length of 2-2$^1/_2$ feet is tipped by nearly 10-12 inch iron plough share (*pansing*). Two or three iron hooks are used to fix the share with the plough. The share needs to be sharpened every three to four years from the blacksmith (*karvomoo*). On the upper end a round shaped wood preferably straight branch of tree is fixed whose other end is connected with the handle (*acham*) to steer the plough. At the middle of the kung where it takes kink shape a beam (*pathing*) of 6-7 feet length is fixed by creating holes and using wooden cork. The wooden yoke (*thokabiyal*) [Figure 5.1(b) is fixed on the other end of the beam with hooks to rest on the shoulders of the pair of bullock. A leather rope (Figure 5.2) (*thong*) is used to tie the beam at the middle of the yoke where it is comparatively curved shaped. The yoke is 3-4 feet length and on its both sides two bamboo rods are fixed vertically so that the bullocks can be tied with rope.

Most parts of plough are prepared by the Lepchas themselves out of best variety of wood available locally except the plough share which they purchase from the market. Two blacksmiths (*karvomoo*) are found only in Pochaok. But their principal occupation is cultivation and both of them fall in the category of owner cultivator (Table 3.3). The owners of the bullocks generally function as ploughmen who usually carry both the plough and bullocks wherever they visit for their service. The bullock which is fixed at the left side of yoke is known as left bullock and that at the right side is right bullock. Left bullock generally cannot be shifted to the right side. Left and right bullocks are fixed to the left and right sides of yoke. Bullocks can understand and obey the orders of their master only.

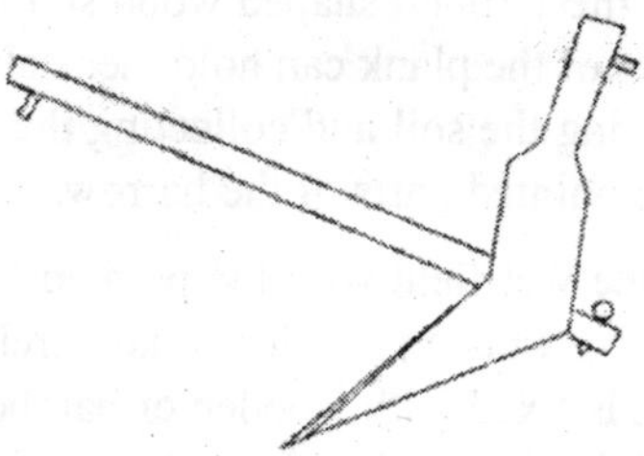

Fig. 5.1(a): Plough (long *kung*)

Fig. 5.1(b): Yoke (*thokabiyal*)

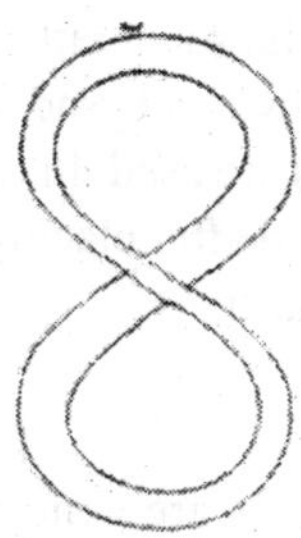

Fig. 5.2: Rope made of leather (*thong*)

Harrowing Implements

After ploughing the next operation is harrowing and levelling for which two types of harrow are used by the Lepchas — pointed harrow (Figure 5.3) (*tset*) drawn by the bullocks and the ordinary wooden harrow or the leveller (Figure 5.4) operated manually.

For harrowing, the same yoke used for ploughing is fixed by the leather rope (*thong*) with the beam (*pathing*) of the pointed harrow. Lepchas generally use 3-4 feet long thick wooden plank to fix 5-8 wooden or bamboo points on one side and two round shaped woods on the two extreme corners of the other side of the plank. Two handles are fixed at the end of these round shaped wood so that two children who sit on the two ends of the plank can hold themselves tightly. *Tset* is also used for harrowing the soil and collecting the roots and other waste articles with the pointed parts of the harrow.

After harrowing the wet field with the pointed harrow, Lepchas use hand driven spade like wooden leveller. A half circle wooden plank with I - 1½ feet length is fixed with wooden or bamboo handle at the middle of the plank. After harrowing the soft clay, the field needs to be levelled so that water can be stored equally at all parts of the field. The leveller can be used for both pulling and pushing clay by an adult male labour.

Sowing and Transplanting Implements

Next agricultural operation is the transplantation of seedlings from nursery bed to the field. In case of dry farming like maize, millet or vegetables, the seeds need to be sown either in row or scattered over the field. It is manually done by hands and for such operation no seed drills or any other implements are used. In case seeds are sown in row, plough is used to make row and after placing seeds on the rows, spade is used to cover seeds with earth.

Weeding Implements

Three types of implements are generally used for weeding — pointed forked hoe with big handle (Figure 5.5) (*foat-krut*), two types of pointed forked hoe with small handle (Figure 5.6 and 5.7)and spade [Figure 5.8(a) and 5.8(b)] (*thakchu*). The iron hoe with three iron points is connected with 2½-3 feet bamboo or wooden handle through a ring holder. It has three iron points but is connected with 6-8 inches wooden handle by a pin sharped iron connector. In one case, the handle is facing the worker like spade while in other case, the small handle is facing against the worker like a shovel. Spade is a 6-8 inch iron plate sharped on the lower side and got a ring holder on the upper end to fix the 2½-3 feet bamboo or wooden handle. The iron parts of all the three implements are purchased from the market while the wooden parts are domestically prepared and fixed by the Lepchas. The paddy and millet field get less weeds and are normally weeded by hands without using much of the appliances. The dry farming needs weeding and where pointed fork is widely used.

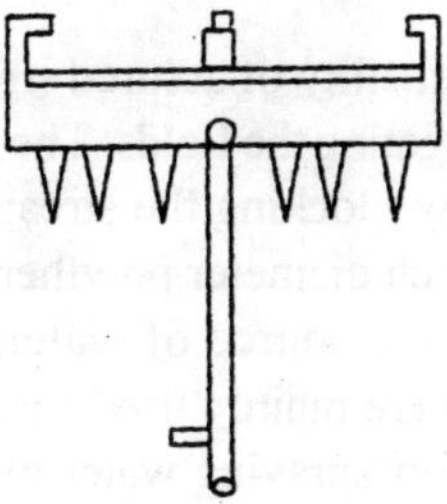

Fig. 5.3 Pointed harrow (*tset*)

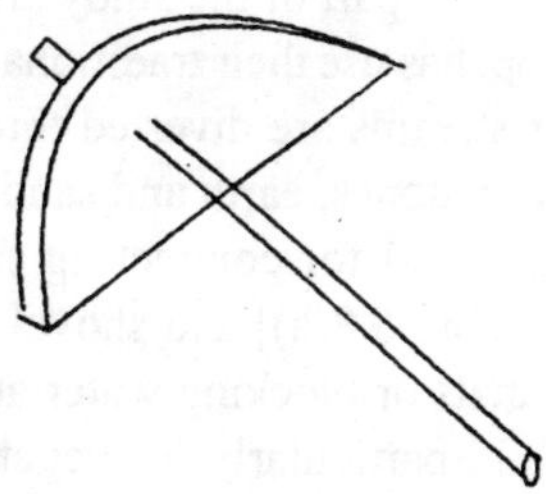

Fig. 5.4 Wooden leveller

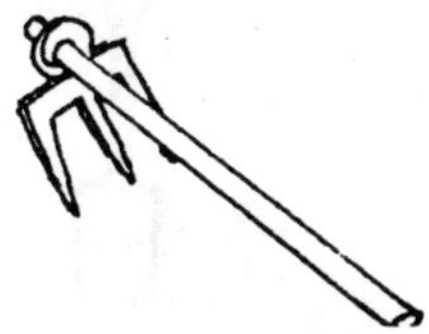

Fig. 5.5 Pointed forked hoe (*foat-krut*)

Fig. 5.6 Pointed forked hoe (*kakchu*)

Fig. 5.7 Pointed forked hoe

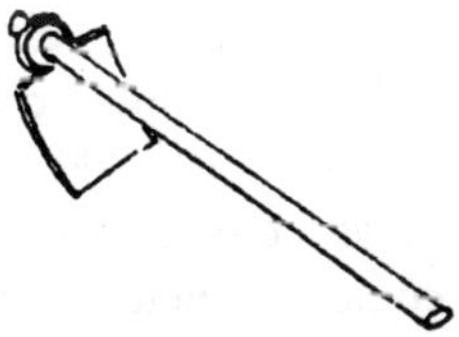

Fig. 5.8(a) Spade (*thakchu*)

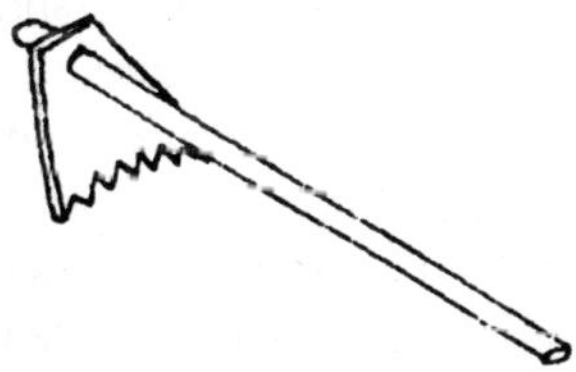

Fig. 5.8(b) Pointed spade

Irrigation Implements

No part of the study area enjoys the facility of assured irrigation. Lepchas use their traditional device in irrigating the fields. The rivulets or streams are diverted through canals by blocking the stream water with stones, earth and sand. Often half inch diameter polythene pipes are used for connecting the field with the source of water. Spade [Figure 5.8(a)] and shovel (Figure 5.10) are mainly used for making canals or blocking water at the source. For spraying water in the dry field particularly for vegetable cultivation, Lepchas use home made sprinklers which are connected by polythene pipes with the water source at the higher heights. The sprinkler is shown in Figure 5.9.

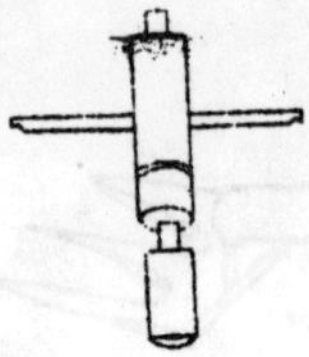

Fig. 5.9 Sprinkler

Fig. 5.10 Shovel *(faat-ghuram)*

The sprinkler is the unique example of indigenous technology which is prepared domestically with the simple things available locally. No parts except the polythene pipe need to be purchased, neither they are available in the market. Some Lepchas are more expert in preparing them and making them available for the others. The Lepchas lend sprinklers without charging anything in return.

Spraying Equipments

Lepchas use modern sprayer for spraying insecticides, pesticides, fungicides and hormone for the cash crops like ginger, gladioli, vegetables. The sprayer is not required for traditional crops like paddy, maize and millet. The price of sprayer varies from Rs. 800/- to Rs. 1200/-. One young Lepcha of Mani Gumpa who brought some parts from Siliguri and assemble them at home could complete the sprayer for Rs.250/- only. The sprayer available in the three villages is shown in Table 5.1. The Lepchas also use other machines without paying them in return. One sprayer has been purchased out of sponsored money of World Vision, the USA based NGO, and is kept at its office at 5 Mile

Lepcha Gaon. The Lepchas at times of requirement can borrow the machine against the payment of Rs. 10/- per week. One machine is sufficient to cater the need of the entire village but in many cases, one household takes the machines for a week but it is used by the others without paying anything either to the World Vision or the household who borrow on rent. These machines are used at the time of cultivation of gladioli in Mani Gumpa, vegetable in 5th Mile Lepcha Gaon and ginger or cardamom in Pochaok.

Table 5.1: Spraying machines available in the three villages

Name of village	No. of machines available	Ownership category	Type of Primary Corps
Mani Gumpa	3	Individuals	Gladioli
5th Mile Lepcha Gaon	1	World Vision, U.S.A. based NGO	Vegetable
Pochaok	11	Individuals	Ginger, Cardamom
Total	15	-	-

Harvesting Implements

The sickle or reaping hook is used by the Lepchas for harvesting. The iron blade of the sickle varies in terms of its arc and length. The sickle used for harvesting paddy [Figures 5.11(a) and 5.11(b)] is generally smaller than those used for cutting the jungles in cardamom field [Figure 5.11(c)]. Lepchas use spade and pointed hoe for digging earth to collect the underground products like potato, ginger, and radish. Harvesting of maize is done manually without any tool.

Threshing Implements

Stalks of harvested paddy or wheat in a form of small bundles are carried to the threshing ground *(zo-laam)* for threshing and winnowing. Lepchas normally use log of wood or wooden plank or seating bench for threshing purposes. A bamboo stick is also used for beating and separating corn from straw. A big oven is used to dry the cardamom and make ready for sale. After plucking, the millet is dried up in sunshine and beaten by wooden rod to get the crop.

Fig. 5.11(a) Sickle used in paddy

Fig. 5.11(b) Sickle used for cutting jungle

Fig. 5.11(c) Sickle used in cardamom

Measuring Device

Lepchas use two types of measurement for agricultural products —*taphu-tungfri* system and the standard metric units. After harvest Lepchas take an account of their products in terms of *taphu-tungfri* system. But they follow metric measurement when they send the product to the market for sale. *Taphu-tungfri* system is used in case of any domestic use of product or any intra-community transaction including loan, payment of wage, and measurement of seed for land. It is also used to measure the quantity and quality of land. Traditionally, lands were measured in terms of seed used or quantity of crops cultivated. The units of measurement as followed by the Lepchas and their metric equivalent are shown in Table 5.2.

Lepcha *taphu* and *tungfri* are the small vessels made up of bamboo, cane, iron copper, bell-metal or brass. There is no separate vessel for *Tungfri — khaa-kaat. Tunggaar* [Figure 5.17(b)] is a bamboo or cane made basket which can be carried on the back after tightening it with the carrier's head by a jute belt. Lepchas also widely use *tung-yaang* [Figure 5.17(a)] for measuring and carrying vegetables, maize, manures. The shape and size of *tung-jyaang* is the same to *tunggaar* excepting that holes are there all around the body of tung-Jyaang and is less costly and of inferior quality. Lepchas are good in handicrafts. They themselves prepare *tunggaar* and *tung-jy*aang with bamboo which are locally available. The *taphu* and *tungfri* are purchased from the market and their cost varies as per the weight of the metal. Most of the Lepchas have their personal *taphu* and *tungfri*.

Table 5.2: Indigenous and metric measuring units

Indigenous Unit	Metric Unit
1 *Taphu*	½ kg.
1 *Tungfri* = 8 *Taphu*	4 kg.
1 *Tungfri* – *khaa-kaat* = 20 *tungfri*	80 kg.
1 *Tungfri* – *Khaa-kaat* = 5 tin	80 kg. (1 tin = 16 kg)
1 *Tungfri* – *Khaa-kaat* = 1 Sack	80 kg.
1 *Tungfri* – *khaa-kaat* = 2 *Tunggaar*	80 kg. (1 *Tunggaar* = 40 kg.)
1 *Tunggaar* = 10 *Tungfri*	40 kg.

For the commercial crop like ginger, cardamom and vegetables, Lepchas use standard steelyard scale and standard metric weights for measurement. Few households have personal scale but others can get it easily from them. The measuring scale is often domestically made from bamboo, cane or wood. In place of the standard weights, the Lepchas use stone or piece of iron or any weighty metals approximately equal to the standard weights for any measurement. The middleman who purchase the product always blame on the Lepcha method of measurement. Suk Tshering Lepcha of Pochaok alleged that "our product always gets reduced by the middlemen and whatever we purchase from them are always under weight". It has been noted that, some middlemen has opened their temporary shelter beside the main road during the harvest of ginger and cardamom. They use wooden balance with two fiat square wooden plank which is rested on a bamboo tripod. They often use local stones as weights in place of the standard weights.

Technique of Husking and Grinding

Lepchas use both traditional and modern technique of husking and grinding for paddy, maize, and turmeric. The wooden morter and pestle (Figure 5.12) (*tuk-tsaam-taaling*) is widely used by the Lepchas for husking paddy, pesting maize, powdering turmeric, chili, wheat or maize. For carrying out the work of husking or grinding or cleaning any grains, Lepchas extensively use the bamboo made winnowing tray [Figures 5.14(a) and 5.14(b)] (*taa-lyoong*).

The morter and pestle has two parts — (i) the morter (*tuk-tsaam*) is approximately three feet wooden stem with a bowl shaped cavity vessel in which grains are to be pounded with, and (ii) a pestle (*taaling*) of six feet long wooden rod with an iron socket in one end to heat the corn placed in the holes of *tuk-tsaam*. Both the morter and pestle are prepared by the respective village carpenters or domestically made from the wood available locally. *Tuk-tsaam* is wicker stool shaped wooden stem with a diameter of 12-15 inch at both the ends but only 8-12 inch in the middle. At the middle of the *taaling* the diameter of the wooden rod has been reduced in such a way that one can grip it tightly. The miniature form of *tuk-tsaam* and *taaling* is used for pesting and powdering articles particularly spices for the kitchen. Recently, Lepchas have begun to use the power driven machine for husking paddy or grinding wheat. As there is no such machine in their village, the Lepchas need to carry paddy at least two kilometres from their villages to avail this facility.

Tukvaar (Figure 5.13) is a pair of circular stones between which grains or other substance is ground. After pouring grains through small holes at the upper plate, *tukvaar* need to be moved thoroughly with the help of a vertically fixed wooden handle. Thus grains enter in between the two stone plates and due to the movement of upper one the grains start grinding or crushing and ultimately come out from all sides of the round shaped bottom stone. The process need to be repeated so long required quality of grinding is not available. Lepchas use *tukvaar* for grinding dal, maize and wheat.

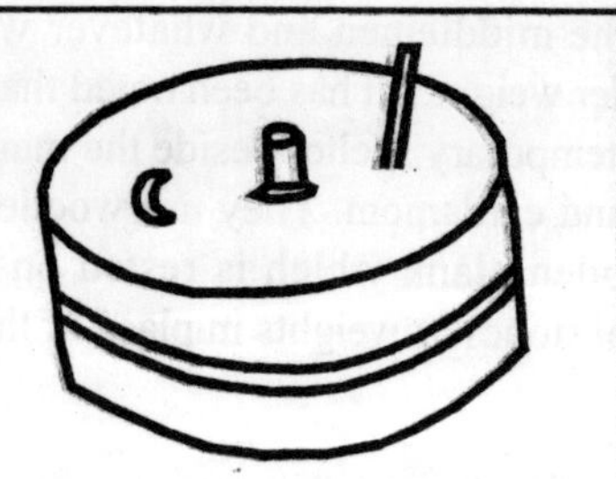

Fig. 5.13 Grinder (*Tuk-vaar*)

Taa-lyoong [Figures 5.14(a), 5.14(b)] is a square or round shaped winnowing tray made up of bamboo used for winnowing chaff from cereals or grains. Beside day to day use in the kitchen, it is also used in the threshing ground (*zo-laam*). It is flat round shaped finely woven mat with bamboo split of 15 inch diameter and whose square boundary is bordered with one inch comparatively thick bamboo split

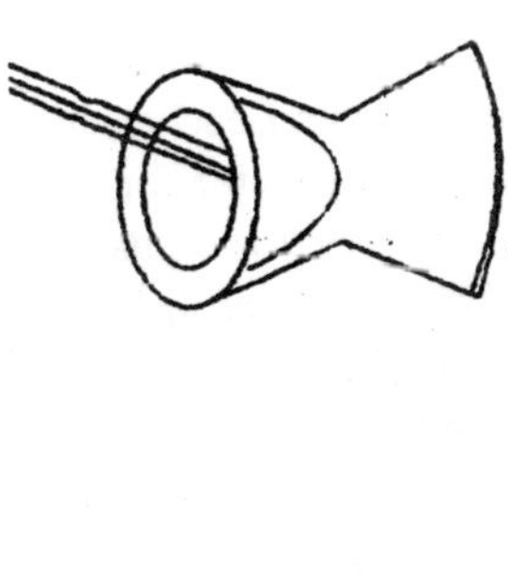

Fig. 5.12 Morter
(*Tuk-tsaam-Taaling*)

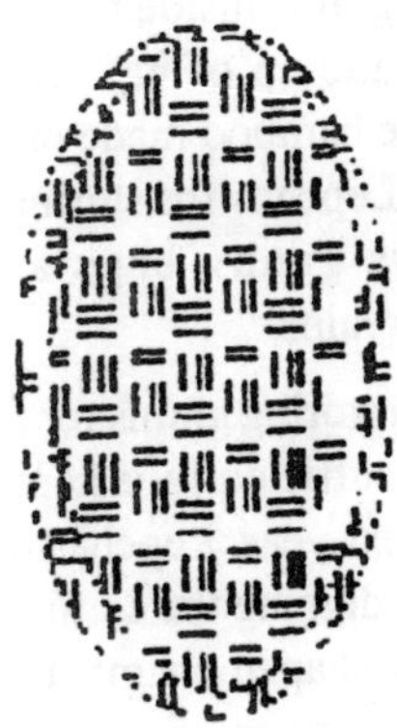

Fig. 5.14(a) Winnowing Tray
(*Taa-lyoong*)

Fig. 5.14(b) Winnowing Tray
(*Taa-lyoong*)

Storing Device

Lepchas preserve their grains particularly paddy in the granary (*zo-baa-hao*). It is a square sized wood or bamboo made store. Lepchas prefer wooden *zo-baa-hao* which reduces wastages of grains from insects. Almost each household keeps pet cats to keep the rats away. A corner under the main Ronglee, Lepcha indigenous house, is selected for the granary whose upper portion is kept open as air passage and that keep paddy dry throughout the year. For other crops like millet, dal and wheat, Lepchas use bamboo basket (Figure 5.15) *tuk-braam*. It is also extensively used both for carrying and keeping the grains inside the house. *Tuk--braam* is made up of both bamboo and cane. But the bamboo made one is widely used by the Lepchas for storing purposes. Now-a-days gunny bags are getting popularity for storing paddy and other grains.

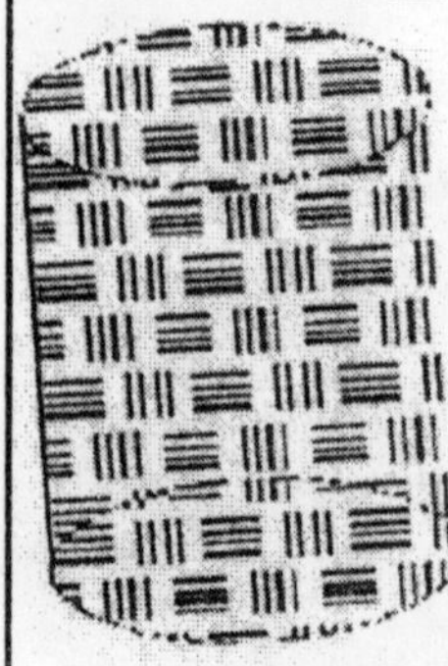

Fig. 5.15 Basket (Tuk-braam)

Each household takes special care in storing grains for the purpose of seed. Best quality paddy, after drying sufficiently, is kept separately in gunny bags as seed (*zo-le*) for the next year. Lepchas of Pochaok keep ginger (*heng*) as seed (heng-le), by digging the earth and making it air-tight. They construct a rectangular shaped chamber as per their requirement. All sides including the bottom of the chamber are carefully covered with banana leaves and paddy straw in such a way that water cannot enter inside. After placing ginger seeds the upper part of the chamber is first covered with wooden plank and then polythene sheet and earth.

Maize (*kun-tsoong*) is a seasonal crop. But Lepchas through their traditional method of preservation made it available for consumption round the year. The matured corn (*kung-tsoong-le*) usually hanged in a hanger made of bamboo (Figure 5.16) in the open air. Lepchas often hang them above the fire place in the kitchen. The smoke of the hearth helps to keep the insects away. The traditional hanger is made by fixing

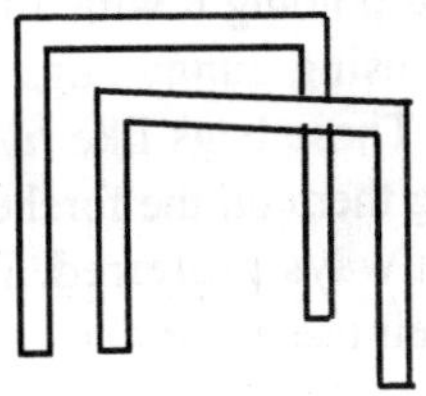

Fig. 5.16 Bamboo hanger

three bamboo poles on each side vertically on the ground. The middle post is about 6-8 inch more in height than the other two which are 6-7 feet high. Each of three poles are connected both sides with bamboo resting parallaly on their top. After preparing the hanger a number of maize cobs hold together in a cluster with their leaves and made them rest on the shelf after slanting on both the sides. One can notice an usual picture of hanging the maize cobs under the cornice in those sides of the house where it receives sufficient sun rays. They are under the shade of the cornice and can be protected from rain water. Good quality of maize are separated and preserved carefully as seed for the next year.

Carrying Method

Tung-jyaang [Figure 5.17(a)] and *tun-ggaar* [Figure 5.17(b)] are the two bamboo and cane made baskets used for carrying agricultural products at different occasions. *Tung-jyaang* is used for maize and vegetable while for paddy or grains *tun-ggaar* is suitable. Both can be prepared at home by thin bamboo splits. *Tun-ggaar* is a product of artistic nature and is prepared from upper portion of bamboo split or cane. In the market their cost varies between Rs.15/- and Rs.20/- for *tung-jyaang* and Rs.90/- and Rs.125/- for *tun-ggaar.*

Fig. 5.17(a) Basket (*tung-jyaang*)

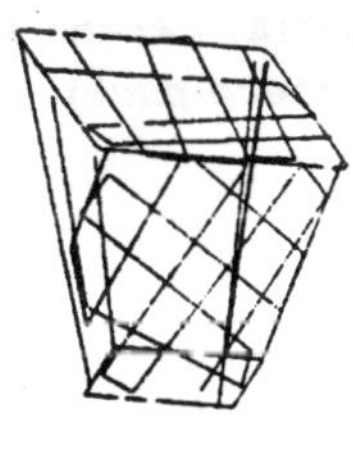

Fig. 5.17(b) Basket (*tunggaar*)

Tung-jyaang is used for carrying manure (*pachyo*) or cow-dung (*biyet*) to the field. For other carrying purposes *tung-jyaang* is widely used. It is carried by resting it on the back and holding it with a jute belt on the forehead. Lepchas are presently using gunny bags for carrying agricultural produce to the market. These bags like *tung-jyaang* are also carried on the back by holding them on the forehead with jute belt. As carrier, male labour is always preferred. For transportation, jeep or truck is available, but their use in the study area is extremely limited.

Beside all the implements and tools mentioned above, the most important one which was traditionally carried by all male members and is a symbol for the Lepchas is a small knife known as *baan-paok* [Figure5.18(a), 5.18(b) and 5.18(c)]. Recently, instead of *Baan-paok, khukri* (Figure 5.19), a Nepali knife, become popular among the Lepchas. No households in the 5th Mile Lepchas Gaon are possessing baan-paok, while few in Mani Gumpa and some in Pochaok are still having it. It is used for making and repairing all types of wooden or bamboo made agricultural implements. While ploughing, the ploughmen carry it for any emergency repairing work and to keep the bullocks under control.

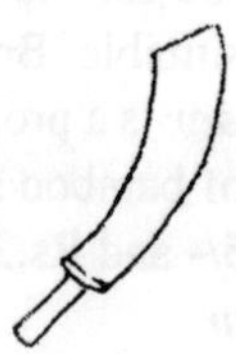

Fig. 5.18(a) Lepcha knife (*baan-paok*)

Fig. 5.18(b) Lepcha knife (*baan-paok*)

Fig. 5.18(c) Lepcha knife (*baan-paok*)

Fig. 5.18(d) Lepcha knife (*baan-paok*)

Agricultural implements used by the Lepchas in the study area conform to the specification of local need and regional culture. The Lepchas are still using the traditional types of plough, yoke, harrow, and sickle. This implies that Lepchas have not been much attracted by the modern tools and techniques of agriculture. Rate of mechanisation in Lepcha agriculture is extremely low and still they are mostly guided by traditional outlook and orientation.

USE OF MANURE AND FERTILISER

It is said, black soil (*farnuk*) is most fertile than either red soil (*farliang*) or white soil (*faryear*). Lepchas normally use black soil for cultivation. They also use different types of manure and fertiliser for different crops. For Lepchas the cheapest and domestically available manure is cow-dung (*biyet*). They deposit it in a rectangular pit throughout the year near the cow shed (*polek*). Lepchas without cattle purchase manure mostly from within the village @ Rs. 10/- per *tung-jgaang* (approximately 15 kg) in Mani Gumpa and Rs. 6/- in 5th Mile Lepcha Gaon. The household who do not have cattle normally exchange millet straw for manure. Unlike plains, no part of cow-dung is used for fuel. Lepchas prefer cow-dung as manure than any other chemical fertiliser. They believe that fertiliser helps improving productivity temporarily but left long-term negative effect on the soil. "Land is our mother and we cannot take any measure which destroys our land in the long-term", opined Sankit Lepcha of Mani Gumpa. An opposite view has been expressed by Choden Tshering Lepcha, a young graduate who introduced gladioli cultivation in the village. He said, "Agriculture is our means of livelihood and modern method of farming is impossible without chemical fertiliser. Economic condition of Lepchas can be changed only by adopting the modern method of agriculture".

Lepchas of all the three study villages, use different chemical fertiliser (Urea, Sufola, Single Super Phosphate, and Potash), pesticides (Metacide, Thioden, and Basathin etc.), fungicides (Indofil, Bavistin, Blitox), plant hormone (Planofix, Thashal, Suptnik, Miracullen etc.) at a limited scale for the cultivation of ginger, cardamom and gladioli. For traditional crops like paddy, millet and maize, Lepchas use only cow-dung. In the bi-cropping plant cycle system, Lepchas use manure once a year, normally for vegetables during the winter season and the second crop that is paddy grows out of the remaining fertility of the soil.

SOURCE OF WATER

Water is one of the most important inputs in agriculture. While all crops do not need equal quantity of water, but some cannot grow without water. The availability of water in field and the actual requirement of water influence the Lepcha cultivators to select the specific crop for growing. Assured irrigation is not at all available to the Lepchas in the study area. They largely depend on rain for cultivation. In some areas, Lepchas make the water available to the field by diverting the hilly streams through indigenous method of canals. Often water is also brought from streams or rivulets (*omkeong*) or from perennial sources of water from a particular spot (*jharong*) through polythene pipes. The World Vision helped in supplying water in 5th Mile Lepcha Gaon and which is used by the Lepchas in cultivation of some crops.

While selecting the terrace for paddy, the Lepchas keep in mind the availability of water and its sources. Areas mostly in close proximity to rivulets or comparatively flat (*taam*) and capable of retaining rain water are selected for paddy cultivation. Ploughing and levelling paddy fields need plenty of water and the Lepchas wait till the monsoon. Sometimes, diverted water is used in preparing the field for re-plantation of paddy seedlings. Sufficient water is required for cardamom cultivation. So, by diverting water through canals or pipes the Lepchas keep the cardamom field marshy throughout the year. Recently, Lepchas have started cultivating vegetables and gladioli during the winter. These two crops need timely supply of water and for which they fetch water from small steams through pipe. Cardamom fields in the upper Pochaok are normally drained either by perennial rivulets or diverting water through canals. Lands in lower Pochaok are comparatively flat and can store water for paddy cultivation. Lepchas depend on monsoon for paddy cultivation.

MANAGEMENT OF ANIMAL LABOUR

In Lepcha agriculture, bullock (*biklong*) is widely used for ploughing and levelling. In the small terraces where the bullock cannot move, the said operations are done manually. Besides their work during the sowing periods normally twice a year, the bullocks are kept idle for the rest of the year. But in season, they need to work continuously in the field for both their owners and neighbours and sometimes they work on rent basis.

Bullocks are inevitable for agriculture. But the proportion of Lepchas having bullocks is only 27.73 per cent. Table 5.3 shows village-wise distribution of bullocks and its ratio with household and land.

Table 5.3: Village-wise statement of Bullocks

Village	Bullocks		Total house-hold	Total landhold-ing	Bullock per	
	No.	%			Household	Land
1	2	3	4	5	6	7
Mani Gumpa	3	9.09	22	22.02	7.33	7.4
5th Mile Lepcha Gaon	3	9.09	21	41.07	7.00	13.69
Pochaok	27	81.82	76	329.96	2.82	12.22
Total	33	100	119	393.23	3.61	11.92

Bullock per household is the highest in Mani Gumpa followed by 5th Mile Lepcha Gaon and Pochaok. Bullocks are mostly busy in 5th Mile Lepcha Gaon while they are least busy in Mani Gumpa. Although the number of bullocks are highest in Pochaok, but they need to cultivate largest quantity of land (329.96 acres) and hence they remain busy in cultivating 12.22 acre of land per pair. Bullocks were ever found to much busy during the survey period of C.A. Bell (1901-03). He observed that on the "average Lepcha uses only one pair of bullock to each 20 acres and the Bhutia one pair to 25 acres, while the Nepali uses one pair to every 15 acres" (1905:25). The proportion of land per pair of bullock has decreased drastically from 20 acres to 11 acres over the last hundred years. But there is no reason to believe that bullocks have been replaced by machines. Bell discussed the reason behind the wide variation in the ratio between land cultivated and bullocks used. He wrote:

A Nepali will attempt to cultivate every available portion of his holding and will keep his bullocks engaged as much as he can; a Bhutia, as a rule, keeps a portion of his holding uncultivated either to give a land a few years rest or to allow jungle to grow for firewood etc.; a Lepcha will not only leave a part of his holding out of cultivation like the Bhutia (though not as much as the latter) but will also cultivate a portion of land with a small spade and spike (1905: 25-26).

Bell's observation faded away with the passage of time when land become much scarce a factor so that no Lepcha can ever think of keeping his holding out of cultivation rather cultivate each portion of his land with a small spade and spike.

A Lepcha village may be considered as a unit as far as the use of bullocks is concerned. A household can easily cultivate land without personal bullock. Matrices of reciprocal exchange of bullocks are shown in Appendices IX and X for Mani Gumpa and 5th Mile Lepcha Gaon respectively. The Matrices show how the bullocks remain busy in cultivating land of the entire village. Reciprocal exchange of bullocks takes place mainly among the Lepcha households. In case, bullocks visit non-Lepcha household, they ask for cash payment. Aspects like genealogy, kinship, and *moo* are not so important in the case of reciprocal exchange of bullocks. A kind of community consideration and a collective feeling of live together, work together, share together in the society is the basis of such exchange. A kind of Lepcha solidarity has been maintained through the reciprocal exchange of bullocks. Village Mani Gumpa is more compact in the sense that as much as twelve households receive the entire bullock in spite of the fact that their average land holding is much less than the other two villages. Sometimes all the three pairs of bullocks work together on a small patch of terrace.

It has been observed that the medium and large sized land holders, and share-croppers are keeping bullocks of their own. These households need additional labour for cultivating their land. A system of exchange of bullocks against labour prevails in the villages. A ploughman with a pair of bullock is exchanged against three labour days of any sex and age. Interestingly, bullock and human labour are considered equally in the Lepcha society. A ploughman gets tea or *chi* and snacks in tiffin and rice, meat, vegetables, *chi* in lunch while bullocks get grass, salted rice water, maize water as food for work.

Timings for bullocks are different from that of human labour. The usual time for ploughing is 6 a.m. to 12 noon while human labour works from 8 am to 5 pm. Deforestation creates scarcity of fodder and the villagers are facing difficulty in tending their cattle.

Cost of a pair of bullock varies between Rs. 4000/- to Rs. 6000/. Veterinary facilities are available locally only for Mani Gumpa and 5th Mile Lepcha Gaon. On an average, the Lepchas use their experience for the treatment of minor diseases of the cattle. Tshering Lepcha of Mani Gumpa informed, "now-a-days, it is hard to get herbs from the local area as medicinal use for both cattle and human beings. Earlier we used to cultivate buckwheat (*kaonthao*) of two varieties–sweet (*aaklem*) and bitter (*aactin*). The bitter variety can be used as medicine and is sure to cure any sort of throat problem of the cattle by applying externally on the affected area. At the time of need we can get buckwheat only from Dip Sing Lepcha in our village who still cultivate it for his cattle". Lepchas take special care for the health and food of their cattle particularly during ploughing season. Bullocks are fed four times a day. The feeding chamber and the floor of the shed are normally cemented and cleaned regularly. To keep the insects, particularly mosquito away, Lepchas arrange smoke near the shed with locally available branches of trees and plants.

CHANGES IN CULTIVATION

In addition to food crops Lepchas are presently cultivating cash crops. Along with the traditional implements and tools a few of them have added sprayer as shown in Table 5.1. No significant change has taken place in the agricultural tools or implements used by the Lepchas.

Some changes have been noticed in the methods of agricultural operation. Broadcasting of seeds particularly in the case of maize has been replaced by a new system of planting seeds in the row. This method minimizes the need of seeds required for a particular plot of land, and also helps growing simultaneously some other crops like vegetables on the same plot. It has been further observed that potato is cultivated in row and at the time of its harvest maize seeds are shown in between rows of potato and thereby helps saving labour and cost of production as well. Monocrop has been replaced by multicropping.

The Lepchas have changed their cropping pattern. Some traditional crops have been replaced by new crops. The Lepchas now no more cultivate dry paddy, large variety of maize and buckwheat. In the list of vanishing crops there are also millet, ginger, orange and cardamom. The newly adopted crops include gladioli, potato and variety of vegetables.

On the whole, no significant change has been taken place in the method and pattern of cultivation of the Lepchas and they mostly adhere to their traditional agricultural practices.

CHAPTER SIX

DISTRIBUTION OF AGRICULTURAL PRODUCE

"Exchange is a surface phenomenon of economic life, reflecting the underlying economic and social organisation of production. Consequently, exchange relations are not general, but specific to each mode of economic organisation that shapes them." [Bhaduri.1984: 1]. In all standard economic theory 'exchange' is a market-based concept where market has taken as precondition for all exchange relations.But in an ideal agriculture based tribal economy 'distribution' rather than exchange may be the most appropriate term to be used and where the crops are produced not for sale in the market but to distribute among different user groups to fulfil different obligations.

Lepchas produce both food and cash crops. The cash crops are made available for sale in the nearby market while food crops are used for the following purposes: i)to fulfil the food requirements of household consumption, ii) to meet the requirement of seed etc. for agricultural purposes, iii) to meet the payment of exchange of labour, iv) to fulfil social obligations, v) to fulfil ritual obligations, vi) to meet miscellaneous obligations.

Let us discuss each of these obligations in brief.

FOOD FOR CONSUMPTION

"We live and work for food. We do not think much for the future. Whatever we earn or produce, we enjoy by consuming together with the family members" -said Gyanthop Lepcha of 5th Mile Lepcha Gaon. Food comprises an important component of domestic life of Lepchas.

They are very hospitable. Hospitality to the guests and care for the household members depend on supply of food available domestically.

Rice is the staple food for the Lepchas. They also consume maize, millet and wheat. The two principal meals (at around 11-12 noon and 7-8 pm) comprise of rice along with green vegetables, pulses and occasionally meat. The morning breakfast comprises of *roti* made of maize, millet and wheat. *Chi*, home made liquor made from fermented millet, is widely used by the Lepchas in different rituals, daily consumption in agricultural field and entertaining the guests.

Lepchas cultivate and select the crops as per their different requirements. They cultivate paddy solely for domestic consumption and never sell it in the market. Budhimaya Lepcha, an 80 year old lady of Mani Gumpa humorously remarked "we cultivate paddy in the plains."

Almost entire production of maize, millet, and wheat are also used for domestic consumption. The maize and wheat are consumed by all household members irrespective of age and sex. Millet is consumed mainly by the elderly male members by preparing *chi*. The Buddhist Lepchas consider *chi* as a symbol of their identity and they prepare it at their home. However, the Christians have some reservation in preparing and consuming *chi*. In Mani Gumpa, eight households prepare *chi* for sale. Inspite of religious restrictions seven households (two UCNI and five RC) in 5th Mile Lepcha Gaon prepare *chi* for their domestic consumption. There is no restriction on preparing and consuming *chi* in Pochaok. On the question of millet, Ong Tshering Lepcha of Mani Gumpa informed, "no household can ever sell millet, on the contrary all have to buy it, because we are using millet widely in a number of occasions like daily consumption, rituals, entertaining guests, agricultural labours. Production of millet is always less than our requirement."

Vegetables are grown both for domestic consumption as well as sale. Most of the households grow vegetables like cabbage, cauliflower, radish, beans, cucumber, pumpkin, lady's-finger, chilli, *raisak* for domestic consumption. Some Lepchas, mainly in 5th Mile Lepcha Gaon, cultivate vegetables on a large scale and for market. Lepchas prefer fresh green vegetables for their kitchen and grow them on small patches of lands wherever are available.

The cash crops of the Lepchas include cardamom, ginger (in Pochaok), vegetables (in 5th Mile Lepcha Gaon) and gladioli (in Mani Gumpa). The entire production of cardamom, ginger, gladioli and a major part of vegetables are made available for sale.

Table 6.1 shows the participation of Lepcha households in the production of cash crop, food crop and both cash and food crops.

The table reveals that larger proportion of households (57.15) are engaged in the cultivation of food crop and only one household in Pochaok is engaged in the production of cash crop. A sizeable section is engaged in the production of both cash and food crops. As food crops are not available for sale so the Lepchas are primarily concerned about those crops necessary to feed their household members.

Village-wise data show that largest percentage of households (71.05) in Pochaok are engaged in producing food crops, another 15.78 per cent consider food crop as their main crop. Lephas of 5th Mile Lepcha Gaon considered food crops as their main crop and which is consumed by the household members. The picture is slightly different in the case of Mani Gumpa where 13.64 per cent household produce cash crop as a main crop. The others are engaged in cultivation of food crops necessary for distribution and consumption.

The food crop and cash crop can further be classified as principal and subsidiary crops. Those crops, which cover more than 50 per cent of the available cultivable area, are identified as principal crop. The need of the household is the prime consideration for the choice of principal and subsidiary crops. Table 6.2 reveals that the three traditional food crops – paddy, maize and millet are considered as principal and most preferred crops by the Lepchas. They prefer the modern cash crops like gladioli, vegetables and cardamom as subsidiary crop. Inspite of a move from traditional to modern crops, Lepchas still consider food crops as their principal crop.

The most preferred principal crop among the Lepchas is maize. It is used both as food as well as fodder. The percentage of household cultivating maize is the highest in Pochaok (78.12) followed by 5th Mile Lepcha Gaon (11.46) and Mani Gumpa (10.42). The second preferred principal crop is millet. It is traditional crop among the Lepchas. Millet is mainly used for preparing *chi*, (indigenous liquor) and used widely

Table 6.1: Village-wise Distribution of households in the production of food crop and cash crop

Name of the village	Food Crop	Cash crop	Engagement in both food and cash crop			Non-cultivator	Total
			Food crop as main crop	Cash crop as main crop	Total		
Mani Gumpa	5 (22.73)	-	12 (54.54)	3 (13.64)	15 (68.18)	2 (9.09)	22 (100.00)
5th Mile Lepcha Gaon	9 (42.86)	-	11 (52.38)	-	11 (52.38)	1 (4.76)	21 (100.00)
Pochaok	54 (71.05)	1 (1.32)	12 (15.78)	8 (10.53)	20 (26.31)	1 (1.32)	76 (100.00)
Total	68 (57.15)	1 (0.84)	35 (29.41)	111 (9.24)	46 (38.65)	4 (3.36)	119 (100.00)

(Figures in the parenthesis indicate percentages)

Table 6.2: Cropping Pattern: Principal and Subsidiary Crop

Village	Total HH	Total cultivator	Paddy		Maize		Millet		Gladioli		Cardamom		Ginger		Vegetables		No Crop	
			P	S	P	S	P	S	P	S	P	S	P	S	P	S	P	S
Mani Gumpa	22 (18.49)	20 (17.39)	14 (33.33)	2 (10.00)	10 (10.42)	5 (20.00)	4 (5.71)	3 (12.00)	10 (100.00)	9 (100.00)	-	-	-	-	2 (20.00)	7 (17.07)	-	2 (6.06)
5th Mile Lepcha Gaon	21 (17.65)	20 (17.39)	18 (42.86)	2 (10.00)	11 (11.46)	8 (32.00)	3 (4.29)	10 (40.00)	-	-	-	-	-	-	8 (80.00)	10 (24.39)	-	-
Pochaok	76 (63.86)	75 (65.22)	10 (23.81)	16 (80.00)	75 (78.12)	12 (48.00)	63 (90.00)	12 (48.00)	-	-	1 (100.00)	28 (100.00)	-	22 (100.00)	-	24 (58.54)	-	31 (93.94)
Total	119 (100.00)	115 (100.00)	42 (100.00)	20 (100.00)	96 (100.00)	25 (100.00)	70 (100.00)	25 (100.00)	10 (100.00)	9 (100.00)	1 (100.00)	28 (100.00)	-	22 (100.00)	10 (100.00)	41 (100.00)	-	23 (100.00)

(Figures in the parentheses show percentage).

Note: P = Principal; S = Subsidiary.

for domestic consumption and ritual purposes. Millet is also used as fodder for pig, hen, and goat. It has observed that 90 per cent of millet is produced in Pochaok. Lepchas of Pochaok are still stick to their old agricultural practice while in other two villages they have recorded a shift from traditional millet to modern crops.

Paddy is another preferred principal crop among the Lepchas. The Lepchas are rice eaters. But paddy can only grow in wet fields and whose availability is somewhat limited. Higher percentage of paddy field is found is 5th Mile Lepcha Gaon followed by Mani Gumpa and Pochaok. In Mani Gumpa some portion of wet fields which were earlier used for paddy cultivation have been later converted to dry field for gladioli cultivation.

Among the non-traditional crops, vegetable is important both as principal and subsidiary crop. In 5th Mile Lepcha Gaon majority (80 per cent) of Lepchas consider it as principal crop. Lepchas of Pochaok (58.54 per cent) rated it as an important subsidiary crop. Vegetables are identified as main cash crop by the Lepchas of 5th Mile Lepcha Gaon. In other two villages they are used mainly for domestic consumption.

Lepchas, thus, still retained their traditional outlook in cultivating the days old food crops – maize, millet and paddy. But no Lepcha consider all the three crops as unprofitable nor have they stopped cultivating them. They consider the use value of all these crops rather than their monetary value. No part of production of these three crops are meant for the market; rather to meet the deficit in consumption, which is most common, Lepchas very often buy them from the market. The entire cultivable amounts of all the three crops are used for household consumption. Obligation towards the kins is the basis of Lepcha cultivation.

Some of agricultural produce particularly fruits and vegetables are sent to the married girls and boys who settled elsewhere. The nearest relatives, neighbours and even visitors are also honoured with the crops available in the field at the time of their visits.

SEED FOR AGRICULTURE

After harvesting, Lepchas preserve a portion of produce of better quality as seed for the next year. Food crops like paddy, maize and millet are grown exclusively from seeds available domestically. Lepchas are aware that at times of sowing the price of seeds gone up. In order to avoid risk and higher cost of seed, they preserve the healthy seeds properly and at times even by curtailing their consumption needs at domestic front. Lepchas prefer to purchase the crop from market for consumption but not the seed. Budha Sing Lepcha of Pochaok told "We do purchase rice for daily consumption but we never consume paddy seeds kept at home. As we take special care for our seed, they are more productive than the seeds available in the market".

Ginger seeds are also preserved under the earth with special care (discussed in ch. 5). The ginger seeds are costly and most Lepchas of Pochaok prefer to use domestic seeds.

Those Lepchas who cultivate potato normally store only a small portion of produce for domestic consumption and sell the major part to the market. They prefer to purchase the potato seed as per their requirement from the local market.

For gladioli, Lepchas preserve both the cormlet and bulb as seeds for next year. The Lepchas cultivating gladioli in Mani Gumpa do not sell the bulb of gladioli. They take special care in storing bulb and cormlet. The Lepchas sell only the gladioli stick not its bulb.

Seeds for the variety of vegetables are mostly available domestically. The households with excess seeds help the neighbours on request without any return. Lepchas allow plants to remain in the field and grow so long the seeds get matured.

Seeds of all the major crops are domestically supplied. Lepchas do not like to take any risk in the matter of seeds. So the harvested crops are sharply divided in two parts: one part they use for domestic consumption and the other part they preserve as seeds.

PAYMENT TO EXCHANGE LABOUR

As no cash/kind payment is made to the exchanged labour, Lepchas take special care to feed them. The breakfast consists of *roti*, vegetable, tea while rice, dal, vegetable, meat, *chi* are some of the essential items of lunch. Lepchas prefer to entertain the exchange labours with the home made food items. A part of the agricultural produce is, thus utilised as meal of labours employed in agricultural works. In addition, the user often needs to supply fodder to the bullocks employed for ploughing or levelling the field. That includes paddy or millet straw, grass, paste maize, rice water, and salt. The by-products like paddy straw are often exchanged against cowdung manure.

If the recipient households can not reciprocate labour in exchange, they are supposed to pay labour charge in terms of paddy immediately after harvesting. Labour per manday is usually paid one *tungfri* (4 kg) of paddy. The rate is same for male, female, child or even bullock. Those Lepchas who do not have wet land prefer to exchange their labour against payment in paddy. In case of other crops labour is exchanged either against labour or cash.

Labour, employed during the harvesting of food crops (other than paddy), receive a handful of harvested crop as gift after the work is over. This is customarily practised during the harvesting of potato or maize when each labour gets a bag (approximately 5 kg) of potato or 8-10 of maize sticks at the end of the work.

Labours engaged in cash crops are generally paid in money. But they are entertained with tea, tiffin, and *chi* and for which millet is widely used. Some prepare liquor from the fermented wheat, maize or millet for those who do arduous work like ploughing.

SOCIAL OBLIGATIONS

Among the Lepchas agricultural produces are used to meet different types of social obligations. It has been noticed that most of the social activities including marriage take place after the harvesting of paddy. The contributions, whatever meagre that may be, are met from the agricultural produce. In each Lepcha village there is a *Kyong Shezeom* (village level unit) who looks after the social activities. Individual household problems of Lepchas are also handled by the *Kyong Shezeom*.

Some of the important social functions where Lepchas contribute their agricultural produce are:

a) Funeral Ceremony (Sung-Lyaon)

Death of any individual is considered as a loss to the whole village and all take part in helping the grief stricken family according to their capacity. All agricultural operations remain suspended at any death in the village. All assemble to the deceased house to extend both sympathy and help to the mourning household. As an immediate help sugar, tea leaf, ghee, incense, flour or cash are made available. The Buddhist Lepchas burn the dead body while the Christian bury them. The firewood etc. required for burning is supplied by the villagers free of cost.

Buddhist Lepchas observe the funeral ceremony (*Sung-Lyaon*) on the 49th day of death. Recently some perform the *Sung-Lyaon* on 21st day and a small function after one year. Besides lighting the lamp on the 3rd, 7th, 14th and 21st days, full plate of rice containing all favourable items of the deceased are to be served in the name of the dead person. Burning of incense throughout the 49 days in the morning and evening is a symbol that somebody has expired in the family.

On the day of funeral ceremony each household in Mani Gumpa contributes Rs.50/- and in Pochaok Rs.40/-to the deceased family. In addition they supply rice, ghee, firewood, flour etc. Earlier the custom was to supply millet compulsorily. Due to low productivity of millet Lepchas have replaced it by supplying cash. *Sung-Lyaon* is one such social function where the Lepchas spend huge money in feeding and performing the rituals. In Mani Gumpa, the villagers at the *Keyong Shezeong* level decided for vegetable meal, which has obviously reduced the cost of the ritual Lepchas of Pochaok entertain the guests by killing domestic ox or cow.

Sung-Lyaon consists of the followings:

a) *Tomugen* and *Mithup*–the reading of Tibetan holy scriptures by the Lamas.

b) *Rong Chyo*–reading of Lepcha religious scriptures by the Lepcha Lama.

c) *Torgen*–raising of Tibetan prayer flags.

The nearest relatives belonging to the same *moo* usually bear the different expenses connected with *Sung-lyaon* and which varies between Rs.500/- and Rs.700/- per item. The relatives in some cases meet this obligation by selling their agricultural produces.

b) Marriage (bri)

Marriage is another function where the Lepchas share the burden collectively. The young Lepchas of the village extend physical labour in the ceremony. In Mani Gumpa 20 out of 22 households jointly came forward in arranging Nima's marriage on 25th April 1999. In this marriage each household supplied one *saptuj* of *chi* (packed dry *chi*), made out of 8-10 kg. of millet, one day advance of the marriage. Villagers also supplied other materials like bamboo, wood required for necessary repair works and in decorating the marriage pandal.

c) New Year Festival (Naam-bun)

Another social function popular among the Lepchas of Mani Gumpa and Pochaok is *Naam-bun*, Lepcha new year day. It is celebrated in the no moon day of *Maa-labo* (December-January). The young Lepchas collect money by singing and dancing from door to door popularly known as *Lasso* dance. After the 7th day of *Naam-bun*, Mani Gumpa arranges a picnic in the village popularly known as *Chongay* where each household needs to contribute millet (3 kg), rice (as required for each family), vegetables (as per availability at home), hen, egg (as per domestic supply) and some cash (Rs.50 – Rs.100 as per capability) for grocery items. The Lepchas of other two villages have organised no such social picnic.

d) Birth-day of Punu Gaeboo Achyok

Lepchas celebrate the birth anniversary of King Gaeboo Achyok each year at Bong Busty on 20th December. The function is organised centrally by the Lepcha Association, Kalimpong. King Gaeboo Achyok is considered the legendary personality of Kalimpong who fought against the Bhutanese and dedicated his life for the upliftment of his loyal followers. Lepchas from far flung villages assemble at Associations headquarters by contributing cash through the *Kyong – Shezeom* towards conveyance and food. Many contribute rice and vegetables for arranging the lunch party. Although there is no compulsion on such payment but Lepchas voluntarily bear the burden of arranging the function. The Buddhist Lepchas are keener in attending this function than the Christians.

e) Muk-Zik-Ding Rum Faat

Another social function organised centrally by the Lepcha Association is *Muk-Zik-Ding Rum-Faat*. It is like that of *Tendong Lho-Rum-Faat* of Sikkim. Usually Lepchas of Kalimpong celebrate *Muk-Zik-Ding-Rum-Faat* on 21st February each year while in Sikkim they celebrate Tondong-Lho-Rum-Faat on 8th August. on this occasion the Lepchas pay homage to the 'mother nature' for her blessings towards favourable natural environment for the human habitat. Lepchas offer different fruits of their orchards or kitchen gardens to nature. Along with fruits they also voluntarily carry with them rice, vegetables, and cash necessary for arranging lunch. This celebration is more popular among the Buddhist Lepchas than the Christians.

f) Lyaang-Run-Faat

It is another type of offering to 'nature' to satisfy her in favour of good and timely rain for agricultural purposes. Lepchas assemble near any river or rivulet and offer prayer to nature as per *Bongthing* tradition. In this community offering the Lepchas need to offer hen, egg, *chi*, fruits to the deity. It is a community picnic where each participant household needs to contribute one hen, two eggs, millet (3 kg.), rice (as per requirement), vegetables (as available) and little cash. The Lepchas assemble for prayer, contribute collectively, cook and eat together and enjoy the day by singing and dancing. As the celebration follows the traditional Lepcha style, the Buddhists are the main followers while the Christians remain off the picture.

RITUAL OBLIGATIONS

Lepchas belong to two religious faiths – Buddhists and Christians. Followings are the important ritual obligations which the Buddhist Lepchas are found to discharge:

a) Mane

In connection with Buddha Jayanti, the villagers of Mani Gumpa assemble in the *Gumpa* for worship and prayer in the month of April-May. They also join the prayer function on full moon day in the month of December-January. The *Gumpa,* out of its income from agriculture bears the costs of organising the prayer and feeding all the members of 68 households belong to Buddhist faith. The cultivated crops on Gumpa land are used for the purpose. The villagers on their own bring oil for lighting, and some token money.

b) Chu chu

On 22nd day of each *Mane*, the Buddhist Lepchas of Mani Gumpa observe *chu chu* in the *Gumpa* twice a year (in May–June and December–January). During *Chu Chu* each household needs to pay Rs.5/- as interest for the loan given by the *Gumpa* to all its members in early days. Tshering Lepcha who possesses the list of members and collects *chu chu* opined "during the initial stage of establishment of this village the *Gumpa* helped all its members by lending them Rs.20/-. Now we are settled and paying Rs.5/- on each *Chu Chu* to run the expenditure of our *Gumpa*."

c) Rum-Chi-Faat

Buddhist Lepchas offer *chi* to *Rum* (God) during sowing and harvesting of paddy (*zo*). Early in the morning before transplanting the paddy seedlings, *Bongthing* offers *chi* to the almighty praying for good crop. After harvesting *Bongthing* once again needs to offer *chi* to God, thanking him for good yield. Traditionally Lepchas used to offer *chi* after the harvest of both wheat (*Kakyo*) and millet (*Moong*). But at present a short cut method has been followed where *chi* is prepared from the first crop and made available to the *Bongthing* for his consumption. *Rum-Chi-Faat* is popular among the Buddhist Lepchas. It requires eggs (3 pieces), *chi* (4 barrels), rice (handful), incense and Rs.10/- (remuneration to *Bongthing*). Chi also offered to Rum by *Bongthing* during construction of new house or for cure from diseases.

d) Lirum-Faat

It is a household ritual performed once in a year individually by Buddhist Lepchas with the help of *Bongthing* as priest. *Lirum* is the deity who protects and guards the household members and cattle from all evils. Buddhist Lepchas in the month of April-May (*Tafaa*) offer *chi*, hen, egg, fish, incense, *forma* (made from maize) to household deity.

e) Sekeor-Rum-Faat

Buddhist Lepchas praise the spirit who looks after and guards the grains stored in the house, and also protects the kitchen garden or orchard from animals and human beings. The ginger cultivators of Pochaok take special interest in observing *Sekeor-Rum* to protect the field from evil eyes of spirits. Lepcha orchards are kept unfenced but no outsider dares to encroach the field out of the fear of Lepcha spirit. In the worship of *Sekeor-Rum, Bongthing* asks for cock, egg, *chi*, fruits, incense, rice as offering and gets Rs.10/- as his personal remuneration.

f) Intensurup

The Buddhist Lepchas offer their first fruits and vegetables to Lord Buddha. Lepchas never consume or sale fruits or vegetables without offering them at first to the *Gumpa*. Now-a-days by keeping some fruits or sale money in the name of God, the villagers consume or sell the rest before *Intensurup*.

The Christian Lepchas distribute their agricultural produce for the following ritual purposes:

a) Sunday donation

On every Sunday at least one member from each household attends on the prayer at Church. He/she donates some money for the service rendered by the Church which ranges between Rs.1/- and Rs.5/- per visit.

b) Tithe

As per the Bible each Christian is supposed to pay ten per cent of his/her income for the cause of Lord. Tithing Christians of both 5th Mile Lepcha Gaon and Pochaok however do not follow any specific rule in this regard. Here someone can pay any amount in the form of *Dhanyavadi*, (thanks giving) while the Lepcha cultivators normally contribute in the form of *Muthidan*, (a handful of anything) in the second week of each month. Any amount in the form of cash or kind is accepted and recorded by the Church.

c) Katni

After harvesting of paddy, Lepchas send some produce to Church. Lepchas of 5th Mile Lepcha Gaon offer their fruits and vegetables at first to the Church before they consume or sale those. Lepchas of

Pochaok supply maize to Church each year on 15th August. *Katni* payment is made in terms of agricultural produce and applicable to both the major food crops (paddy, maize, millet, wheat) and fruits or vegetables. Often *Katni* is paid in cash after selling the crops.

d) Membership

Each adult Christian needs to pay his membership fee (Rs.36/-) to Church in monthly, quarterly or yearly terms. All new born babies or after marriage bride and groom must visit the Church and get membership. As the Lepchas are mostly agriculturists, they pay the membership fees in cash by selling their agricultural produce.

e) Death Relief Fund

After any death, Church normally helps the deceased family by offering it a sum of Rs.600/- from the Death Relief Fund created out of collection from its members regularly. Beside this help received from the Church each Lepcha in his individual capacity helps the deceased family by providing daily necessities like sugar, tea leaf, wheat flour, milk.

f) Prayer Class

Villagers at individual capacity often arrange prayer class at home. The elderly persons from the Church also attend this prayer. On such an occasion the host household needs to provide tea and snacks to the assembled guests who attend prayer.

MISCELLANEOUS OBLIGATIONS

Lack of alternative source of income compels the Lepchas to meet up all sorts of expenses or obligations from agricultural income only. Sometimes they directly pay in produce but often they meet up these expenses in cash by selling their crops in market. Followings are some of the prevailing arrangements of obligation management:

- Lepchas procure the grocery items like salt, sugar, oil either by selling or exchanging, the agricultural produce with the grocers (particularly in Pochaok).
- Clothes for the family members are purchased in cash from the money earned from agricultural produces.

- Expenditure on education, whatever meagre the amount may be, is adjusted with the agricultural produces.
- Medical expenses, although negligible an amount, share some part of agricultural produces.
- Construction, repair of household, cattle shed are carried out of the agricultural income.

CHAPTER SEVEN

CONCLUSION

The present study aimed at identifying the social formation or socio-economic formation among the Lepchas. After discussing the theoretical concept of social formation in the introductory chapter, we have discussed at length about the mode of production of Lepcha agriculture in Third, Fourth and Fifth Chapters. The last chapter has been devoted to show how the Lepcha economy is socially embedded.

For identifying Lepcha social formation the following points are worth mentioning.

Economically, the Lepchas are dependent on agriculture. Irrespective of age and sex they are involved in agriculture in different capacities. In the contemporary period the Lepchas have settled down in terrace based cultivation. But it is said that their ancestors were shifting cultivators. A Lepcha acquires agricultural knowledge through practice and involvement. All that are required in agriculture i.e. land, labour, finance, manure, seed, tools etc., are simple and supplied by the households.

Most of the Lepchas are small landowners who manage and cultivate the land of their own. Share-cropping is practiced mainly in the cases of institutional (*Gumpa*) lands where the deal has been informally settled. In cases of leasing out of land for particular period or crop, several arrangements of cultivation have been noticed but these have neither been institutionalised nor do they follow any regular pattern.

At the outset individual ownership of land may appear to negate Lepcha tribal character based on the central proposition of Marxist theory that "private property and exploitation are just two sides of the same coin" [Bloch, 1985: 24]. A tribal society should be free from exploitation and a private ownership of land may extend the possibility of exploitation. But if we visualise the ownership right from the angles of right to use and right to transfer, the ownership pattern of Lepcha lands are not individualistic. In Lepcha society a landowner does not always exclusively enjoy the right to use his own land. The labour (by consuming crop), the neighbours (by using land as pasture or road), the sharecropper (by managing and cultivating) directly or indirectly establish their right to use others land. The village level Lepcha organisation uses individual land either temporarily for celebrating different community functions or permanently for constructing road, church, *gumpa* and school. Land is transmitted hereditarily on male lines. In this transmission *moo* (clan) plays an important role. Most of the lands in Lepcha villages belong to few *moos*. A system of corporate use and transfer of land within the kin groups is marked among the Lepchas. Against the emergence of such a kin based arrangement, Bloch has offered a reason. He says, "With settled agriculture........ land becomes communal property, specially because of the need to defend it from other tribes" [1985 : 34].

Lepchas depend heavily on household labour for cultivation. Like any other peasant, for Lepchas also "family is the main unit of production" [Thorner, 1963: 323]. But during peak agricultural season they go for exchange labour within the community itself without keeping any detailed record. In Lepcha agriculture the sources of labour have not been restricted to Chayanov's "non-wage family labours to the family household farm" [Harrison, 1982: 246–247]. It goes beyond the family unit and becomes a community based collective activity. All works are governed and carried out by cherished social values and obligations. This is more a tribal feature than peasant one. The relations between those who work and for whom they work are direct and personal. Unmarried children of both the sexes and the adopted male child are two peculiar potent sources of labour in a Lepcha household.

Lepchas use simple tools and techniques in their agricultural operations. They apply traditional means in exploiting natural resources with minor changes here and there. They do not employ any mechanical tools or power driven appliances except a few manually operated sprayers. Wooden plough, leveller, spade, sickle etc., are commonly used. Technologically, the Lepchas belong to the category of non-capitalist society where they like the "peasant community .... applied many of the techniques which had previously been used for tribal societies in order to elucidate the community's cultural and social configuration" [Smith, 1995 : 220]. According to some scholars "peasant agriculture is conducted with its own equipment" [Gavin, 1982: 383]. In case of Lepchas, agricultural equipment may be individually owned but shared by the community.

Lepchas are subject to low level of technological development in agriculture and prefer to stick to their traditional method of cultivation. As a result, the Lepcha economy is 'under-developed'. There is no clear cut work specialisation and division of labour among the Lepchas. We know that tribal societies are under-developed because of the absence of specialisation and division of labour.

Lepchas carry forward tribal character of 'subsistence economic system' and simple living. Eat, drink and enjoy are the basic motive of their livelihood. Economically, they are more concerned about their present consumption than the future. The concept of saving or hoarding is absent among the Lepchas. We all know that "in a peasant economy the first concern of the production units is to grow food crops to feed themselves" [Thornor, 1971: 205]. It is equally true in the case of Lepchas.

Our penultimate chapter shows how the Lepcha economy is socially embedded. Their economic organisation is intertwined with the social structure. A type of social correlation has been established between the type of socio-economic transactional mode and the degree of social distance. Some institutions like marriage, religion, ethnic association play important role in influencing the Lepcha economy. The social institutions to which he belongs sway Lepcha economic behaviour. Their production organisation is intimately related with the social structure.

At the community level a strong sense of fraternity and interdependence is maintained through social process of production and distribution. They follow the strong kinship obligations in social and economic spheres of life like in transfer of landed property, distribution of agricultural produce and reciprocal labour exchange. *Moo*, as the highest order of kinship, plays an important role in holding landed property and its transmission.

Now, considering all these several aspects of their agrarian character, Lepchas can be identified as 'tribal peasants'. In our introductory chapter we have grouped all societies under the simple binary classification of capitalist and pre-capitalist. Any pre-capitalistic society is basically based on agriculture and its economy can be identified as 'peasant economy'. All settled tribes due to their dependence on agriculture are likely to fall under the category of tribal peasants. The other types of peasantry like feudal peasants etc. are rare among the tribes. The Marxian concept of 'primitive communism' is a concept of the past and is no more practiced by any community. Same is the case with Sahlin's 'band' where they normally moved from one place to another in a group. By now, most tribes have settled down and behave like peasant. So tribe as a separate category should preferably not be used for wild speculation. Ghosal's observation of shifting from tribe to peasant among the Lepchas [1990: 208-219] is neither plausible theoretically nor carries much significance. Lepchas are peasant looked at from their economic behaviour and practices but they are tribes as well from their social attitude and interaction.

In addition to tribal peasantry, some rudimentary elements of capitalism have also been observed among the Lepchas in production and marketing of modern cash crop. Like capitalist farming, production of cash crop is guided by profit motive and they in some respects act like a farmer. The outlook and behavioural pattern of the Lepchas differ in case of the production and distribution or exchange of food and cash crops. Even the same individual behaves differently in producing these two types of crops.

Let us now specify the elements of capitalist farming and tribal peasant mode of production in Lepcha society.

Three villages have accepted three different crops as their cash crops: gladioli in Mani Gumpa, vegetables in 5th Mile Lepcha Gaon and cardamom in Pochaok. Peculiarly, each of the three villages has been specialised in the production of one crop where the production of other two varieties is absolutely nil. But there is no reason to believe that all three crops cannot grow in all three villages which are located in almost the same geo-climatic conditions. As against this, all the villages are homogeneous in the production of food crop - paddy, maize and millet are the three common crops among the Lepchas. Both food and cash crops are grown in all the villages.

Land under cash crop is organised and managed by the educated young Lepchas while food crop is grown by the comparatively elderly persons with traditional outlook. Very recently, some young Lepchas have started leasing in land on contractual basis either by paying cash or kind. These lands are used absolutely for the production of cash crop. In case of traditional share cropping, food crop is most common. The traditional monocrop has been replaced by multi-cropping, which includes modern variety of cash crops. More and more lands are being brought under the cultivation of cash crops at the cost of food crop.

Lepchas employ wage labour from outside the community and the village for the modern cash crop. The rate of wage varies as per age and sex. But they cultivate food crops with reciprocal exchange of labour where labour of any age and sex from within the village is treated equally. In addition to the obligation to reciprocate labour, each household needs to entertain all those who extend labour with tiffin and lunch. But no such customary arrangements are there to regulate the interaction with the wage labour. The work timings for exchange labour are not rigidly fixed while wage labour works for standard eight hours a day. Further, as against exchanging human labour for bullock, Lepchas have started using bullocks on rent. Bullocks need to be served with fodder etc. in the traditional system but no such obligations are maintained with the cultivation of cash crops.

Both females and children take active part in carrying out different processes of traditional cultivation. As there is no specialisation of work all are absorbed in agriculture either as principal or subsidiary sector of their engagement. On the contrary, almost all works are assigned to the young males in connection with the different agricultural operations of cash crop. Females and children are, thus, released from the land used for cash crop and are found to concentrate exclusively in the cultivation of food crop. A sort of division of labour has been created on the basis of age and sex in operating cash crop.

The requirement of finance is very negligible for the food crop because of which the households or the community are generally capable of supplying it of their own. Cash crop needs more capital and the Lepchas, in many cases, manage it from outside sources like traders and middiemen who indirectly charge interest on their capital. As against domestic manure and seed, Lepchas use chemical fertiliser, pesticides and HYV seeds for cash crop. The indigenous tools and implements are sufficient for food crop while they use some, although as yet negligible, mechanical device like spraying machine for the new crops.

Traditional *taphu-tungfri* (measuring vessels) system is used for taking accounts of the crops cultivated. The area or productivity of land is measured in terms of *taphu-tungfri* of crops grown in the field. Any intra-community transaction of crops like loan, payment of labour, measurement of seed is done with this indigenous system. On the other hand, the standard metric unit is used to measure all the cash crops.

The basic purpose of cultivation of food crop is to meet the household and social obligations while cash crops are meant for the market. Usually no part of the food crop is exchanged for money while no part of cash crop is used domestically and the entire amount is sold in the market. The basic objective of cultivation of these two varieties of crops is thus diametrically opposite. Lepchas fulfil different social and religious obligations with food crop while cash crop is free from such obligations and meet the cash requirement of the cultivator.

Lepchas follow as recommended by Karl Polanyi all the three transactional modes of agricultural produce under three distinct forms – reciprocity, redistribution and market exchange. This again can broadly be classified as (a) 'socio-economic transactional mode' comprising of reciprocity and redistribution and (b) 'economic mode' like market exchange. It should be noted that while economic mode has little or no social embeddedness, socio-economic transactional mode is socially related. Lepchas cultivate food crops (paddy, maize and millet) mainly to meet up diverse social and economic needs. It is carried forward reciprocally in the form of gift giving between kin and friends and also redistribution in the form of obligatory payment to Lepcha Association and religious institutions like church or *gumpa*. Cultivation of cash crops (like cardamom, ginger, gladioli) is basically oriented towards the economic mode of market transaction.

One can thus witness two different social formations in Lepcha agricultural society: tribal peasantry and capitalistic farming. Their economy is partially barter and partially monetised. They adhere to "non-monetised barter system of exchange economy" [Beteille, 1977: 12-13] within their own community and go for monetary payment with the outsiders.

But there is no theoretical contradiction in simultaneous existence of more than one social formation in the context of any community. A similar view has been endorsed by Bernardo Berdichewsky who says that a society may be "constituted by more than one mode of production, one mode being dominant" [1979: 9]. Sometimes, socio-economic formation of any society may apparently contradict with the particular mode of production by which the society is recognised. Socio-economic formation of "other modes beside the dominant mode of production, whether as hangovers from the past or precursors of the future" [Melotti, 1977: 4] may be present simultaneously. Some has identified this type of simultaneous existence of two or more modes of production as a manifestation of 'hybrid socio-economic formation'.

The co-existence of different forms of society has also been observed by J.H.Boeke (1953), the Dutch economist, in the context of his socio-economic studies in Indonesia. Beside the 'homogeneous society' which is exclusively dominated by one system, Boeke observed dual or plural society where two or more social systems may appear simultaneously but each one can be clearly distinguished from the other. Every society in its progression will show, beside the prevailing social system, the remains of the preceding and the beginning of the future social style. Boeke described such types of society as 'social dualism' which is more common among the developing countries. "Social dualism is the clashing of an imported social system with an indigenous social system of another style. Most frequently the imported social system is high capitalism. But it may be socialism or communism just as well, or a blending of them" [Boeke, 1953: 3-5].

The Lepcha society can be identified as an example of social dualism where "an imported western capitalism has penetrated into the pre-capitalistic agrarian community" [Ibid]. By virtue of their tribal peasant character Lepchas are pre-capitalist. Capitalism has entered into the Lepcha society through production and exchange of cash crop and "have gained its existence in the new environment without being able to oust or to assimilate the divergent social system that has grown up there" [Ibid]. As a result neither of them becomes 'general and characteristic' for the Lepcha society. The co-existence of two separate social systems makes their economy a sort of 'dualistic economy'.

But Lepcha social dualism is different from that of Boeke's where the "essence of social dualism is the clash between an imported and an indigenous social system of divergent character" [Ibid]. But in Lepcha society the two separate social systems (tribal peasantry and capitalism) co-exist simultaneously without creating any 'clash'. Lepchas irrespective of their acceptance of or divergence from the imported social system (capitalism) are maintaining perfect harmony in the society without creating any tension among them whatsoever. The peace-loving Lepchas have accommodated all changes without ever making any challenge or protest.

A further peculiarity with the Lepcha dualism is that unlike what is generally understood, the divergent social systems are not prevalent in two separate sectors of their society. More specifically, a Lepcha behaves like a peasant when he produces food crop but acts like a capitalist farmer in his cultivation and exchange of cash crop. The same Lepcha performs a dual role and, therefore, dualism need not necessarily occur at the level of two or more mutually exclusive subsets of any society. Lepcha society is thus an example of integrated social dualism where the imported capitalistic farming of cash crop has penetrated into the divergent pre-capitalistic cultivation of food crops, and both co-exist simultaneously without creating any tension or clash in the society. It could have been both interesting and instructive if the Lepcha agriculture were studied against this perspective in detail. But since this study was designed to be diagnostic, it would, it is hoped, serve its purpose if it helps future studies on these people to be more focussed. This is a task which has become important because the veil of 'tribes' has the tendency to make all studies of them monotonous, making it difficult to integrate the existing theories with the varied reality.

BIBLIOGRAPHY

BAGCHI, G.C. (1982), 'From Semi Nomadism to Settled Agriculture: An Appraisal of Lepcha Economy' in K.S. Singh, (ed.), *Economics of Tribe and TheirTransformation.* Concept Publications, New Delhi.

BAILEY, K. (1971), 'Chayanov and the Theory of Peasants as a Specific Type of Economy' in Theodor Shanin, ed., *Peasants and Peasant Society.* Penguine Education.

BASNET, L.B. (1974), Sikkim: *A Short Political History.* S. Chand and Co. (Pvt.) Ltd., New Delhi.

BELL, C.A. (1905), *Final Report on the Survey and Settlement of the Kalimpong Government Estate in the District of Darjeeling – 1901-1903.* Bengal Secretariate Press, Culcutta.

BERDICHEWSKY, B. (1979), 'Anthropology and Peasant Mode of Production' in Bernardo Berdichewsky, ed., *Anthropology and Social Change in Rural Areas.* The Hague Mouton Publishers.

BETEILLE, A. (1977), 'The Definition of Tribe' in Ramesh Thapar, ed., *Tribe Caste and Religion in India.* Macmillan Company of India Ltd., Meerut.

BHADURI, A. (1984), *The Economic Structure of Backward Agriculture.* Macmillan India Limited, New Delhi.

BLOCH, M. (1985), *Marxism and Anthropology.* Oxford University Press, Oxford, New York.

BOEKE, J.H. (1953), *Economics and Economic Policy of Dual Societies.* New York.

BOHANNAN, P. and DALTON, G. (1968), ed., *Markets in Africa.* Third Edition, North Western University Press.

BOTTOMORE, T. and OTHERS. (1983), ed., *A Dictionary of Marxist Thought.* Oxford University Press, New Delhi.

CAMPBELL, A. (1840), 'Note on the Lepchas of Sikkim with a

Vocabulary of Their Language' in *Journal of Asiatic Society of Bengal IX*. Part 1, Culcutta.

CHATTOPADHYAY, K.D. (1978), *Tribalism in India*. Vikash Publishing House Pvt. Ltd., New Delhi.

CHATTOPADHYAY, T. (1990), *Lepchas and their Heritage*. B.R.Publishing Corporation, New Delhi.

CHAYANOV, A.V. (1987), *The Theory of Peasant Economy*. Edited by Daniel Thorner and others. First Indian Edition, Oxford University Press, New Delhi.

COHEN, S. (1967), 'Economic Analysis and Economic Man' in Raymond Firth, ed., *Themes in Economic Anthropology*. Tavistock Publications, London.

CENSUS OF INDIA. (1961), *West Bengal*. Vol.XVI, Part V-A (ii), Special Tables on Scheduled Tribes.

CENSUS OF INDIA. (1961), *Village Survey Monograph on Upper Pedong*. Vol. XVI, Part VI (10), West Bengal and Sikkim.

CENSUS OF INDIA. (1971), *West Bengal, Special Table on Scheduled Tribes*.

CENSUS OF INDIA. (1971), *Tripura, Social and Cultural Table*. Part II C(I) – VA, Special Tables on SC and ST.

CENSUS OF INDIA. (1981), *West Bengal*. Series-23, Part IX (IV), Special Tables for Scheduled Tribes.

CENSUS OF INDIA. (1991), *District Census Handbook: Darjeeling*. Series-26, Part XII-B, West Bengal.

CENSUS OF INDIA. (1991), *Village and Town-wise Primary Census Abstruct, Darjeeling District*. District Census Handbook, Part XII, B, Series-26, West Bengal.

DAHAL, D.D. (1984), *Sikkim Ka Rajnaitik Itihas* (in Nepali). Subba Prakashan, Gangtok, Sikkim.

DALTON, E.T. (1872), *Descriptive Ethnology of Bengal*. Govt. Printing Press, Culcutta.

DALTON, G. (1971), *Economic Anthropology and Development: Essays on Tribal and Peasant Economics*. Basic Books, Inc. Publishers, New York.

DAS, A.J. (1947), *Bengal District Gazetteers, Darjeeling*. Bengal Govt. Press, Alipur, Bengal.

DAS, A.K. and BANERJEE, S.K. (1962), *The Lepchas of Darjeeling District*. Tribal Welfare Department, Govt. of West Bengal.

DAS, A.K. (1978), *The Lepchas of West Bengal*. Indian Editions, Culcutta.

DESAI, A.R. (1971), 'Tribes in Transition' in Ramesh Thapar, ed., *Tribe, Caste and Religion in India.* Macmillan Company of India Ltd., Meerut.

DONALDSON, F. (1900), *Lepcha Land or Six Weeks in the Sikkim Himalayas*. Sampson, Low Marston, London.

DOZEY, E.C. (1916), *A Concise and Complete History of the Darjeeling District since 1835*. Darjeeling.

ELWIN, V. (1943), *The Aboriginals*. Oxford University Press, Bombay.

FIRTH, R. (1939), *Primitive Polynesian Economy*. George Routledge, London.

- (1967), *Themes in Economic Anthropology*. Tavistock Publications, London.

FONING, A.R. (1987), *Lepcha: My Vanishing Tribe.* Sterling Publishers Pvt. Limited, New Delhi.

FRANKENBERG, R. (1967), 'Economic Anthropology' in Raymond Firth, ed., *Themes in Economic Anthropology*. Tavistock Publications, London.

GAVIN, W. (1982), 'Taking Part of Peasants' in John Harriss, ed., *Rural Development Theories of Peasant Economy and Agrarian Change*. Hutchinson University Library, London.

GHOSAL, S. (1990), *Lepchas of Darjeeling and Sikkim: A Study in Cultural Ecology and Social Change*. Unpublished Ph.D. Thesis, North Bengal University, Darjeeling, West Bengal.

GHURYE, G.S. (1995), *The Scheduled Tribes*. Popular Prakashan, Bombay.

GODELIER, M. (1977), *Perspectives in Marxist Anthropology*. Cambridge University Press, Cambridge.

GORER, G. (1938), *The Lepchas of Sikkim*. Reprint 1984, Central Publishing House, New Delhi.

GOWLOOG, R.P. (1995), *Lingthem Revisited: Social Change in a Lepcha Village of North Sikkim*. Har Anand Publications, New Delhi.

GREWAL, D.S. (1992), *Aka and their Kindred in Arunachal Pradesh: An*

Enquiry into the Determinants of their Identity. Unpublished Ph.D.Thesis, Centre for Himalayan Studies, North Bengal University, Darjeeling, West Bengal.

HARRISON, M. (1982), 'Chayanov's Theory of Peasant Economy' in John Harriss (ed.), *Rural Development: Theories of Peasant Economy and Agrarian Change*. Hutchinson University Library, London.

HOOKER, J.D. (1855), 'Notes of a Naturalist in Bengal, The Sikkim and Nepal Himalayas, The Khasi Mountains & C' in *Himalayan Journal*. Vol. 2, Murry, London.

HUNTER, W.W. (1876), *A Statistical Account of Bengal*. Vol.X, Trubner & Co., London, Reprint, 1984, Concept Publishing Company, New Delhi.

HUTTON, J.H. (1931), *Census of India*. Vol.II, Reprint, 1986, Gyan Publishing House, New Delhi.

KATTAKAYAN, J.J. (1983), *Social Structure and change among the Tribes: A Study among the Uralies of Idukki District of Kerala*. D.P.Publications, New Delhi.

KLOSS, H. and MECONNELL, G.D., (1989), *The Written Languages of the World: A Survey of the Degree and Modes of Use*. International Centre for Research on Bilingualism, Latal, Canada.

LEPCHA, P. (1999), *A Study of the Scottish Mission Work in Kalimpong Sub-division with Special Reference to the Lepcha Tribe*. Unpublished Thesis for the degree of Bachelor of Divinity, Faculty of the Union Biblical Seminary, Pune, Maharashtra.

LEPCHA, S.W. (1979), *The Process of Detribalisation of an Indian Tribe and Problems of Modernisation: A Sociological Study of the Lepchas of Darjeeling District*. Unpublished Ph.D. Thesis, Department of Sociology, Bhagalpur University, Bihar.

MAHARAJA, H.H. and MAHARANI DOLMA OF SIKKIM. (1908), *History of Sikkim*. Unpublished Manuscript.

MAINWARING, G.B. (1876), *A Grammar of the Lepcha (Rong) Language*. Reprint 1971, Manjusri Publishing House, New Delhi.

MALLICK, M.R. (1995), *West Bengal Land Reform Act 1955 with West Bengal Land Reform Rules 1965*. Kamal Law House, Calcutta.

MARSHALL, G. (1998), *ed., A Dictionary of Sociology*. Oxford University Press, Oxford, New York.

MEIER, G.M. (1970), *Leading Issues in Economic Development: Studies in International Poverty*. Second edition, Oxford University Press, Oxford.

MELOTTI, U. (1977), *Marx and the Third World*. Translated into English by Pat Ransford, Edited by Malcolm Coldwell, Macmillan Press, London.

NAKANE, C. (1966), 'A Plural Society in Sikkim: A Study of the Interrelations of Lepchas, Bhotias and Nepalis' in C.V.Furer Haimendorf, ed., *Caste and Kin in Nepal, India and Ceylon*. Asia Publishing House, Bombay.

NAYEK, T.B. (1988), 'Tribe? What is a Tribe?' in S.B.Chakraborty, ed., *Social Science and Social Concern*. Mittal Publications, New Delhi.

NEBESKY, R.V.W. (1956), *Where the Gods are Mountains: Three Years among the People of the Himalayas*. Translated from German by Micheal Bullock Weildenfeld and Nicolson, London.

NIROULA, B.P. (1988), 'Caste/Ethnic Composition of Population of Nepal' in *CNAS Journal*. Vol. 25, No.1, January, Kathmandu, Nepal.

O' MALLEY, L.S.S. (1907), *Bengal District Gazetteers: Darjeeling*. The Bengal Secretariate Book Depot, Reprint, 1989, Logos Press, New Delhi.

PATHY, J. (1984), *Tribal Peasantry: Dynamics of Development*. Inter India Publications, New Delhi.

PHILPOT, H.C.V. (1925), *Final Report on the Survey and Settlement of Kalimpong Government Estate – 1919-1922*. Bengal Secretariate Book Depot, Culcutta.

POLANYI, K., ARENSBERG, C.W. & PEARSON, H.W. (1957), *Trade and Market in the Early Empires*. Glencoe, III, Free Press.

PORTER, A.F. (1931), ed., *Census of India: Bengal and Sikkim*. Part II, 1933, Central Publishing Branch.

RISLEY, H.H. (1891), *Tribes and Castes of Bengal Ethnographic Glossary*. Vol. II, Bengal Secretariate Press, Culcutta, Reprint, 1981, Firma Mukhopadhyay, Culcutta.

RISLEY, H.H. (1894), *The Gazetteer of Sikkim*, Bengal Government Secretariate, Culcutta.

SAHLINS, M.D. (1965), 'On the Sociology of Primitive Exchange' in M. Bouton, (ed.), *The Relevance of Models for Social Anthropology*. As A Monography-1, Tavistock Publications, London.

SANKRITYANAYAN, R. (1950), *Darjeeling Parichay* (in Hindi). Adhunik Pustak Bhawan, Culcutta.

SHANIN, T. (1975), 'A Russian Peasant Household at the turn of the Century' in Teodor Shanin, ed., *Peasants and Peasant Societies*. Harmandsworth, Penguin Book.

SIINGER, H. and RISCHEL, J. (1967), *The Lepchas: Cutural and Religion of a Himalayan People*. Part I, II, The National Museum of Denmark Copenhagen.

SINGH, K.S. (1996), *Peoples of India, The Schehuled Tribes*. National Series, Vol.III, Anthropological Survey of India, Oxford University Press, New Delhi.

STOCKS, C.DE.B. (1925), 'Folk-lore and Customs of the Lep-chas of Sikkim' in *Journal and Proceedings Asiatic Society of Bengal*. New Series, Vol. XXI, No.4., Issued on 6th May 1927.

TAMSANG, K.P. (1983), *The Unknown and Untold Reality about the Lepchas*. Luen Sun Offset Printing Co. Ltd., Hong Kong.

TAMSANG, L.S. (1997-2002), Editor, *Aachuley*. A Quaterly Lepcha Bilingual News Magazine. The Lepcha Literary Organisation, Kalimpong, Darjeeling.

TEMPLE, R. (1875), 'Two Diaries of Travels in Sikkim' in S.K. Sharma & Usha Sharma, ed., 1997, *Encyclopedia of Sikkim and Bhutan*. Anmol Publications Pvt. Ltd., New Delhi.

THAKUR, R.N. (1988), *Himalayan Lepchas*. Archives Publishers, Distributors, New Delhi.

THORNER, D. (1971), 'Peasant Economy as a Category in Economic History', in Teodor Shanin, (ed.), *Peasants and Peasant Studies*. Penguin Educations.

WADDELL, L.A. (1899), *Among the Himalayas*. Constable, London. Reprint, 1978, Ratna Pustak Bhandar, Kathmandu, Nepal.

WITCZYNSKI, J. (1981), ed., *An Encyclopaedic Dictionary of Marxism, Socialism and Communism*. Macmillan Reference Books, Macmillan Press Ltd., London.

APPENDICES

APPENDIX I

Statement of Adopted Children in the Study Area

Sl. No.	Name of head of theHH	Name of village	Details of adopted children					
			Name	Sex	Age	Education	Occupation	Lepcha/ Non-Lepcha
1	Ongu Tshering Lepcha	Mani Gumpa	Pandi Tshering Lepcha	M	35	Class VIII	Agriculture	Non-Lepcha
2	Lha Tshering Lepcha	5th Mile Lepcha Gaon	Do Tshering Lepcha	M	30	B.Sc. (Agri)	State Govt. Service	Non-Lepcha
3	Jormen Lepcha	5th Mile Lepcha Gaon	Habil Lepcha	M	40	Class V	Agriculture	Non-Lepcha
4	Odila Lepcha	5th Mile Lepcha Gaon	Mitho Lepcha	M	56	-	Agriculture	Non-Lepcha
5	Subash Lepcha	5th Mile Lepcha Gaon	Gayboo Lepcha	M	45	-	Agriculture	Non-Lepcha
6	Gay Tshering Lepcha	5th Mile Lepcha Gaon	Raju Lepcha	M	45	B.A.	Agriculture	Non-Lepcha
7	Barsing Lepcha	5th Mile Lepcha Gaon	Keshar Lepcha	M	36	-	Carpentry	Non-Lepcha
8	Keshar Lepcha	5th Mile Lepcha Gaon	Hezel Lepcha	F	16	VII	Student	Non-Lepcha

APPENDIX II

Details of Land awarded to Girl Child or Adopted Child in the Study Area

Sl. No.	Name of Head of the household	Name of the Village	Details of land awarded			
			Name	Relation with the head	Quantity	Use of land
1	2	3	4	5	6	7
1	Dawa Tshering Lepcha	Mani Gumpa	Aimit Lepcha	Daughter	4 decimal	Dwelling
2	Ongu Tshering Lepcha	Mani Gumpa	Pandi Lepcha	Adopted Son	3.20 decimal	Dwelling & agriculture
3	Kam Dorjee Lepcha	Mani Gumpa	Dodimit Lepcha	Daughter	1.22 decimal	Agriculture
4	Jorman Lepcha	5th Mile Lepcha Gaon	Habil Lepcha	Adopted Son	2 decimal	Dwelling
5	Kandu Lepcha	5th Mile Lepcha Gaon	Luysa Lepcha	Daughter	4 decimal	Dwelling
6	Dakrip Lepcha	5th Mile Lepcha Gaon	Sangmit Lepcha	Daughter	3 decimal	Dwelling
7	Rekha Lepcha	5th Mile Lepcha Gaon	Runchi Lepcha	Daughter	0.59 decimal	Dwelling

APPENDIX III
Copy of *Khatian*

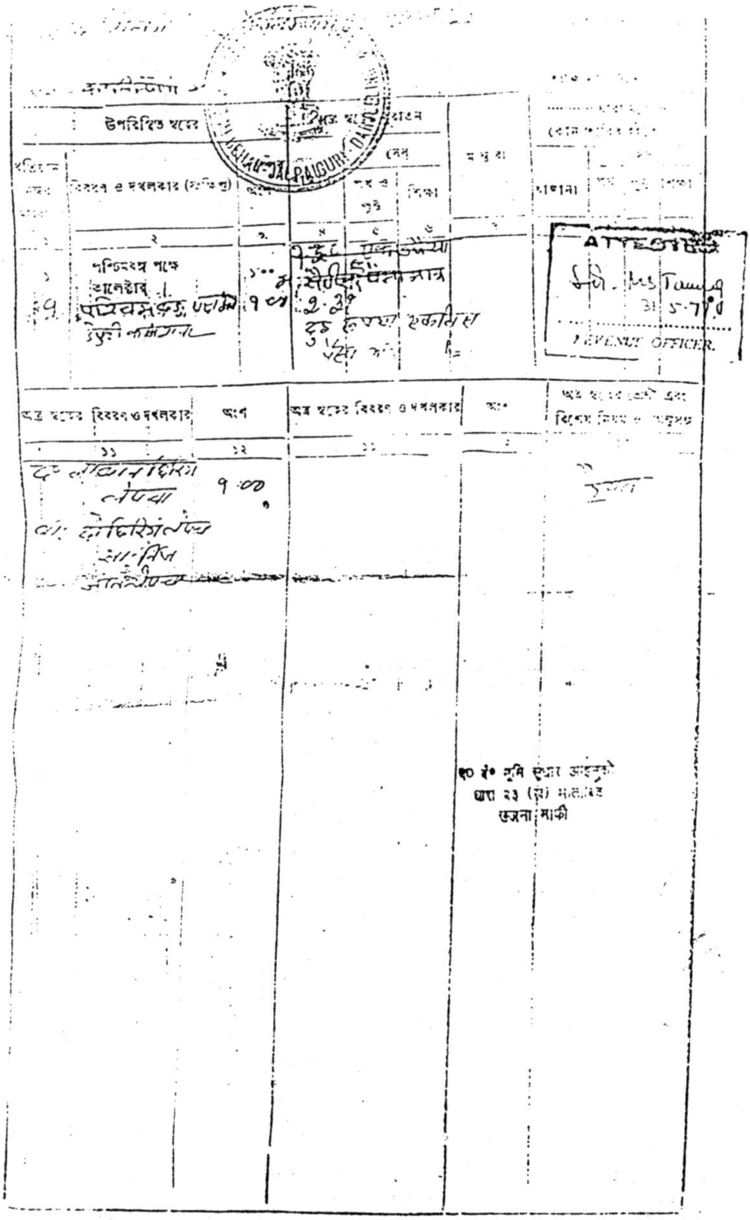
ATTESTED

REVENUE OFFICER.

খতিয়ান নং		এই খতের নিজ দখলীয় জমি							
দাগ নং	জমির শ্রেণী	মন্তব্য	দাগের মোট পরিমাণ (এ.)	(শ.)	দাগের মধ্যে অত্র স্বত্বের অংশ	দাগের মধ্যে অত্র স্বত্বের অংশের পরিমাণ (এ.)	(শ.)		
৭৬৬৬	सुरवासात 2		–	০৭	9240/3338	–	০7		
৭৬৬২	पाखिमेत 2		–	76	9240/3338	–	০8 .w		
৭৬63	मिसखोरी		–	৭৭	9240/3338	–	০3		
৭৬৬৪	पाखिमेत 2		2	৪৪	9240/3338	–	২০2		
৭৬৭6	मिसखोरी		–	৭৪	9240/3335	–	০2		
৭৬৭৭	घरेरी	घरा	–	৭৭	9240/3338	–	০3		
৭৬৭৮	सुरवासात 1		৭	৭৪	9240/3338	–	3২		
৭৬০6	घरेरी	घरा अनुमति [illegible] मायाँ [illegible] [illegible] बहादुर [illegible]	–	০8	9240/3338	–	০7		
৭৭০৫	सुरवासना 2		–	৭৫	9240/3338	–	০2		
		নিজ দখলীয় জমির মোট পরিমাণ				–	[illegible]		
[illegible]		অধীনস্থ স্বত্বের বিভিন্ন খতিয়ানের নং					৭ ৪২		
		২২							
		অধীনস্থ স্বত্বের মোট পরিমাণ							
		সর্ব মোট				৭	৬৫		

[illegible] ৩/3/77

Appendix IV
List of Unmarried Children Crossing Marital Age

Sl. No.	Name of village	Name of child	Name of head of household	Relation with head of household	Sex	Age	Occupation Principal	Subsidiary
1	2	3	4	5	6	7	8	9
1	Mani Gumpa	Phurba Lepcha	Aghi Lepcha	Daughter	F	30	Household	Agriculture
2	Mani Gumpa	Choden Lepcha	Palden Lepcha	Brother	M	35	Agriculture	-
3	Mani Gumpa	Ramit Lepcha	Tanmit Lepcha	Daughter	F	42	Household	-
4	Mani Gumpa	Marmit Lepcha	Tangmit Lepcha	Daughter	F	40	Household	-
5	Mani Gumpa	Dongmit Lepcha	Dawa Tshering	Daughter	F	45	Service	Agriculture
6	Mani Gumpa	Dorjee Tshering	Dawa Tshering	Son	M	30	Service	Agriculture
7	Mani Gumpa	Nim Lhamu Lepcha	Nim Lhamu Lepcha	Self	F	70	Household	Agriculture
8	Mani Gumpa	Nimkit Lepcha	Nim Lhamu Lepcha	Sister	F	60	Agriculture	Household
9	Mani Gumpa	Jamit Lepcha	Nim Lhamu Lepcha	Sister	F	50	Agriculture	Household
10	Mani Gumpa	Chomit Lepcha	Nim Lhamu Lepcha	Brother's daughter	F	25	Agriculture	Household
11	Mani Gumpa	Mayal Lepcha	Nim Lhamu Lepcha	Sister	F	20	Agriculture	Household
12	Mani Gumpa	Som Tshering	Tshemit Lepcha	Son	M	34	Driver	Agriculture
13	Mani Gumpa	Gen Tshering	Tshemit Lepcha	Sister	M	31	Agriculture	-

(Contd.)

1	2	3	4	5	6	7	8	9
14	Mani Gumpa	Sangmit Lepcha	Songdil Lepcha	Daughter	F	22	Agriculture	Household
15	Mani Gumpa	Northen Lepcha	Chenchu Lepcha	Son	M	22	Agriculture	-
16	Mani Gumpa	Ongden Lepcha	Mingma Lepcha	Son	M	32	Agriculture	-
17	Mani Gumpa	Susang Lepcha	Mingma Lepcha	Daughter	F	23	Household	Agriculture
18	Mani Gumpa	Emang Lepcha	Mingma Lepcha	Daughter	F	20	Service	-
19	Mani Gumpa	Imit Lepcha	Tshering Lepcha	Sister	F	57	Household	Agriculture
20	Mani Gumpa	Ugen Lepcha	Tshering Lepcha	Son	M	21	Lama	-
21	Mani Gumpa	Sangmit Lepcha	Prem Tsh.Lepcha	Sister	F	42	Agriculture	Household
22	Mani Gumpa	Dugel Lepcha	Prem Tsh.Lepcha	Sister	F	24	Agriculture	Household
23	Mani Gumpa	Nima Lhamu Lepcha	Dipsing Lepcha	Sister	F	41	Agriculture	Household
24	Mani Gumpa	Songden Lepcha	Dipsing Lepcha	Son	M	20	Agriculture	-
25	Mani Gumpa	Dodimit Lepcha	Kam Dorjee Lepcha	Daughter	F	48	Agriculture	Household
26	5th Mile Lepcha Gaon	Do Thshering	Lha Tshering Lepcha	Adopted Son	M	30	Govt. Service	-
27	5th Mile Lepcha Gaon	Lamit Lepcha	Lha Tshering Lepcha	Daughter	F	26	Household	Agriculture
28	5th Mile Lepcha Gaon	Danial Lepcha	Lha Tshering Lepcha	Son	M	24	Agriculture	-

29	5th Mile Lepcha Gaon	Elizabeth Lepcha	Lha Tshering Lepcha	Daughter	F	22	Household	Agriculture
30	5th Mile Lepcha Gaon	Duklas Lepcha	Run Tshering Lepcha	Sister	F	35	Nurse	-
31	5th Mile Lepcha Gaon	Renu Lepcha	Run Tshering Lepcha	Daughter	F	30	Teacher	-
32	5th Mile Lepcha Gaon	Aju Lepcha	Run Tshering Lepcha	Daughter	F	25	Teacher	-
33	5th Mile Lepcha Gaon	Marshy Lepcha	Run Tshering Lepcha	Daughter	F	23	Govt. Service	-
34	5th Mile Lepcha Gaon	Yugen Lepcha	Bar Sing Lepcha	Son	M	45	Agriculture	-
35	5th Mile Lepcha Gaon	Ruben Lepcha	Bar Sing Lepcha	Son	M	30	Agriculture	-
36	5th Mile Lepcha Gaon	Sudan Lepcha	Bar Sing Lepcha	Son	M	28	Paster Training	
37	5th Mile Lepcha Gaon	Anu Lepcha	Bar Sing Lepcha	Son	M	25	Govt. Service	-
38	5th Mile Lepcha Gaon	Paul Lepcha	Goel Sing Lepcha	Son	M	28	Paster	-
39	5th Mile Lepcha Gaon	Yohanna Lepcha	Goel Sing Lepcha	Son	M	24	Driver	-
40	5th Mile Lepcha Gaon	Sushang Lepcha	Goel Sing Lepcha	Daughter	F	23	Household	Agriculture

(Contd.)

1	2	3	4	5	6	7	8	9
41	5th Mile Lepcha Gaon	Nabi Lepcha	Goel Sing Lepcha	Son	M	20	Agriculture	-
42	5th Mile Lepcha Gaon	Sofia Lepcha	Odila Lepcha	Daughter	F	41	Service	Agriculture
43	5th Mile Lepcha Gaon	Mithu Lepcha	Odila Lepcha	Son	M	56	Agriculture	-
44	5th Mile Lepcha Gaon	Gynatho Lepcha	Odila Lepcha	Son	M	31	Service	Agriculture
45	5th Mile Lepcha Gaon	Fabina Lepcha	Odila Lepcha	Daughter	F	36	Church Sister	-
46	5th Mile Lepcha Gaon	Chipen Lepcha	Chypen Lepcha	Son	M	20	Agriculture	-
47	5th Mile Lepcha Gaon	Gayboo Lepcha	Subash Lepcha	Adopted Brother	M	45	Agriculture	-
48	5th Mile Lepcha Gaon	Anjuna Lepcha	Rabi Lepcha	Daughter	F	24	Teacher	Agriculture
49	5th Mile Lepcha Gaon	Runjana Lepcha	Rabi Lepcha	Daughter	F	21	Household	Agriculture
50	5th Mile Lepcha Gaon	Seon Tshreing Lepcha	Gay Tshering Lepcha	Son	M	30	Service	-
51	5th Mile Lepcha Gaon	Gayboo Lepcha	Gay Tshering Lepcha	Son	M	25	Agriculture	-

52	5th Mile Lepcha Gaon	Raju Lepcha	Gay Tshering Lepcha	Cousin	M	45	Agriculture	-
53	5th Mile Lepcha Gaon	Dokiamit Lepcha	Laban Tshering Lepcha	Daughter	F	26	Household	Agriculture
54	5th Mile Lepcha Gaon	Gaymit Lepcha	Laban Tshering Lepcha	Daughter	F	23	Household	Agriculture
55	5th Mile Lepcha Gaon	Danmit Lepcha	Yahan Tshering Lepcha Gaon	Daughter	F	29	Teacher	-
56	5th Mile Lepcha Gaon	Aimit Lepcha	Yahan Tshering Lepcha Gaon	Daughter	F	27	Household	-
57	5th Mile Lepcha Gaon	Dawat Lepcha	Sakath Sing Lepcha	Son	M	39	Service	-
58	5th Mile Lepcha Gaon	Merry Lepcha	Sakath Sing Lepcha	Daughter	F	35	Agriculture	Household
59	5th Mile Lepcha Gaon	Denma Lepcha	Sakath Sing Lepcha	Daughter	F	33	Agriculture	Household
60	5th Mile Lepcha Gaon	Sarah Lepcha	Sakath Sing Lepcha	Daughter	F	25	Service	-
61	5th Mile Lepcha Gaon	Mangalmit Lepcha	Mikma Tshering Lepcha	Sister	F	56	Household	Agriculture
62	5th Mile Lepcha Gaon	Elias Lepcha	Mikma Tshering Lepcha	Son	M	43	Driver	Agriculture
63	Pochaok	Rutmit Lepcha	Indising Lepcha	Daughter	F	22	Agriculture	Household
64	Pochaok	BudhasingLepcha	Indising Lepcha	Brother	M	40	Agriculture	-

(Contd.)

1	2	3	4	5	6	7	8	9
65	Pochaok	Samit Lepcha	Barsing Lepcha	Daughter	F	22	Household	Agriculture
66	Pochaok	Nilu Lepcha	Thomas Lepcha	Daughter	F	28	Nurse	-
67	Pochaok	Dominik Lepcha	Thomas Lepcha	Son	M	24	Agriculture	Household
68	Pochaok	Carmila Lepcha	Thomas Lepcha	Daughter	F	22	Agriculture	-
69	Pochaok	Silvester Lepcha	Thomas Lepcha	Son	M	20	Agriculture	-
70	Pochaok	Sushama Lepcha	Thomas Lepcha	Sister	F	52	Agriculture	Household
71	Pochaok	Junmit Lepcha	Eizidar Lepcha	Daughter	F	21	Household	Agriculture
72	Pochaok	Joseph Lepcha	Richard Lepcha	Brother	M	32	Agriculture	-
73	Pochaok	Peter Lepcha	Barmit Lepcha	Son	M	24	Agriculture	-
74	Pochaok	Marsing Lepcha	Sammuel Lepcha	Son	M	39	Agriculture	-
75	Pochaok	Sashi Lepcha	Sammuel Lepcha	Son	M	30	Agriculture	-
76	Pochaok	Simsong Lepcha	Dukli Lepcha	Daughter	F	25	Household	Agriculture
77	Pochaok	Yangjong Lepcha	Mikram Lepcha	Brother	M	53	Agriculture	-
78	Pochaok	Pius Lepcha	Lewis Lepcha	Daughter	F	22	Household	Agriculture
79	Pochaok	Libina Lepcha	Lewis Lepcha	Sister	F	38	Agriculture	Household
80	Pochaok	Som Tshering Lepcha	Sanchu Lepcha	Brother	M	32	Agriculture	-
81	Pochaok	Barnabas Lepcha	Paul Lepcha	Son	M	25	Agriculture	-

82	Pochaok	Albert Lepcha	Paul Lepcha	Son	M	20	Agriculture	-
83	Pochaok	Pius Lepcha	Gonam Lepcha	Son	M	27	Agriculture	-
84	Pochaok	Yukman Lepcha	Gonam Lepcha	Brother	M	54	Agriculture	-
85	Pochaok	Gomansing Lepcha	Gonam Lepcha	Brother	M	24	Agriculture	-
86	Pochaok	Julinia Lepcha	MarkusLepcha	Daughter	F	21	Household	Agriculture
87	Pochaok	Alpharse Lepcha	MarkusLepcha	Son	M	28	Agriculture	-
88	Pochaok	Edward Lepcha	Lucus Lepcha	Son	M	29	Agriculture	-
89	Pochaok	Piasca Lepcha	Lucus Lepcha	Daughter	F	26	Household	-
90	Pochaok	Albarto Lepcha	Donadus Lepcha	Daughter	F	20	Household	-
91	Pochaok	Michael Lepcha	Deodutt Lepcha	Brother	M	35	Agriculture	-
92	Pochaok	Sonam Lepcha	Nap Tshering Lepcha	Son	M	23	Agriculture	-
93	Pochaok	Sanumit Lepcha	Anchoy Lepcha	Daughter	F	21	Household	Agriculture
94	Pochaok	Martha Lepcha	Timba Lepcha	Sister	F	65	Sister in Church	-
95	Pochaok	Fanas Lepcha	Norbot Lepcha	Son	M	20	Agriculture	-
96	Pochaok	Suksing Lepcha	Tobgoy Lepcha	Son	M	26	Agriculture	-
97	Pochaok	Phursing Lepcha	Tobgoy Lepcha	Son	M	21	Agriculture	-
98	Pochaok	Leonad Lepcha	Tanje Lepcha	Son	M	32	Agriculture	-
99	Pochaok	Lendup Lepcha	Tanje Lepcha	Son	M	30	Agriculture	-
100	Pochaok	Mangal Lepcha	Tanje Lepcha	Son	M	23	Agriculture	-
101	Pochaok	Michael Lepcha	Maria Lepcha	Son	M	36	Agriculture	-

(Contd.)

1	2	3	4	5	6	7	8	9
102	Pochaok	Jona Lepcha	Maria Lepcha	Daughter	F	38	Household	Agriculture
103	Pochaok	Philip Lepcha	Maria Lepcha	Son	M	31	Agriculture	-
104	Pochaok	Airin Lepcha	Maria Lepcha	Daughter	F	28	Household	Agriculture
105	Pochaok	Zilbert Lepcha	Maria Lepcha	Son	M	24	Agriculture	-
106	Pochaok	Tshering Lepcha	Laku Tshering Lepcha	Son	M	23	Agriculture	-
107	Pochaok	Gregory Lepcha	Kathring Lepcha	Son	M	35	Agriculture	-
108	Pochaok	Helen Lepcha	Joseph Lepcha	Sister	F	50	Household	Agriculture
109	Pochaok	Patvisia Lepcha	Joseph Lepcha	Sister	F	48	Agriculture	Agriculture
110	Pochaok	Temba Lepcha	Joseph Lepcha	Brother	M	46	Agriculture	-

Appendix V
Matrix of Reciprocal Exchange of Labour for Agriculture
Name of the Village: Mani Gumpa

HOUSE HOLDS RECEIVE LABOUR (columns); HOUSEHOLDS EXTEND LABOUR (rows)

Sl.No.	1	2	3	4	5	6	7	8	9	10	11	12	13	14	15	16	17	18	19	20	21	22	Total
1																							-
2																							-
3																							-
4				√		√	√	√		√			√	√			√	√	√		√		11
5																							-
6				√		√	√	√		√				√	√		√	√	√	√			11
7				√		√		√		√				√	√		√	√	√	√	√		11
8				√		√	√			√				√	√		√	√	√	√	√		11
9				√		√	√	√		√				√	√		√	√					9
10				√		√	√	√		√				√					√				7
11			√	√	√	√	√	√		√			√	√			√	√					11
12						√	√	√		√													4
13																							-
14				√		√	√	√		√					√				√				7
15				√	√	√	√	√		√				√	√		√	√	√	√	√	√	14
16			√		√	√	√	√		√				√	√		√						9
17				√		√	√	√		√			√	√	√		√	√	√	√	√	√	14
18			√	√			√	√					√				√	√	√	√	√	√	11
19																							-
20							√	√		√				√	√		√	√					7
21				√										√	√		√	√		√		√	7
22								√						√	√			√	√			√	6
Total	-	-	3	12	3	12	13	14	-	13	-	-	4	13	11	-	12	12	10	7	6	5	150

Appendix VI
Matrix of Reciprocal Exchange of Labour for Agriculture
Name of the Village: 5th Mile Lepcha Gaon

HOUSEHOLDS RECEIVE LABOUR (columns); HOUSEHOLDS EXTEND LABOUR (rows)

Sl.No.	1	2	3	4	5	6	7	8	9	10	11	12	13	14	15	16	17	18	19	20	21	Total
1	√	√	√			√	√		√		√					√	√		√	√	√	12
2	√		√	√			√					√										5
3	√	√		√		√						√										5
4		√				√	√		√						√							5
5																						-
6				√			√				√	√		√	√							6
7	√	√		√		√			√												√	6
8				√			√	√				√										4
9	√							√			√	√		√	√	√			√	√		9
10																						-
11	√			√		√	√	√	√			√		√	√	√				√	√	12
12	√	√	√		√	√	√	√	√		√	√	√	√		√	√		√	√	√	17
13						√						√		√								3
14							√	√				√	√	√						√		6
15																						-
16	√					√	√					√		√			√		√			7
17																						-
18				√			√							√		√	√		√			6
19											√	√		√					√			4
20																						-
21	√										√				√				√	√	√	6
Total	9	5	3	7	1	8	10	5	5	-	6	11	2	9	5	5	4	-	7	6	5	113

Appendix VII
Matrix of Reciprocal Exchange of Labour for Purposes other than Agriculture
Name of the Village: Mani Gumpa

HOUSEHOLDS EXTEND LABOUR (rows) / HOUSEHOLDS RECEIVE LABOUR (columns)

	HOUSEHOLDS RECEIVE LABOUR																						
Sl.No	1	2	3	4	5	6	7	8	9	10	11	12	13	14	15	16	17	18	19	20	21	22	Total
1	√	√	√	√	√	√	√	√	√	√	√	√		√	√	√	√	√	√	√	√	√	21
2	√	√	√	√	√	√	√	√	√	√	√	√		√	√	√	√	√	√	√	√	√	21
3						√		√		√					√			√					5
4						√		√		√					√			√					5
5						√		√		√					√			√					5
6	√	√	√	√	√	√	√	√	√	√	√	√	√	√	√	√	√	√	√	√	√	√	22
7	√	√	√	√	√	√	√	√	√	√	√	√		√	√	√	√	√	√	√	√	√	21
8						√		√		√					√			√					5
9						√		√		√					√			√					5
10	√	√	√	√	√	√	√	√	√	√	√	√	√	√	√	√	√	√	√	√	√	√	22
11	√	√	√	√	√	√	√	√	√	√	√	√		√	√	√	√	√	√	√	√	√	21
12						√		√		√					√			√					5
13						√		√		√					√			√					5
14	√	√	√	√	√	√	√	√	√	√	√	√		√	√	√	√	√	√	√	√	√	21
15						√		√		√					√			√					5
16						√		√		√					√			√					5
17	√	√	√	√	√	√	√	√	√	√	√	√		√	√	√	√	√	√	√	√	√	21
18						√		√		√					√			√					5
19	√	√	√	√	√	√	√	√	√	√	√	√		√	√	√	√	√	√	√	√	√	21
20	√	√	√	√	√	√	√	√	√	√	√	√		√	√	√	√	√	√	√	√	√	21
21						√		√		√					√			√					5
22						√		√		√					√			√					5
Total	10	10	10	10	10	22	10	22	10	22	10	10	2	10	22	10	10	22	10	10	10	10	272

Appendix VIII

Matrix of Reciprocal Exchange of Labour for other than Agriculture Operation

Name of the Village: 5th Mile Lepcha Gaon

HOUSE HOLDS RECEIVE LABOUR

Sl.No.	1	2	3	4	5	6	7	8	9	10	11	12	13	14	15	16	17	18	19	20	21	Total
1	√	√	√	√	√	√	√				√					√	√	√	√	√	√	14
2	√	√	√	√	√	√	√				√					√	√	√	√	√	√	14
3	√	√	√	√	√	√	√				√					√	√	√	√	√	√	14
4	√	√	√	√	√	√	√				√					√	√	√	√	√	√	14
5	√	√	√	√	√	√	√				√					√	√	√	√	√	√	14
6	√	√	√	√	√	√	√				√					√	√	√	√	√	√	14
7	√	√	√	√	√	√	√				√					√	√	√	√	√	√	14
8								√	√	√	√	√	√	√	√						√	9
9								√	√	√	√	√	√	√	√						√	9
10								√	√	√	√	√	√	√	√						√	9
11								√	√	√	√	√	√	√	√						√	9
12								√	√	√	√	√	√	√	√						√	9
13								√	√	√	√	√	√	√	√						√	9
14											√										√	2
15								√	√	√	√	√	√	√	√						√	9
16	√	√	√	√	√	√	√				√					√	√	√	√	√	√	14
17	√	√	√	√	√	√	√				√					√	√	√	√	√	√	14
18	√	√	√	√	√	√	√				√					√	√	√	√	√	√	14
19	√	√	√	√	√	√	√				√					√	√	√	√	√	√	14
20	√	√	√	√	√	√	√				√					√	√	√	√	√	√	14
21	√	√	√	√	√	√	√				√					√	√	√	√	√	√	14
Total	13	13	13	13	13	13	13	7	7	7	21	7	7	7	7	13	13	13	13	13	13	247

HOUSEHOLDS EXTEND LABOUR

Appendix IX
Matrix of Reciprocal Exchange of Bullocks
Name of the Village: Mani Gumpa

	HOUSEHOLDS RECEIVE LABOUR BULLOCKS																						
Sl.No.	1	2	3	4	5	6	7	8	9	10	11	12	13	14	15	16	17	18	19	20	21	22	Total
HOUSEHOLDS EXTEND BULLOCKS																							
1																							
2																							
3																							
4																							
5																							
6																							
7																							
8				√		√	√	√		√	√	√		√	√		√	√		√	√	√	14
9																							
10																							
11																							
12																							
13																							
14																							
15				√	√	√	√	√		√				√	√		√	√		√	√	√	13
16																							
17				√		√	√	√		√				√	√		√	√	√	√	√	√	13
18																							
19																							
20																							
21																							
22																							
Total	-	-	-	3	1	3	3	3	-	3	1	1	-	3	3	-	3	3	1	3	3	3	40

Appendix X
Matrix of Reciprocal Exchange of Bullocks
Name of the Village: 5th Mile Lepcha Gaon

HOUSE HOLDS RECEIVE BULLOCKS (columns); HOUSEHOLDS EXTEND BULLOCKS (rows)

Sl.No.	1	2	3	4	5	6	7	8	9	10	11	12	13	14	15	16	17	18	19	20	21	Total
1	√	√	√			√	√		√		√					√	√		√	√	√	12
2																						-
3																						-
4																						-
5																						-
6																						-
7																						-
8																						-
9																						-
10																						-
11																						-
12	√	√	√		√	√	√	√	√		√	√	√	√		√	√		√	√	√	17
13																						-
14																						-
15																						-
16																						-
17																						-
18																						-
19																						-
20																						-
21	√										√				√				√	√	√	6
Total	3	2	2	-	1	2	2	1	2	-	3	1	1	1	1	2	2	-	3	3	3	35

Index